The Thrill of fear

The Thrill of fear

250 Years of Scary Entertainment

Walter Kendrick

GROVE PRESS
NEW YORK

Published by Grove Press
A division of Grove Press, Inc.
841 Broadway
New York, NY 10003-4793

Published in Canada by General Publishing Company, Ltd.

Library of Congress Cataloging-in-Publication Data

Kendrick, Walter M.
The thrill of fear : 250 years of scary entertainment / Walter Kendrick.—1st ed.
p.   cm.
Includes bibliographical references.
ISBN 0-8021-1162-9
ISBN 0-8021-3246-4 (pbk.)
1. Horror tales, English—History and criticism.   2. Horror tales, American—History and criticism.   3. Popular literature—History and criticism.   4. Horror films—History and criticism.   5. Horror in literature.   6. Death in literature.   7. Amusements—History.
I. Title.
PR830.T3K4   1991
823'.0873809—dc20   91-11495
CIP

Manufactured in the United States of America

Printed on acid-free paper

Designed by Irving Perkins Associates

First Edition 1991

First Evergreen Edition 1992

1   3   5   7   9   10   8   6   4   2

For M.

Acknowledgments

Many friends and colleagues helped me write this book—reading drafts, suggesting sources, letting their ideas bump heads with mine. For these and other kindnesses, I owe special thanks to Dan Applebaum, Aileen Baumgartner, Walt Bode, Flip Brophy, Karen Burke, Mark Caldwell, Robert Cornfield, Mary Erler, Michael Feingold, Richard Goldstein, Connie Hassett, Mary Anne Kowaleski, M. Mark, Rebecca Martin, Perry Meisel, Erika Munk, Art Murray, Debra Pearl, Lloyd Rose, Dave Sanjek, Ralph Sassone, Larry Stempel, and Joan Ungaro.

Thanks also to the staffs of the Fordham University and New York University libraries for their unfailing generosity and assistance.

Unless otherwise indicated in the source notes, all translations are my own.

Contents

Introduction:
Fear Is the Same

With all or almost all animals, even with birds, Terror causes the body to tremble. The skin becomes pale, sweat breaks out, and the hair bristles. The secretions of the alimentary canal and of the kidneys are increased, and they are involuntarily voided. . . . The breathing is hurried. The heart beats quickly, wildly, and violently; but whether it pumps the blood more efficiently through the body may be doubted, for the surface seems bloodless and the strength of the muscles soon fails. . . . The mental faculties are much disturbed. Utter prostration soon follows, and even fainting. . . . I once caught a robin in a room, which fainted so completely, that for a time I thought it dead.

These were the symptoms of terror in 1872, as Charles Darwin described them in *The Expression of the Emotions in Man and Animals.* More than a century later, though the world is vastly different, terror hasn't changed. Birds, cats, dogs, and people, when they are frightened, continue to tremble, break out in cold sweats, and faint dead away. Whatever name you give it—fear, fright, terror, horror—the emotion may vary in intensity but remains in essence the same. You may not understand a syllable of

xi

a man's language; his customs may be wholly foreign to you; but when his eyes widen, his mouth hangs open, and his hands uncontrollably shake, you can read fear written all over him. The language seems universal among human beings; it also links us to animals, reminding us of our kinship with them. And we can assume that, ten thousand years ago, our remote ancestors joined us in feeling their hair stand on end when they were afraid. In all ages, nations, and even species, fear is the same.

Darwin speculated that fear's instinctual symptoms evolved, like all other features of life, because they aided survival. Fear was a response to some threat in the environment, especially to the approach of a predator. Standing hairs, for instance—or "the erection of the dermal appendages"—may make a threatened creature look "larger and more terrible to its enemies or rivals." An animal that exhibits such behavior would be more likely to win a mate and to escape being eaten; the trait would then be passed on to later, better-adapted generations. Even an apparently self-defeating maneuver like passing out cold can be accounted for in Darwin's view, because some carnivores will not bite an animal that seems dead already. Animals that play dead—as several species do—avoid real death by faking it.

The Expression of the Emotions is still a primary source for behavioral scientists, who still study the relation between animals' behavior and what they presumably feel. Nowadays, "piloerection" replaces both Darwin's clumsy "erection of the dermal appendages" and the more homely "goose-skin," as he occasionally called fear's characteristic prickle. But the phenomenon endures, and science goes on probing it—to small effect as far as I can see. Scientists freely admit that though we know fear when we feel it or see its symptoms, we may never be able to measure it precisely or mark it off clearly from the spectrum of emotions to which it belongs. Uncertainty grows when we consider the varieties of fear, from mild anxiety to out-and-out terror, for which we also have words. Like "fear" itself, these words do not guarantee the existence of any identifiable condition of body or mind. They blend into one another; one man's frisson may be another man's stark horror or a third man's occasion for belly laughs.

In human beings (whom most of us find more compelling than robins), the body may do what animals do, but the mind is likely to be otherwise engaged. Discussing the erection of the hair, Darwin cited a case reported to him by Dr. J. Crichton Browne, the head of a large insane asylum:

> For instance, it is occasionally necessary to inject morphia under the skin of an insane woman, who dreads the operation extremely, though it causes very little pain; for she believes that poison is being introduced into her system, and that her bones will be softened, and her flesh turned into dust. She becomes deadly pale; her limbs are stiffened by a sort of tetanic spasm, and her hair is partially erected on the front of the head.

The symptoms were plainly those of intense fear, which sufficed for Darwin's purposes. He therefore passed over the most human aspect of the poor woman's case. She was terrified, just as a cat or a bird might be, yet her fear had no object or at best a wholly imaginary one. What frightened her was not so much the morphine or even the needle as a vision that only she could see, the spectacle of her body rotting away.

Neither Darwin nor Dr. Crichton Browne disputed the power of such a vision to bring on the symptoms of terror. There was nothing insane about the woman's response; madness lay in the lack of correspondence between her imagination and reality. A couple of centuries earlier, any preacher might have informed the learned gentlemen that their inmate was wiser than they. Her mistake was merely to suppose that morphine and needles would do the trick; nothing so drastic, only time, was required. Her bones indeed would soften; her flesh would turn to dust; so would the learned gentlemen's, for that matter. They would all die, in whatever way, at whatever moment, inevitably. The preacher might have urged the scientist and the doctor to heed the woman's vision, instead of calling it madness or gauging what it did to her hair. She glimpsed eternal truth; they saw mere phenomena.

It has often been said—though a proper survey remains to be taken—that human beings are the only species who know they must die, who can conjure up the event as if it were happening now and react accordingly. Animals fear death, but the fear seems to come on them only when death immediately threatens. They do not brood upon it; for animals, death is an endemic surprise. Dr. Crichton Browne's madwoman reminds us that human beings can also imagine being dead, a very different thing from death and perhaps a more frightening one. Deprived of soul, spirit, force, whatever you may call it (this fear requires no religion), human flesh is meat, and it goes meat's way. Few seventeenth-century preachers would have balked at summoning up the madwoman's vision in their congregations' minds. Then, as in all prior Christian centuries, the lesson was plain and familiar: Put your faith in flesh and you'll end up feeding worms; put your faith in spirit, subdue the ephemeral flesh, and you'll transcend the grave.

Well into the eighteenth century such lessons went on being preached, but they sharply dwindled after 1750, and I know of no one who preaches in that style now. By 1872, the idea that the flesh will rot seemed as horrifying as ever, to mad and sane alike. The idea, however, had long since lost its religious usefulness; though it could still frighten, it no longer admonished. Indeed, decorum hardly admitted notions of deadness into public discourse. Fond as they were of funerals and all the panoply of mourning, the Victorians exhibited a thoroughly modern squeamishness in regard to the symptoms of being dead. They continued a development that began at the end of the seventeenth century and has not ceased—hiding deadness away, cosmeticizing corpses, denying ever more strenuously that anything nasty happens to the body after death. The gaudy American funeral industry that Evelyn Waugh lampooned in *The Loved One* (1948) and Jessica Mitford lambasted in *The American Way of Death* (1963) is only the most grotesque by-product of a long, slow, immensely complex process of deliberate forgetting.

It may seem paradoxical that death itself, especially violent death, has remained immune to the taboo against deadness. In their newspapers, melodramas, and popular fiction, the Victorians exhibited the same fervent interest in the varieties of dying that their Elizabethan and Jacobean ancestors had gratified at bloody stage plays and public executions. We have inherited that interest, and we cultivate it, if possible, with even greater fervor. But our interest fades once the deed is done; what happens to the corpse thereafter belongs in a different zone, a shadowy one, where we, like the Victorians, would prefer not to tread. Those Elizabethans and Jacobeans (and the generations before them) exhibited a very different attitude, one that must strike a modern observer as callous, revolting, utterly incomprehensible, or perhaps all three. Before the eighteenth century, though decay was horrible enough to induce repentance, it was not strange; it did not bring on the peculiarly modern sensation of terror at the very idea of being dead.

The roots of any such large-scale change are impossible to locate with precision. Our recoil from deadness may be just one aspect of the overall tidying up that has been going on in Western culture for the last two hundred years. Frequent baths, efficient disposal of garbage and excrement, the banishing from ordinary view of all things that smell bad—these and many other apparently hygienic practices have reached a high degree of thoroughness in the most advanced Western nations, and the sequestering of the dead may merely have moved alongside them. This is probably progress; certainly no one would wish any of it undone. But progress, as Sigmund Freud was fond of pointing out, exacts costs that often work unseen. By the end of the eighteenth century, deadness had entered the realm it still inhabits: Being dead had joined the ranks of what Freud, in a famous 1919 essay, called "The 'Uncanny.' "

Freud's point works better in German: *Das Unheimliche* literally means "the un-home-like" and suits itself well to Freud's definition as "that class of the frightening which leads back to what is known of old and long familiar." It may also, however, be something "that ought to have remained secret and hidden but comes to light." As might be expected, Freud proceeds to discover a good deal of castration anxiety in the business, along with survivals of primitive beliefs and emotions. With these tried-and-true formulas he manages to answer a number of questions. Yet he never quite smooths out the apparent discrepancy between those two possible meanings of *das Unheimliche.* Nor does he satisfactorily explain a classic occasion for the feeling, though he cites it more than once: "doubts whether an apparently animate being is really alive; or conversely, whether a lifeless object might not be in fact animate."

"Since almost all of us still think as savages do on this topic," says Freud (evidently not including himself in that majority), "it is no matter for surprise that the primitive fear of the dead is still so strong within us." Perhaps so, but older cultures feared the dead as vengeful spirits, not as rotten, reeking things. And that old fear was grounded in belief; it could be met and mastered by rituals designed for the purpose. Modern fear of deadness gets no solace from worn-out platitudes about heaven and the afterlife. We may believe that we'll end up sitting on clouds, strumming harps; we may cherish some subtler notion of the soul's survival, or none at all. Whatever happens to the soul, it cannot save the body, which will turn to clay and can be seen already moving in that direction before death. Nothing can console this modern fear—which is why, on the whole, we prefer not to discuss the subject.

Yet, of course, we know it well. We can picture what goes on underground, in those gleaming, satin-lined caskets, especially if we've never seen it. Such secret knowledge renders the subject un-home-like in both of Freud's senses: familiar and strange, hidden and blatant, all at once. And the fear it inspires is focused on just the instance of the uncanny that Freud cited without exploring it: the line, if there is one, between being alive and being dead. When the loved one dies and is buried or cremated, we wish that only her ethereal aspect survive—her soul perhaps, her memory certainly. At the same time, we remember that she lingers on in a more material form, even if it's only a handful of dust. And we may well be made uneasy by the mysterious kinship between the human being she once was and the hidden thing some part of her is now. Maybe the difference between being alive and being dead is not so absolute as our wishes would make it. Maybe the dead retain more of life than we care to acknowledge; there may be more of death in life than we can think of without a shudder.

NOTHING TO FEAR

At the end of the twentieth century, these are literally unspeakable matters. We have been born into a late stage of a process, more than two centuries old, that has almost totally removed the after-effects of death from most Western experience, leaving them to cavort in the imagination. We do not discuss the frailty and ultimate dissolution of our flesh, and when the fact leaps at us, as the AIDS epidemic has made it do, it elicits redoubled horror thanks to the entrenched strength of our denial. Even as we deny that our flesh must decay, however, we surround ourselves with fictional images of the very fate we strive to hear nothing about. They are every-where: in books, films, and TV, in advertising, in toys and games for all ages, in children's breakfast food. No American child (even one lucky enough to escape Count Chocula) can grow up without learning what a vampire is—an undead creature, uncannily both living *and* dead, that rises from his coffin in the after-midnight hours to drain our blood and to make us his own. The vampire belongs to a lively crew of ghouls, ghosts, zombies, and man-made monsters, all of which seem, with their insistent display of what death does, to deny our very denial.

They don't, of course. In the midst of a culture hell-bent on saying no to deadness, vampires and their ilk fit smoothly, as if they had always been there. No contradiction follows from the pitting of fictional ghastliness against a scoured and would-be-immortal real life. There is no debate, and one side does not correct or even impinge on the other. As in late-twentieth-century American politics, these apparent opposites agree at bottom on practically everything. The tireless repetition of the horrors of being dead has grown into an enormous international industry, which it never would have done if its message were simply *"You will die and rot."* That might have sufficed for an eighteenth-century preacher, whose audience half-believed him; in any case, the audience was a captive one, and the preacher held out salvation as the eventual reward for enduring him. But twentieth-century readers, moviegoers, and TV-watchers, who pay good money for the opportunity to be scared by walking corpses, cannot be so cheaply satisfied. They demand entertainment, and somehow the thought they abhor beyond all others has been wrenched into a way of amusing them.

It looks paradoxical at best—psychotic at worst—that one might go from an hour on the Nautilus machines or in an aerobics class, where the body is urged to the acme of aliveness, directly to a screening of *Night of the Living Dead*, which pits animated corpses against the living and lets the corpses win. If this were the fourteenth century, the spectacle of death's ravages would admonish pride of life. The admonition might go unheeded—people might go on living pridefully, as they evidently did after the plague had claimed a third of Europe—but there would at least be a coherent relation between the two experiences. In the late twentieth century, there seems to be none. Pride of life has carried the day; death's ravages are bearable now only because they have been processed to enhance that pride instead of mortifying it. From Count Chocula and the cutesy rituals of Halloween to the most vomit-provoking splatter film, scary entertainments can entertain only because even as they apparently violate the taboo against showing the aftereffects of death, they transform them into affirmations of the body's impregnability.

Many commentators have expressed surprise, often tinged with outrage, that gut-wrenching scenes of violence are greeted by today's horror-movie audiences with laughter. Viewers imagine with alarm that these audiences—usually composed of less genteel people than the alarmists themselves—would respond to a real scene of carnage in much the same way: Rather than calling 911, such callused folk would guffaw and walk on by. No satisfactory evidence of that behavior has ever been found, but the callus-building effect of exposure to violence on the screen, large or small, seems logical and therefore necessary. The analogy with pornography is exact. In both cases, evidence of a cause-and-effect link is lacking, yet the desire to find one remains so strong that research goes on unstoppably.

In both cases, what the researchers have missed is the simple fact that, at the end of the twentieth century, anyone who sees a film or videotape knows the difference between a picture of a thing and the thing itself. The point seems too elementary to be worth making; it ought to be so. Yet cultural commentators at all levels of sophistication, from the unaccountably august Susan Sontag to the Cincinnatians who sweated in the summer of 1990 over the harm caused by Robert Mapplethorpe's photographs, evidently fret still about the danger that lurks in pictures. In the case of horror and violence, to make a simple equation between the image and the reality is to miss the most characteristic trick of horror entertainment, perhaps the only thing that makes it entertaining. Horror films and stories are fiction and admit it; they revel in being *made* articles, presenting themselves to an audience that knows the fact well and is ready to play the game on those terms.

The game isn't subtle, though it's easily missed by naive or horrified observers. It simply entails the entertainer's constant endeavor to catch the audience off guard—to show it on film, for example, something so gross or alarming that its experience of horror fiction offers no precedent. The audience, in response, counters each move with a burst of hilarity that says, "You can't fool *us.*" Reality has little to do with the proceedings; what's at stake is fictional experience, most importantly that of other horror films. Today, this cat-and-mouse game has reached such a high degree of sophistication that horror films are among the archest, most self-conscious products of contemporary culture. In many cases, they are little more than technological showpieces, extravagant displays of imitation human bodies getting mauled in ever more outlandish ways. The audiences that applaud such films do honor first of all to the special-effects designer, who has brilliantly tried to outwit them—though, of course, he has failed.

In this way, the horror of death and dying is rendered safe; it is turned into a celebration of being permanently alive, forever immune to decay. Death and dying are made to provide pleasure— not of an intellectual sort or even exactly an emotional one, but the gut thrill of deep breaths, shouts, and half-serious clutches at the viewer in the next seat. Fear of deadness has become a reliable reservoir of muscular innervation that can be tapped at any time, without much inventiveness or, it seems, any anxiety that it will ever run dry. The cleverest horror films may offer political commentary, even social criticism, thereby winning the approval of those who would otherwise never glance at a horror movie. But such things are extras; they're far from necessary, and they sometimes threaten to impede horror's fundamental errand—to assure the viewer that his flesh will always remain firm and intact, that for all this display of rot and carnage, there is nothing to fear.

HORROR'S HISTORY, HISTORY'S HORROR

Vampires, zombies, and the like come to us so tightly woven into the fabric of everyday culture that they appear natural and inevitable. Most portrayals present them as unfathomably ancient, mankind's dogged companions since the first days when there was such a group as mankind. In Bram Stoker's *Dracula* (1897), for instance, the king vampire is said to be five hundred years old at least. There must have been vampires before then for him to get that way, but Stoker leaves the matter vague. When Anne Rice, in *The Queen of the Damned* (1988), felt obliged to reveal the origin of vampires, she set the event in prehistoric Egypt, and even then there is a demon, older than the dunes, who brings it about.

Scholars of frightening fictions enjoy imagining that if a contemporary film or novel introduces a vampire, it aligns itself with a
tradition so old we might as well call it human nature. Throughout
history, the comforting story runs, people have loved to sit around
the flickering fire, chilling one another's blood with tales of monsters and the vengeful dead.

The scenario is certainly plausible. As everyone knows and Darwin documented, human fear acts much like fear in animals. Animals don't, so far as we know, tell each other scary stories, but then
human beings are gifted with imagination, and they probably always used it much as we do now. Anthropologists have gathered
plenty of ancient myths, from cultures all over the world, that make
an anthropologist's hair stand up and seem to have the same effect
on those who believe them. Classic Western literature, from Homer
to Shakespeare, is studded all over with episodes of horror. They
are only episodes—the first full-fledged horror stories seem to have
appeared only in the nineteenth century—but the impulse must
have been present long before, though somehow its realization got
delayed.

Modern horror stories are often set in the distant past, a more
credulous, differently haunted age. Even when the setting is contemporary, as Stoker's and Rice's are, the horror usually comes
from long ago and far away. The first English vampire story, John
Polidori's "The Vampyre," appeared as late as 1819, but there is
evidence of a much older tradition of belief in undead blood-
suckers. In his introduction, Polidori attached "The Vampyre" to
that venerable line: "The superstition upon which this tale is
founded is very general in the East. Among the Arabians it appears
to be common; it did not, however, extend itself to the Greeks until
after the establishment of Christianity," and so on, a weighty pedigree for a pretty slight piece of work. A typical Westerner, Polidori
seemed to think that Arabs in 1819 were more ancient than medieval Christians; his own research apparently extended no further
than a 1732 issue of the *London Journal*, which reported a case of
vampirism in Hungary.

Whatever its literary merits, "The Vampyre" came into the world
as a thoroughly up-to-date, commercial article, ca. 1819. It was
published in the *New Monthly Magazine*, which had been founded
only five years before, one of the many British periodicals born in

the first decades of the nineteenth century. The *New Monthly* aimed to please upper-middle-class readers with literary tastes—a class that, until quite recently, hadn't existed in sufficient numbers to make such enterprises profitable. And Polidori's tale looked little different from the run of magazine short fiction: The vampire gimmick was new, but the gloom-and-doom atmosphere was commonplace, and the bloodsucking Lord Ruthven amounted to only a slight twist on that popular favorite, the depraved aristocrat. Yet Polidori claimed a direct connection between his calculated money-maker and Hungarian folk legends.

There was nothing new about that strategy either: It had been popular among more careful, honest writers at least since Horace Walpole's *Castle of Otranto* more than half a century earlier, and it remains a staple of fictions that intend to raise gooseflesh. In fact, nothing linked "The Vampyre" to folk legends, Hungarian or otherwise. The only connection was a predatory, even vampiric one: A would-be commercial writer, prowling after material that would gratify a proven contemporary taste, hit upon some old legends and molded them in modern form. Unlike the folksy Hungarians, Polidori's intended readers did not believe in vampires, nor did he expect them to do so. "The Vampyre" solicited no belief; it was an entertainment, and a minor one at that, a half hour's diversion for urban, affluent readers in search of a pleasant little chill. Polidori's credulous Hungarians had responded quite differently to *their* vampire: Several, he reports, had been "tormented" by him; four had died from his attacks.

For Polidori and his readers, there was something scary about the past itself, especially the distant past, and most of all when it wore the exotic trappings of eastern or southern European Catholicism. He and other gooseflesh mongers sought to draw on that source of chills as well, and their successors go on tapping it today. Fear of deadness is closely related to fear of the past; both took on their modern form at the same time, about the middle of the eighteenth century, when Gothic buildings (which had been moldering in quiet neglect for centuries) were suddenly found to provide delicious chills. Decayed walls and towers made the perfect milieu for ghosts, skeletons, and the like; by the turn of the nineteenth century, they had become standard fixtures of scary entertainments, and they play the same role today. But exploiting the past for its gooseflesh value establishes no meaningful bond between the exploiter and his materials. In no way does it make the modern version a continuation of its old sources. From the middle of the eighteenth century onward, there may be a certain continuity in the tradition of wringing pleasure out of fear, though it is full of gaps and bouts of wholesale amnesia. There is no continuity, however, between those entertainments and the myths, legends, and superstitions on which they draw. Indeed, our steadily growing alienation from the past has helped to make such entertainments possible.

Nevertheless, scholars who write about horror fiction love to describe it in mythic, legendary terms, as if there were any plausible resemblance between a postindustrial American teenager, screaming in delight at a monster movie, and some medieval peasant who trembled in the dark for fear a ghost would get him. Perhaps the scholars worry that the horror tradition has produced too few masterpieces to justify the labor of studying it. If so, they're right. By ordinary academic standards, a very short shelf will hold all the goosefleshy works worth looking at, and we've already had enough glum essays on *Frankenstein*. When they've been gussied up as "popular culture," such things still need to be read psychoanalytically, psychosexually, or in some other way that makes them symptoms of forces higher and better than themselves. Otherwise, the embarrassed scholar sinks in a morass of throwaways, churned out for profit and scanned at idle moments, then junked. Even now, when the academic canon has been nearly kicked to pieces, these are not the building blocks of a scholar's reputation.

Scary entertainment, as we know it today, showed its first stirrings in the middle of the eighteenth century, when deadness and pastness began to acquire the eerie aura they possess yet more powerfully 250 years later. But this aura alone would not have led to Gothic novels, horrid melodramas, magazine ghost stories, horror movies, or any of the other shows that try to frighten their audiences. These have all been commercial ventures; they would not have been launched without a public that wished to be entertained by playing on its own emotions, even unpleasant ones, simply for the sake of exercise. That public made its earliest appearance toward the end of the eighteenth century and has grown steadily since, until it now includes virtually every inhabitant of Western

Europe and the industrialized Americas. Increasingly, this potential audience has been urban, secular, cut off from any religious or ethnic tradition. Such people's hair may prickle in fright just as a medieval peasant's did, but modern fright is a kind of connoisseurship, a deliberate indulgence that recognizes no aim beyond itself.

This attitude toward one's own feelings is another eighteenth-century invention. It first became fashionable in the rarefied, polite circles that had the time and money to be frivolous, but it soon invaded the middle class and has spread along with it ever since. As early as 1802, in the preface to *Lyrical Ballads*, William Wordsworth felt moved to voice a complaint we haven't heard the end of:

> a multitude of causes, unknown to former times, are now acting with a combined force to blunt the discriminating powers of the mind, and unfitting it for all voluntary exertion to reduce it to a state of almost savage torpor. The most effective of these causes are the great national events which are daily taking place, and the increasing accumulation of men in cities, where the uniformity of their occupations produces a craving for extraordinary incident, which the rapid communication of intelligence hourly gratifies. To this tendency of life and manners the literature and theatrical exhibitions of the country have conformed themselves. The invaluable works of our elder writers . . . are driven into neglect by frantic novels, sickly and stupid German Tragedies, and deluges of idle and extravagant stories in verse.

It was our world already, nearly two centuries ago.

Like generations of artists after him, Wordsworth deplored these developments, both because they seemed to deaden the soul and because they gave his own work small chance of widespread success. Like later generations of social commentators, he saw contemporary life as a pathological state resembling drug addiction: Each shock of the new made the citizen's skin a little thicker, and ever higher voltages were needed to make him feel anything at all. Instead of trying to cure the disease—as, needless to say, Wordsworth's poetry did—novels, plays, and poems merely imitated the outside world, furnishing stronger and stronger jolts to their audiences' jaded nervous systems. The result was universal degradation, reversion to savagery, the loss of all sense of the past in a frantic, sickly, and stupid rush after the next cheap thrill.

As Wordsworth's distant heirs, we can hardly help admiring him for describing our own cities so far ahead of the fact. His indictment of the popular culture of 1802 also applies pretty well to ours. But Wordsworth missed—he could not afford to notice—the immense vitality and invention displayed by the shows he found so pernicious. He was witnessing, on a very small scale, the defining habits of an entertainment industry: shameless imitation and pandering to the fad of the moment, desperate recycling of what has just scored a success until it wears out and gets discarded. Commercial culture of all sorts continues to operate in just these ways. It has spawned few masterpieces, but for all its slavishness, it makes an amusing show in its own right. And if we feel that Wordsworth's vision of a savage society has at last been realized, we should remember that he thought it had already happened two hundred years ago.

Except for a few canonized novels and stories, scary entertainment has been confined throughout its history to the commercial run of the mill. Perhaps this is because the effects it aims at, no matter how skillfully they are handled, remain physical: cold sweat on the brow, upstanding hairs on the nape of the neck, involuntary gasps and shudders. Intellectual activity has little to do with the experience and may even spoil it. For most of its history—until very recently, in fact—commercial chills always came mingled with other more or less automatic responses, like guffaws at the antics of bumpkins and tears at the plight of an imperiled heroine. From Gothic novels and melodramas to horror films of the 1920s and 1930s, even fictions that were known for scariness usually went after a range of widely different feelings as well. Late-century horror mavens, taking as their standard the relatively singleminded films that came into vogue after the 1950s, often turn up their noses at such apparent bastards as the spooky-house comedy, which might send the buffoonish East Side Kids into a haunted mansion and expect to wring both chuckles and shrieks from the encounter.

Unfortunately for purists, hodgepodges like *The Ghost Creeps* adhered more faithfully to the scary tradition than did highly admired later films like *The Texas Chainsaw Massacre*, with its nearly relentless drive toward raising gooseflesh. The same "tradition," however, applied to two centuries of scary fictions, is a misnomer, since for most of that time practitioners of the trade had only the dimmest sense that they possessed precursors or that their own work continued anything. They were opportunists, most of them, laboring moment by moment in the interest of providing momentary pleasure and (especially) getting paid for it. They used what came to hand, dropped it when profits fell, and seldom complained about the oblivion that overtook them and their products. Only since the 1920s has scary entertainment—usually called "horror"—become self-conscious about its past and anxious about its future.

Now, the would-be entrant on the horror field can refer to dozens of anthologies and scholarly studies of the genre; he can rent or buy a videocassette of nearly every relevant film, radio broadcast, or TV show; he is catered to by a glut of magazines and newsletters that specialize in the most arcane details of horror's manufacturing. At the end of the twentieth century, horror has grown so aware of itself that it threatens to die of effeteness. Now may be the best time to tell horror's story, because horror seems about to emit its last gasp.

THE STORY SO FAR

Last gasps, however, are habitual gestures in this genre that is not one. Victims and villains have been emitting them nonstop for more than two centuries, and though the forms have varied wildly, the urge that enlivens them seems stronger now than it ever was. The forms have burgeoned and died, too, but the desire to be scared—along with its twin, the desire to be scary—never fails to rise again, providing new generations of buyers and sellers of fear. Mild physical exercise brings pleasure, and artificial fear puts muscles and glands into a special kind of play that, so long as it remains play, leaves behind delicious after-the-game euphoria. That joy is innocent; I would hate to see it fade. So long as we remain without faith in a bodily afterlife yet unable to believe that when the soul departs it, the body really returns to the earth, spectacles of carnage and rot will go on furnishing occasions for these ghastly aerobics. Right now it seems that, exhausted by repetition and self-consciousness, horror fiction cannot go on. It will go on.

In the meantime, it may look as if I've set up the story of scary

entertainment as both a gruesome business and, if you like continuity or meaningfulness, no story at all. In fact, for its whole 250-
year history, the business of scaring and being scared has formed
one of the most vivacious sideshows of our culture. The fire might
be fueled by the grimmest of fears, but it has burned bright and
spanned a gorgeous spectrum. From dour eighteenth-century
preachers, lured against their wills into amusement as well as
instruction, the trail leads to horror mavens of the 1990s, who haunt
video stores in search of the latest breakthrough in phony gut-
spilling. Along the way, we meet infatuated collectors, mad self-
dramatizers, scrambling hacks, stern remonstrators, fools, gulls,
lunatics, and occasionally a genius. The road meanders, peters
out, starts up again from an unexpected spot; if it fails to make a
story, it makes a fine display.

No moral comes tagged on at the end; there are no heroes and no
villains. Instead of adopting the standard family tree of scariness,
I've explored how fear blends into other feelings and cohabits with
them. Instead of forcing run-of-the-mill work to yield up deeper,
richer, more stable meanings, I've tried to read culture's throwaways on their own terms—not as unconscious folklore, unwitting
criticism of gender roles, unsuspected assaults on the status quo,
or any of the other blind ingenuities with which critics of popular
culture try to credit them. I've gone in search not of meanings but of
feelings, those momentary prickles of the scalp and sudden intakes
of breath that provide mysterious pleasure. For good or ill, and
whether we remember it or not, we live in a culture that plays on
our bodies more than our minds—steadily more, it seems, till the
mind becomes a vestigial organ like an appendix, better off gone.
That culture has been slowly, irregularly in the making since the
eighteenth century, and artificial fear has counted among its trust-
iest instruments. In the process, it may have ruined us for Wordsworth, but it's given us two centuries of incomparable fun.

The Thrill of Fear

In the Middle Ages, the dead weren't scary, though they could be decorative. Bones of the Cappuccine monks, Cappuccine Monastery-Mortuary Chapel, Rome, Sta. Maria of the Conezione. (ALINARI/ART RESOURCE)

1

Into the Crypt

"I LOVE DEAD"

Bride of Frankenstein (1935) is a bottomless reservoir of the scenes and situations that define the horror movie. Scores of later films have drawn on or simply copied it; it also sums up the nearly two centuries of scary entertainments that went before. Even academic critics—who usually scorn such frankly commercial work—recognize *Bride of Frankenstein* as an accomplished piece of moviemaking. And horror mavens grow nearly hysterical admiring it.

Among its numerous merits, *Bride of Frankenstein* has the wisdom never to slow down long enough for the viewer to ponder what's going on. After a stately prologue, in which impossible versions of Lord Byron, Percy Bysshe Shelley, and Mary Wollstonecraft Shelley lounge about a Regency drawing room the size of Grand Central Station, the film picks up where the 1931 *Frankenstein* left off and careens practically nonstop to its explosive close. There are a few tedious stretches, like the episode of the Monster and the blind violinist, but even that maudlin interlude serves the plot by explaining how the Monster learns to speak and to overcome his fear of fire. Besides, the sequence is so extravagant in its kitsch-Christian sentimentality that it's fully in tune with the grand-operatic bravado of the whole movie.

But the next sequence seems to last much longer than either plot or character requires. Driven from the hermit's hut, pursued by irate, torch-wielding villagers, the Monster flees into a graveyard—the same one, evidently, where *Frankenstein* began. It is a desolate place, shrouded in mist while the rest of the landscape is clear, barren except for a few dry and stunted trees, one of which the raging Monster tears down. Everything exudes a miasma of extreme and long-standing neglect. Here and there in the gloom, statues tilt at crazy angles, as if they've been sagging for centuries and might tip over any night now. Toppling the effigy of a bishop, the Monster breaks open what appears to be a sarcophagus sunk in the earth and finds a staircase leading down. He follows it into a burial vault of surprising dimensions, considering that no trace can be seen aboveground.

It is cavernous, much larger than the modest needs of the village could require (but then all the sets in *Bride of Frankenstein* seem built to accommodate giants). And unlike the graveyard, it shows signs of recent activity; many of the coffins that lie about on the floor look new. The Monster pries one open to reveal the unde-cayed corpse of a beautiful young woman, her face clearly visible through a diaphanous shroud. In a grotesquely pathetic moment—cut by British censors for its necrophiliac overtones—he passes his gross hands over her, plaintively growling, "Friend?" The hermit, who could not see the horror of his appearance, taught him this word; but, sadly, the Monster will never find another friend among the living. Neither alive nor dead in any proper sense, he has tried his best to seek living love, but those who are truly alive always recoil from him. Soon he will have no choice but to turn to the dead—or to another monster.

In case the viewer feels inclined to wonder what sort of friendship the Monster might establish with that pretty corpse, pathos is soon interrupted by black comedy. Noisily gabbing and clanking down the vast staircase, Dr. Pretorius and his assistants, Karl and Rudy, arrive on their own errand. The Monster hides and watches while they enter a barred enclosure and approach another coffin, this one considerably less fresh. Blowing the dust from its lid, Karl reads that the occupant, Madelina Ernestine, died in 1899, aged nineteen years, three months.

The date contradicts the stately prologue, which pretends that the story is being told by Mary Shelley on a thundery night in 1816. The accoutrements of the rest of the film, along with the quasi-medieval notions of science held by both Pretorius and Henry Frankenstein, also suggest a period much more distant than this could be, if Madelina has been moldering for several years since 1899. But *Bride of Frankenstein*, like many of its precursors and imitators, is set in an indeterminate past full of anachronisms. It is merely long ago and, in this case, very far away from anything the viewer knows firsthand. And all the spookier for that reason.

Karl and Rudy wrench open Madelina's coffin, exposing (to judge from Karl's groan and from the oblique, dim glimpse the viewer gets of it) a body well advanced in decay. "I hope her bones are firm," says Pretorius, who has doffed his overcoat to reveal a white lab smock. He has brought along various metal implements of unspecified purpose. The villains set about their work, which the viewer does not see but which is evidently the extraction of Madelina's skeleton for use in the female monster Pretorius plans to construct. When the ghastly business is done, Karl and Rudy quickly take their pay and scurry off. Pretorius, however, lingers; "I rather like this place," he says.

Alone (he thinks) among dust, rot, and skeletons, Pretorius unwraps a little meal and lays it out atop Madelina's coffin lid, where he has also set two large, drippy candles and a neat arrangement of clean white bones, apparently Madelina's. The Monster now emerges from the shadows and approaches, but instead of turning vicious as other living men have done, Pretorius urbanely welcomes him, offers him a cigar, and engages him in conversation. The outcome is that the two monsters become allies. When Pretorius asks if the Monster knows who Henry Frankenstein is, the Monster grimly replies: "He made me from dead. I love dead. Hate living." "You're wise in your generation," returns the unflappable doctor.

To love the dead and hate the living is perhaps understandable in a creature sewn together from bits of corpses. The source of Pretorius's necrophilia—if it can be called that—is much less clear. Even Karl and Rudy, both murderers, show abhorrence for the precincts of the dead; this, the film assumes, is the normal reaction of any living person, no matter how depraved he may otherwise be. But Pretorius feels comfortable among corpses. Worse yet, when his grisly job is done, he proceeds to eat where he just delved into putrid human flesh. (It's a nasty little joke that the entrée, which the Monster crunches into, appears to be roast chicken, bones intact.) Such behavior must constitute a health risk, to say the least, yet of course it's much more chilling than that. It verges on a kind of abomination for which we have no name. Not necrophilia: Pretorius doesn't love the dead or betray any sexual arousal by them. He merely enjoys the peace of their abode and finds their remains congenial. He is horrible because he feels no horror; the dead neither frighten nor disgust him. He commits the unnamed crime of failing to recognize any distinction between the living, the dead, and an intermediate creature like the Monster.

Of course, it would be silly to expect from the characters in *Bride of Frankenstein* anything resembling plausible psychology. They are, as all twelve-year-olds in today's culture know well, generic figures, drawn with strong, simple strokes and intended not to mimic reality but to stimulate certain responses in those who watch their stories. In Pretorius's case, the horror one might be tempted to feel is contained and neutralized by Ernest Thesiger's bravura performance: Comically effete, birdlike, and quite mad, Thesiger's Pretorius behaves in such an outlandish manner that Boris Karloff's Monster looks all the more touchingly human by his side. Pretorius's weirdly funny nonhumanity also allows him to perform actions and express opinions that would otherwise have been unportrayable on the screen, at least in 1935.

The only place where Pretorius feels at home—the only place he can relax and enjoy himself—is this bizarre subterranean hall, where the dead are both populous and readily accessible. *Bride of Frankenstein* flouts history and common sense to put him there, in a scene that looks just as unreal as he does. Few moviegoers, today or in 1935, have ever entered such a chamber; most probably suppose that it is no less fantastic than the "science" Pretorius practices. Yet the vault remains a familiar scene, even to those who know it only from fiction. There is something like it in Bram Stoker's *Dracula* and in most of the novel's film adaptations, from F. W. Murnau's *Nosferatu* (1921) to John Badham's *Dracula* (1979). Edgar Allan

Poe's stories present several of them, including the copper-sheathed former dungeon in "The Fall of the House of Usher" (1839), luridly visualized in Roger Corman's *House of Usher* (1960).

Some features of *Bride of Frankenstein*'s vault—notably the fenced-in area where Madelina Ernestine's coffin rests—suggest that art director Charles D. Hall had some actual places in mind as he supervised the construction of this scene's set. Maybe not, though. He and his designers might have remembered burial vaults only from fiction, and they might have been unable to name any particular story or film in which they'd seen them. Like the film's other sets and all its characters, the vault is generic, an imitation of imitations, whose real original—if there was one—may work all the more powerfully when it has been forgotten. Just as no one has ever met a person who resembles Dr. Pretorius, though any twelve-year-old knows what he's meant to make you feel, so the vault comes to the viewer already invested with an emotional charge that need have nothing to do with real or even possible experience.

Pretorius and the vault have more in common than their generic qualities. They suit each other perfectly, though *Bride of Franken-stein* takes the match for granted and never bothers to explain it. There's no reason to suppose that the makers of the film paused to analyze it either; their culture had bequeathed it to them, and they have passed it on to us, all of a piece. Yet it's far from obvious why ghoulishness and gloomy archways should belong together, or why Pretorius's nonchalance in the company of corpses should chill even murderers' blood. The desire to get frightened by fiction may be an eternal human urge; perhaps our cave-dwelling ances-tors enjoyed a tingling spine as much as we do. But there's nothing eternal about the paraphernalia of scary fiction—the crypts, char-nel houses, ghouls, and monsters that our entertainment media endlessly dish out for us as if we could never get our fill. We have learned to be frightened by these things; they have a history.

THE GRAVE

There was a time when crypts and coffins were believed to have nothing inherently scary about them, when they inspired very dif-ferent, nearly contrary emotions. But around the middle of the eighteenth century, a new attitude began to show itself, one that has helped determine how we now regard the trappings of mortality in both fact and fiction. The change has rendered some eighteenth-century literature virtually incomprehensible. In 1743, for instance, Robert Blair (1699–1746) published a blank-verse poem entitled *The Grave*, which won enduring fame for its stern morality and rigorous religious teaching. The poem's repute among sober-minded Christians (especially Scots) is reflected in James Boswell's praise:

> He [Samuel Johnson] told me that "so long ago as 1748 he had read *'The Grave*, a Poem,'* but did not like it much." I differed from him, for though it is not equal throughout, and is seldom elegantly correct, it abounds in solemn thought, and poetical imagery beyond the common reach. The world has differed from him; for the poem has passed through many editions, and is still much read by people of a serious cast of mind.

In 1791, when Boswell published these remarks in his *Life of Johnson*, some readers, somewhere, must have still been taking *The Grave* as its devout clerical author intended; as late as 1808, there were enough such readers to justify an illustrated edition, with engravings based on drawings by William Blake. But for the heirs of *Bride of Frankenstein*, that intention is almost impossible to follow.

The Grave isn't quite unreadable even now, though it takes stamina. Some of it, especially the first hundred lines or so, elicits an automatic though apparently inappropriate response. Literary scholars may observe that the poem is pseudo-Miltonic, pseudo-Popean, altogether derivative, but even scholars must fight off another reaction when they encounter lines like these:

> The sickly Taper
> By glimmering thro' thy low-brow'd misty Vaults,
> (Furred round with mouldy damps, and ropy Slime,)
> Lets fall a supernumerary Horror,
> And only serves to make thy night more irksome.

Today's readers must blot out the influence of a 250-year-old tradition if they wish to understand Blair as he understood himself and as his first readers took him.

The Grave won't help. In the next lines, Blair addresses the yew tree. Its accoutrements are eerily familiar:

Chearless, unsocial plant! that loves to dwell
'Midst Sculls and Coffins, Epitaphs and Worms:
Where light-heel'd Ghosts, and visionary Shades,
Beneath the wan cold Moon (as Fame reports)
Embody'd, thick, perform their mystick Rounds.

Few twentieth-century visitors to cemeteries, though yews flourish
there, see them amid skulls, coffins, and worms, let alone ghosts.
We know the scene well, however, from fiction. It's as if, despite the
antiquated style, we knew already what *The Grave* is about.

Blair reinforces the feeling:

The Wind is up: Hark! how it howls! methinks
Till now, I never heard a Sound so dreary:
Doors creak, and Windows clap, and Night's foul Bird
Rook'd in the Spire screams loud: The gloomy Isles
Black-plaster'd, and hung round with Shreds of 'Scutcheons
And tatter'd Coats of Arms, send back the Sound
Laden with heavier Airs, from the low Vaults
The Mansion of the Dead. Rous'd from their Slumbers
In grim Array the grizly Spectres rise,
Grin horrible, and obstinately sullen
Pass and repass, hush'd as the Foot of Night.
Again! the Screech-Owl shrieks: Ungracious Sound!
I'll hear no more, it makes one's Blood run chill.

For the two and a half centuries since these lines were written, and
in defiance of Robert Blair, Western blood has run chill at sights
and sounds like these.

If this is our only response to *The Grave*—and it's the only one
that comes easily to a latter-day reader—we're doomed to miss the
entire point of Blair's poem. After its first hundred lines, *The Grave*
turns into a catalogue of proud men, licentious women, and other
stereotypes of worldliness, all of whom get their comeuppance
from death. Near the end, when Blair arrives at the "Good Man," his
real message declares itself:

Thrice welcome *Death!*
That after many a painful bleeding Step
Conducts us to our Home, and lands us safe
On the long-wish'd for Shore. Prodigious change!

> Our Bane turn'd to a Blessing! *Death* disarm'd
> Loses her Fellness quite: All Thanks to him
> Who scourg'd the Venom out.

The Grave seeks to transform death's horrors into the joyous promise of an afterlife; fear is a mere preliminary to joy. If the poem's
original readers took that second step, as most evidently did, they
read *The Grave* on Blair's own terms.

All we know of Blair—and we know little—testifies that he was a
modest, retiring, utterly sincere clerical gentleman; *The Grave* is a
versified sermon, meant to be read for the ancient lesson it conveys. No one but scholars reads *The Grave* today, but it did not sink
into total oblivion as most devotional verse has done. Instead it got
misread, radically revised, and transformed into something both
commonplace and strange. It became a precursor of a modern
industry whose only product is an emotion—fear.

THE GRAVEYARD SCHOOL

The Grave and other poems of its ilk belonged to a transient
fashion that has become known as the Graveyard School. The
label—a nineteenth-century invention—is misleading on several
counts. For one thing, the Graveyard poets, most of whom wrote
during the 1740s and 1750s, didn't consult one another as the
members of a self-conscious school would do. There were back-
and-forth influences, but on the whole each Graveyard poet worked
independently. Only posterity has lumped them together. And
though their works featured graveyards, these were only backdrops; the poets' true purpose transcended tombs and skulls.
Though the horrors they invoked were those of the flesh, they
desired to admonish the spirit.

Graveyard poetry had some Continental precursors, including Andreas Gryphius's grisly *Kirchhofsgedanken* (Churchyard
Thoughts, 1657), but its eighteenth-century flowering seems to
have been an English phenomenon. It inspired a flurry of imitations
in Germany, Italy, America, and elsewhere, becoming a minor
international craze and reinforcing England's reputation as a chilly
place whose melancholy natives are prone to suicide—rather like
Scandinavia's reputation today. The earliest work commonly as-

signed to the school is "A Night-Piece on Death" by Thomas Parnell (1679–1718), which was first published, posthumously, in 1721. Unlike most of his successors, Parnell was not a clergyman; perhaps for that reason, "A Night-Piece" is rather jaunty at times and relatively brief. But it contains all the features that would later identify the school, including the yew tree:

> Now from yon black and fun'ral Yew,
> That bathes the Charnel-House with Dew,
> Methinks I hear a *Voice* begin;
> (Ye Ravens, cease your croaking Din,
> Ye tolling Clocks, no Time resound
> O'er the long Lake and midnight Ground)
> It sends a Peal of hollow Groans,
> Thus speaking from among the Bones.

Death itself delivers the poem's last lines, intending not to frighten but to deliver a consoling message for "pious Souls":

> On Earth, and in the Body plac'd,
> A few, and evil Years they waste:
> But when their Chains are cast aside,
> See the glad Scene unfolding wide,
> Clap the glad Wing, and tow'r away,
> And mingle with the Blaze of Day.

Nothing in "A Night-Piece" (or in Parnell's other poetry) is at all original. Along with most of his English contemporaries, Parnell staggered under the influence of John Milton (1608–1674); the main literary source for "A Night-Piece" is Milton's "Il Penseroso" (1631), which uses the same eight-syllable line and also glories in darkness and silence. Milton, in turn, drew on Robert Burton's *Anatomy of Melancholy* (1621), a compendium of ancient and modern learning on its title subject. Parnell's great near-contemporary Alexander Pope (1688–1744) aimed to evoke a similar gloomy mood in "Eloisa to Abelard" and "Elegy to the Memory of an Unfortunate Lady" (both 1717). Like any cultural phenomenon, the Graveyard School borrowed bits and pieces from the culture of the past, and every bit and piece has a long, branching history of its own.

Funeral elegies, for instance: They were enormously popular throughout the seventeenth century both in England and on the

Continent. The scenes they evoke often strongly anticipate those of Blair and Parnell. Some, in fact, are far more ghastly than anything to be seen in Graveyard poetry—like this 1653 "Elegie" by Christopher Burrell:

> The chambers there with Coffins planched sure
> Corruptions sap will not let long indure;
> These worn and torn, in time renew'd again,
> The cost of future Funerals maintain:
> The lower floor's of earth, most rooms be ful,
> Loe here the dead mens bones, and there a skul.

Later, Burrell tops himself by describing Death as a

> raw bon'd carcass, of his Head the *haire*
> And *flesh* is falne, and left the *skul* all bare;
> His *eyes* no *eyes*, cannot be seen nor see,
> Worm-eaten *nose*, one *jaw*, no *teeth* hath he . . .

According to John W. Draper, pioneering historian of the genre, "a more perfect example of the funeral elegy is hard to find." It reads like a guide for today's special-effects technicians.

As their generic label suggests, however, funeral elegies were composed on the occasion of a particular death. Burrell's appeared in a volume, *Suffolk's Tears*, commemorating the lamented Sir Nathaniel Barnardiston. Copies of such poems were distributed to mourners, and, in the case of illustrious demises, broadsides decorated with grim woodcuts went on sale. This tradition can be traced back even further, in both the verbal and the visual arts, to the famous gruesomenesses of the fourteenth and fifteenth centuries. Burrell's poem is horrific and was no doubt intended to be; like the tradition of funerary art that lies behind it, however, it also provides a fairly realistic description of a contemporary burial site and, personified as Death, a typical resident.

The same is true of the gruesome art of earlier centuries: It is both graphic in its realism and precise in its reference either to a particular death, like Burrell's "Elegie," or to a specific occasion of death, like the plague. A fashion for macabre funerary art swept Europe in the fourteenth century and lingered well into the next. Some scholars attribute this wave of horrific imagery to the successive plagues of 1348, 1363, and 1374, which wiped out perhaps 80 percent of the population in some cities. Millard Meiss, in his classic study of late-medieval art, remarks that the last years of the fourteenth century "were the most gloomy in the history of Florence and Siena, and perhaps of all Europe." He draws special attention to a painting by Giovanni del Biondo, in which "there is a representation entirely unprecedented in Tuscan art: a decayed corpse, consumed by snakes and toads. A bearded old hermit points to it with an admonishing gesture, while a man and his dog recoil in terror."

The admonition was already ancient—and it would continue unaltered through the Graveyard poets and somewhat beyond, till modernity stifled it—but the terror was apparently new (except in the dog's case, which was wishful thinking). Perhaps it reflected the feelings of those who had seen death close up, too frequently, and who knew decay well. If so, it stiffened and stylized the terror, adapting it to the old emblems of death, bringing experience into conformity with tradition. As Johan Huizinga remarked in 1924:

> Ascetic meditation had, in all ages, dwelt on dust and worms. . . . To render the horrible details of decomposition, a realistic force of expression was required, to which painting and sculpture only attained toward 1400. At the same time, the motif spread from ecclesiastical to popular literature. Until far into the sixteenth century, tombs are adorned with hideous images of a naked corpse with clenched hands and rigid feet, gaping mouth and bowels crawling with worms. The imagination of those times relished these horrors, without ever looking one stage further, to see how corruption perishes in its turn, and flowers grow where it lay.

In fact, flowers never grew where most medieval corruption lay, inside the walls and under the floors of churches; it would take centuries before they brightened the typical graveyard. Huizinga succumbed to a modern bias when he chided the medieval imagination on this point.

And, despite what Huizinga says, the Western imagination did move beyond the symptoms of corruption—but not to flowers. Before the middle of the eighteenth century, orthodox Christians believed that on Judgment Day their souls would be reunited with their bodies, all intact, whatever decay might have ravaged those bodies during life or after death. That belief, codified in the eleventh century as the Apostles' Creed but evidently prevalent much earlier, took this form in a 1963 Catholic missal: "I believe in the Holy Ghost, the Holy Catholic Church, the communion of saints, the forgiveness of sins, the resurrection of the body, and life everlasting." Probably no one in 1963 gave bodily resurrection any credence; in earlier ages, expectation of it had led to a paradoxical combination of reverence for the dead and matter-of-factness toward their remains. The corrupting corpse was venerable and disgusting, disposable and eternal, loathsome and wonderful, all at once.

The most significant achievement of Parnell's "Night-Piece"— the reason it both founded a school of poetry and signaled a shift in cultural attitudes—is that Parnell wrote a funeral elegy without a funeral. "A Night-Piece" has no true affinity with ancient cere- monies of mourning, or indeed with grief of any kind. Parnell chose the grave as a scene of instruction and, though he doesn't say so, pleasure. For all his work's resemblances to the elegiac and funerary traditions, he broke new ground by detaching grief from any occasion, turning it into poetry, and selling it for delecta- tion and profit. This was his difference from the past and his likeness to the future. He began a process—which the later Grave- yard poets continued—of turning the trappings of death into ob- jects of aesthetic appreciation. His successors would transform them further, until tombs and skulls lost whatever connection they once had to anybody's real death and became the icons of a new kind of entertainment.

Parnell's "Night-Piece" predated Blair's *Grave* by twenty years, and there is no evidence that the two poems are more than coinci- dentally related. Yet *The Grave* reads like an immensely blown-up version of "A Night-Piece": the same nocturnal churchyard setting, the same gloomy yew, above all the same doleful speaker. There is a significant difference, however, between the two first-person narrators. Parnell's, exasperated with scholarly reading, puts down his books to go "Where Wisdom's surely taught *below*"—that is, down in a graveyard. Blair's narrator has a vaguer motive:

> Whilst some affect the Sun, and some the Shade,
> Some flee the City, some the Hermitage;
> Their Aims as various, as the Roads they take
> In Journeying thro' Life; the Task be mine
> To paint the gloomy Horrors of the *Tomb* . . .

Parnell's narrator at least offers a reason—slight though it is—for his grim wanderings. Blair's offers none. Parnell's narrator seeks out tombs in search of wisdom; Blair's simply *likes* them.

If the works that make up the ramshackle Graveyard School have a single feature in common, it is not so much the charnel-house tableau as this figure of the doleful, graveyard-seeking narrator. Most often, as in *The Grave*, he claims that his arbitrary decision to visit charnels at midnight is quite natural. The most arbitrary case is Beilby Porteus's "Death: A Poetical Essay" (1759). The poem is stilted, verbose, and clumsy throughout its mercifully short extent. But it makes no excuses:

> At this hour,
> This solemn hour, when Silence rules the world,
> And wearied Nature makes a gen'ral pause,
> Wrapt in Night's sable robe, through cloysters drear
> And charnels pale, tenanted by a throng
> Of meagre phantoms shooting cross my path
> With silent glance, I seek the shadowy vale
> Of DEATH.

If Nature is making a general pause (the modern reader might ask), what's this man's problem?

Of course it's an anachronistic question. The bulk of "Death" bears witness to the future bishop's chaste, admonitory intentions. Yet for a twentieth-century reader, the various members of the Graveyard School insistently pose this problem. Bombast aside, it's impossible to read them now without wondering what drove them to praise behavior that the twentieth century inevitably associates with madmen like Dr. Pretorius. How did eighteenth-century piety get split into two modern forms—mental aberration of a particularly repellent kind and a genre of entertainment that pleases millions of presumably sane people all over the world?

If this question pollutes the modern reader's experience of Parnell and Blair, it virtually prevents the reading of another, also clerical member of the school, Edward Young. Young (1683–1765) was a clergyman of an elevated kind—he became chaplain to George II—who did not take religious orders until 1730, when he was forty-seven, the same year of his marriage. Before then, he had been a moderately successful playwright and a friend of the leading literary and scientific authorities of his time. Young's entry into the Graveyard School occurred in 1742, when the deaths of his son-in-law, daughter-in-law, and wife, in quick succession, supposedly inspired his masterpiece, *The Complaint; or, Night-Thoughts on Life, Death, and Immortality.*

Published in nine installments between 1742 and 1745, *Night Thoughts* was by far the longest (nearly ten thousand lines) and the most admired of the poems later pigeonholed as examples of the Graveyard School. It is also, to a modern reader, the most difficult to account for. One can, perhaps, imagine dour Scotsmen savoring the moldy pomposity of Blair or Porteus, but the whole of Western culture seems to have gone mad for Young, and his reputation remained exalted well past the middle of the nineteenth century, when his compeers had been forgotten. Even Samuel Johnson, who dismissed Blair out of hand, had praise for Young: "In his *Night Thoughts*, he has exhibited a very wide display of original poetry, variegated with deep reflections and striking allusions; a wilderness of thought, in which the fertility of fancy scatters flowers of every hue and of every odour." So, at least, Johnson told Boswell, who—as usual when he liked something—waxed furious over *Night Thoughts*, rating it "a mass of the grandest and richest poetry that human genius has ever produced."

"Mass," however, even from the wide-eyed Boswell, conveys less than total praise, and Johnson's "wilderness of thought" comes close to describing a modern reader's impression, should a modern reader venture into the thickets of *Night Thoughts*. It is a vast, rambling, seemingly planless poem that holds together at all only because it obsessively returns to the same ancient, simple lesson taught by the other Graveyard poets: Human life is nasty, brutish, and quite as long as it needs to be; death, its inevitable end, would render life both disgusting and futile if death were not redeemed by the promise of immortality.

Night Thoughts also contains, at least in proportion to its length, far less charnel-house furniture than Parnell, Blair, and Porteus provide. Until rather near the end, in fact, Young largely avoids the horrors of *The Grave* and of "Death"; when he does invoke them, he treats them with scorn:

> The knell, the shroud, the mattock, and the grave;
> The deep, damp vault, the darkness, and the worm;
> These are the bugbears of a winter's eve,
> The terrors of the living, not the dead.

That last line somewhat spoils the point, since no one ever suggested that the dead were frightened by their own props; the flat-footedness is typical of *Night Thoughts*. But, though he disdains the trappings, Young insists upon the Graveyard School's favorite paradox with such fervor that he raises, in the modern reader's mind, even graver suspicions.

Much of *Night Thoughts* is addressed to a vague personage called Lorenzo, a thoroughly worldly, perhaps atheistical pleasure seeker who unaccountably possesses the patience to endure night after night of nonstop haranguing. Again and again, the narrator exhorts him to dwell on thoughts of death:

> Lorenzo! no; the thought of death indulge;
> Give it its wholesome empire! let it reign
> That kind chastiser of thy soul in joy;
> Its reign will spread thy glorious conquests far,
> And still the tumult of thy ruffled breast;
> Auspicious era! golden days begin!
> The thought of death shall, like a god, inspire.

True wisdom, as well as true happiness, lies just where it does for Parnell, Blair, Porteus, and the other graveyard haunters:

> The man how bless'd, who, sick of gaudy scenes
> (Scenes apt to thrust between us and ourselves!)
> Is led by choice to take his fav'rite walk
> Beneath Death's gloomy, silent, cypress shades,
> Unpierc'd by Vanity's fantastic ray;
> To read his monuments, to weigh his dust,
> Visit his vaults, and dwell among the tombs!

Night Thoughts merges the two-step reading aimed at by Blair and Porteus into a nonstop upsurge, embracing death's horror and pooh-poohing it in a single gesture. Mid-eighteenth-century readers seem to have excelled at this maneuver, and for more than a century after *Night Thoughts* was published, Young's eminence held firm. Yet it crumbled: A century later still, most libraries don't possess a copy of *Night Thoughts*, and the poem looks both verbose and trivial.

Changes in taste are impossible to explain, but in Young's case there was a definite turning point: George Eliot demolished him, in an 1857 essay that testifies to both his extraordinary reputation at that late date and the developing modern taste that would soon sink him. "Worldliness and Other-Worldliness: The Poet Young," published in the impeccably intellectual *Westminster Review*, oozes scorn from first word to last. Its irony is so merciless, in fact, that a reader ignorant of Young (virtually any twentieth-century reader) can't help wishing to defend the squirming victim. According to Eliot, Young was "a sort of cross between a sycophant and a psalmist":

> He is equally impressed with the momentousness of death and of burial fees; he languishes at once for immortal life and for "livings"; he has a fervid attachment to patrons in general, but on the whole prefers the Almighty. . . . If it were not for the prospect of immortality, he considers, it would be wise and agreeable to be indecent, or to murder one's father; and, heaven apart, it would be extremely irrational in any man not to be a knave. Man, he thinks, is a compound of the angel and the brute: the brute is to be . . . frightened into moderation by the contemplation of death-beds and skulls; the angel is to be developed by vituperating this world and exalting the next; and by this double process you get the Christian.

Eliot's chief complaint—with which it's hard to disagree—is that Young was radically insincere: He "is never bent on saying what he feels or what he sees, but on producing a certain effect on his audience; hence he may float away into utter inanity without meeting any criterion to arrest him."

There can be little doubt, especially if you take Young's long, well-padded life into account, that *Night Thoughts* expresses next to nothing about the poet's true feelings. Personal grief may have occasioned the poem, but grief is barely discernible in these ten thousand lines of unmitigated rant. There are no characters to speak of in the poem and scarcely the hint of a setting; Young provides nothing but endless exhortations to poor Lorenzo—and the poor reader—that he must feel, feel, feel, always at fever pitch and never with a shred of good reason.

So it struck George Eliot in 1857, and she turned against Young with violence. For her, however, this meant the rejection of her own earlier judgment: "The sweet garden-breath of early enjoyment lingers about many a page of the 'Night Thoughts,' " she confessed, "giving an extrinsic charm to passages of stilted rhetoric and false sentiment." To demolish Young was also to dispose of the young woman who called herself Mary Ann Evans and who endured too many inconvenient surges of the heart. For the twentieth-century reader, who probably escaped youthful attachment to the poem, only mold clings to *Night Thoughts*. The poem is certainly insincere; it's difficult to conceive how such a gigantic gush of bombast could express any heartfelt emotion. But we'd be unwise to attack it on that account. After all, no one supposes that the writers of "General Hospital" or *A Nightmare on Elm Street 4* express through those fictions the yearnings of their souls. Most of what's called mass or popular culture consists of entertainments designed to make their audiences feel certain clearly defined emotions; in popular culture, as in Young, sincerity is irrelevant.

In fact, a handy way of distinguishing mass culture from elite culture, for the last 150 years or so, might be simply this: Elite culture expresses, mass culture manipulates—or tries to. Elite opinion still follows George Eliot (who followed the Romantics) in judging that manipulative art hardly deserves to be called art. At its best, manipulation produces kitsch or stuff of anthropological interest; at its worst, it spawns the pornography of sex or violence. This distinction, this ranking, was not available to the first readers of *Night Thoughts* and the other poems of the Graveyard School. For those readers, these poems lost no artistic value because they tried to instill strong feelings that their authors might never have felt. Boswell's swoony response to Blair and Young was probably typical: He loved how they made him feel, for the feeling's sake, regardless of the reality of the poets' lives or his own.

By 1857, when George Eliot assaulted Young, Boswell's adult pleasure had become child's play—or the delight of the ignorant masses, whom elite commentators, like Dr. Livingstone among the savages, continue to regard as overage children. The transformation is fascinating, and we'll see it again. Elite (or at least respectable) entertainment of certain kinds gets degraded, first to mass level, then to that of children, and at last it disappears into the archives, eventually to be retrieved by scholars, who make it a professional matter.

The process is especially beguiling—and clear-cut—in the case of the Graveyard poets, because they became the rude forefathers of today's horror movies by taking an old popular tradition and making it elite, with the result that it turned popular again in a very different way. They came at the end of one tradition and the beginning of a new one. Like the funeral elegies of the seventeenth century, the macabre funerary art of the fifteenth and sixteenth centuries, and the elegiac tradition that dates from the beginnings of Western culture, their poems invoked the horrors of the tomb as a chastening reminder to heedless living souls. But starting already in Parnell and reaching a crazy extreme in Young, they separated horror (along with any other emotion) from its home, offered it to the reader's whim, and turned it into entertainment.

Not only that, of course, but the Graveyard poets' style, as Samuel Johnson saw, is feeble, and readers who want Miltonics are better off going to Milton. The Graveyard poets were inferior by any standard—so inferior that just one work of the school has entered the modern literary canon. Thomas Gray's "Elegy Written in a Country Churchyard" (1751) is the only such poem routinely included in twentieth-century anthologies and therefore the only sign to most modern readers that the Graveyard School ever existed. Gray's modern critics are understandably reluctant to include his famous "Elegy" in that tacky company, but it belongs there.

The opening stanza unmistakably recalls Parnell and Blair, along with a hint of Young:

> The curfew tolls the knell of parting day,
> The lowing herd winds slowly o'er the lea,
> The ploughman homeward plods his weary way,
> And leaves the world to darkness and to me.

This is the voice of the same arbitrary tomb seeker who speaks in the rest of the Graveyard poems, and other familiar accoutrements soon join him. There is a gloomy owl in "yonder ivy-mantled tower," and

Beneath those rugged elms, that yew-tree's shade,
Where heaves the turf in many a mouldering heap,
Each in his narrow cell for ever laid,
The rude forefathers of the hamlet sleep.

If the "Elegy" is properly called a Graveyard poem, as I think it is, why should it be the only one that lives?

For one thing, Gray turns memorable phrases that have been quoted and requoted for more than two centuries, until they have become clichés. The poem's survival, however, is also due to an accidental fact: Modern readers can recognize Gray's churchyard and stand a good chance of ending up in one like it. The place is a little strange—the turf in modern graveyards doesn't heave, and no moldering is visible—but we can recognize the image of corpses laid forever in narrow, private spaces. Despite the frequent appearance of the phrase in reviews of modern horror films and fiction, I doubt that many late-twentieth-century people know what a "charnel house" is—or was. And can anyone imagine today how eighteenth-century people felt when they came across a moldy skull lodged in the dirt or a human thighbone sticking up from freshly turned earth?

The gloomy precincts imagined in the other Graveyard poems look alien, bizarre, and lurid. Indeed, they look made up, like *Bride of Frankenstein*'s improbable crypt. But they were not. Clunkily as Parnell, Blair, Young, and Porteus phrased their descriptions of misty vaults and ropy slime, they didn't fantasize such things. They had seen them, and the experience wasn't exceptional. Today, you can visit such places in only two ways: on excursions to the few sites that have preserved (in a highly sanitized condition) the remnants of obsolete burial customs, or else when you enter the deliberately disturbing landscape of scary entertainment.

Most Graveyard poetry was so bad, even by the standards of its time, that the future would have junked it anyway. But it also came at a point of transition from an ancient attitude toward death to a new one. The new attitude found death frightening, but that wasn't and isn't the worst. The worst is just what the Graveyard poets and their precursors held up as death's negation: the hope or belief that the dead will rise, bodies and all, on the Day of Judgment. Trust in that rising gave way, within two generations of the Graveyard poets, to a fear that has not abated: that the dead will rise and in fact do rise, all the time, the moment you turn your back on them.

We no longer bury our dead as they were buried in the middle of the eighteenth century. We no longer conceive of death as people did then, and we carry about with us—even if we never call it to consciousness—a very different notion of what our bodies do after they die. Dimly, fearfully, we're aware that our bodies lose form, disintegrate, stink. In the past, people knew these things well, because they lived among the dead, in fact as well as in thought, day by day. For us, the moment of death has become grossly immediate: John F. Kennedy was assassinated while cameras rolled, Lee Harvey Oswald took a mortal wound as we watched, the maimed and dying in every hometown, ghetto, and Third World famine are taped for us, heroes and villains both fictional and real fall before our eyes, continually. The moment of death doesn't chill us, but its aftermath does—and all because, even as we revel in death, we have recoiled from the idea of being dead.

INTO THE CRYPT

I don't mean to downgrade the Graveyard poets by suggesting that their work was merely a premonition of changes in the way dead bodies were put into the ground. But I do think their sudden, brief flowering signified more than a wavelet in the history of poetry. They sentimentalized churchyards at the very moment when churchyards, as they had been known since the Middle Ages, were disappearing. Some hints of the coming transformation can be found in James Hervey's *Meditations among the Tombs*, first published in 1745. This essay, framed in approved eighteenth-century style as "a letter to a lady," went through at least twenty-five editions by 1791 and was published in French as late as 1827; even in 1938, Montague Summers remarked that it was "yet regarded with affection by certain old-fashioned people."

Very old-fashioned people, no doubt. Hervey's style is lively and curdles into few of the ponderous periods that have made much eighteenth-century prose unbearable to later readers. Yet *Meditations* offers the same pairing of ghastliness and deep feeling that marks the other entries in the Graveyard School, and it does so with a circumstantial chattiness that makes it far more revealing of the reality to which, in spite of themselves, the Graveyard poets referred. Hervey (1714–1758) was also a clergyman, which lends some excuse to the *Meditations*. As he tells the lady, he had recently found himself with time to spare in a Cornish village, so he visited the local church. He came to "an ancient pile; reared by hands, that, ages ago, were mouldered into dust; situate in the centre of a large *burial ground.*" Entering in, he felt a "sort of *religious dread*" that "stole insensibly on my mind, while I advanced, all pensive and thoughtful, along the inmost aisle." What then caught his eye and instantly gets moralized presents a curiosity to most modern readers:

> The next thing which engaged my attention, was the *lettered floor.* The pavement, somewhat like *Ezekiel's* roll, was written over from one end to the other. . . . They seemed to court my observation; silently inviting me to read them. And what would these dumb monitors inform me of? "That, beneath their little circumferences, were deposited such and such pieces of clay, which once *lived*, and *moved*, and *talked*, that they had received a charge to preserve their names and were the remaining trustees of their memory."

Modern-day tourists in European cathedrals may tread floors like that, and they may emit something like Hervey's sigh: "Ah! said I, is such my situation? The adorable Creator around me, and the bones of my fellow-creatures under me!"

But the adorable Creator is less likely to occupy a modern visitor's mind than is the unnerving nearness of those bones. Hervey makes the scene yet stranger when he checks the parish record book: "I found the memorials of a *promiscuous* multitude. They were huddled, at least they rested together, without any regard to rank or seniority." Hervey goes on at great length about "these confused relics of humanity," moralizing to the top of his bent on how earthly distinctions are leveled by death: "Perhaps their crumbling bones *mix*, as they *moulder*: and those who, while they lived, stood aloof in irreconcilable variance, here fall into mutual embraces, and even incorporate with each other in the grave." The sentiments are admirable; the scene, however, gives pause. Modern bones do not mix, and the very idea of skeletons embracing underground is simply horrific. Yet Hervey contemplates the spectacle and finds it cheering.

The tour continues:

> Yonder entrance leads, I suppose, to the *vault*. Let me turn aside, and take one view of the habitation, and its tenants. The sullen *door* grates upon its hinges; not used to receive many visitants, it admits me with reluctance and murmurs. What meaneth this *sudden trepidation*, while I descend the steps, and am visiting the pale nations of the dead? . . .
>
> Good heavens! what a solemn scene! How dismal the *gloom*! Here is perpetual darkness and night even at noon-day. How doleful the *solitude*! Not one trace of cheerful society; but sorrow and terror seem to have made this their dreadful abode. Hark! how the hollow dome resounds at every tread. The *echoes*, that have long slept, are awakened; and lament; and sigh along the walls.
>
> A beam or two finds its way through the grates, and reflects a feeble glimmer from the nails of the *coffins*. So many of those sad spectacles, half concealed in shades, half seen dimly by the baleful twilight, add a deeper horror to these gloomy mansions.

In both scenery and sentiments, Hervey is a typical Graveyard poet, though without the poetry. He had read Parnell, Blair, and Young (he praises them in footnotes), and he portrays himself as their kind of meditative man, touring the realms of the dead in search of uplift. But because he takes the trouble to describe those realms in detail, we can see in the *Meditations* just how different that scenery was from anything we know in today's reality, how exactly it resembles what for us has become a fantasy landscape.

Unlike the country folk in Gray's "Elegy," Hervey's dead are buried inside the church, and their memorials do not indicate the exact spot where their remains can be found. Indoor burial such as Hervey describes was regarded, until the middle of the eighteenth century and even later in some regions of Europe, as a privilege of rank or wealth—because it was burial *ad sanctos*, "among the saints." Second best was burial in the churchyard, the area that surrounded and adjoined the church, and the closer the better. "Churchyard" is an ancient English word, dating from the twelfth century at least; it corresponds more or less to the German *Kirchhof* and the French *aître*, which means "atrium," the church's court. "Graveyard" entered the English language much later, not till the 1820s in England, though as early as the 1770s in America.

The Graveyard poets should be known as the Churchyard poets, because the scene of their transports looks nothing like what we now call a graveyard, much less a modern cemetery. In modern usage, "graveyard" and "cemetery" mean spaces reserved for the permanent interment of the dead. Such spaces may feature special chapels, but the dead do not huddle in and around modern parish churches as they did for most of Western Christian history. Cemeteries are set both apart and aside: They are located as far as conveniently possible from city centers—though in many cases, like Père-Lachaise in Paris (founded in 1804) and Mount Auburn in Cambridge, Massachusetts (1831), cities have spread out to engulf them. And in the cemeteries of the nineteenth and twentieth centuries, tombstones mark the exact spots where the dead they name are lying—in perpetuity, as the contractual phrase runs.

In *The Hour of Our Death*, his monumental history of Western attitudes toward the one thing we know for certain, Philippe Ariès describes a profound change that began at the very end of the seventeenth century, accelerated in the eighteenth, and has determined even our deepest feelings today. Before the change, in the millennium and more governed by what Ariès calls "tame death," Western people regarded death with fear, even dread, but they did not deny its inevitability. Nor did they shy away from its physical effects. They could hardly hope to do so, given the primitive sanitary arrangements of those ages. Yet Ariès suggests that modern sanitation, on which we pride ourselves so highly, was developed not on rational grounds but because, at some point and for undiscoverable reasons, Western people began to fear death and the dead in a new way.

Ariès accumulates a vast heap of evidence to show with what astonishing casualness Western Europeans used to handle the remains of their dead. He focuses on the Parisian cemetery Les Saints-Innocents, which was established in the Middle Ages and closed only in 1780; it was a very large cemetery adjacent to a very small church, and it had an international reputation, but in many ways it was typical. For one thing, corpses did not linger in the ground of Les Innocents: Its fame—and its nickname, "flesh-eater"—derived from the supposedly miraculous qualities of its soil, which was said to reduce a body to bare bones within twenty-four hours. When the process was completed, and sometimes before, the remains were disinterred to make room for fresh corpses, and the bones were put on display in the *charniers* (charnels), covered galleries that surrounded the churchyard and made popular places for strolling.

Properly speaking, a charnel or charnel house was neither a secret nor a haunted place but a public one. Disjointed skeletons lay piled up there for passersby—devout or not—to admire. Before the eighteenth century, the wee hours would have been an unlikely occasion for such visits; noonday was the proper time, when many other diversions were also available:

> In the seventeenth and eighteenth centuries, les Innocents was a kind of commercial arcade. Idlers strolled there just as they did in the arcades of the Palais-Royal, where there were also booksellers and people selling notions and linens. Both the town hall and the church, being public places, attracted shops and customers. Two out of the four charnels were named after the kinds of business that were done there.

To show that at least some seventeenth-century visitors recognized the incongruity, Ariès quotes a censorious comment of 1657: "In the midst of all this confusion, a funeral was going on. The gravediggers proceeded to open a grave and take out bodies that had not yet decomposed, although even in the heart of winter the soil of the cemetery gave off noisome odors."

Evidently, the carnivorous soil of Les Innocents didn't always meet expectations; but gravediggers went on acting as if it had, and few of the living complained. Real or imagined, its flesh-eating properties were highly prized both in France and abroad, and the churchyard became an early tourist attraction. The contrast with modern practices could hardly be sharper: Since the nineteenth century, we have regarded cemeteries, whatever else they might be, as both discrete and permanent. Not only do the dead not mingle, they also remain in place forever, or at least indefinitely. We have seen Hervey praise their mingling; perhaps even more surprising to a modern observer is how highly Western people used to value graves that held their inmates for the shortest possible time.

Shakespeare's *Hamlet* has been acted in front of modern audiences so often that nothing in it can surprise us anymore. Yet the famous "graveyard scene," Act V, Scene 1, ought to look stranger than it does. It's set, first of all, in a churchyard, not a graveyard, and the term "gravedigger" (though it had been used before 1603) does not appear. The gravediggers are "clowns"—rustic people, but these two are not far from bozos in the modern sense. They've been assigned to dig a grave for the recently self-slaughtered Ophelia, and at first one of them shows some reluctance to give a suicide "Christian burial." He quickly gives in to the other clown, however, and soon he's singing while he works, tossing up both earth and skulls. Hamlet strolls by and has, of course, a comment:

> That skull had a tongue in it, and could sing once: how the knave jowls it to the ground, as if it were Cain's jaw-bone, that did the first murder! It might be the pate of a politician, which this ass now o'er-reaches; one that would circumvent God, might it not?

Hamlet goes on at some length in this vein, as the clowns dig and more bones come into view—this skull might have belonged to a fine lady ("my Lady Worm"), that one to a lawyer—until the First Clown identifies the skull of Yorick, Hamlet's father's jester.

Now the prince turns fully serious. He picks up Yorick's skull (which has been in the ground twenty-three years) and delivers his well-known address to it:

> Where be your gibes now? your gambols? your songs? your flashes of merriment, that were wont to set the table on a roar? Not one now, to mock your own grinning? quite chap-fallen? Now get you to my lady's chamber, and tell her, let her paint an inch thick, to this favour she must come; let her laugh at that.

Take away the mordancy, the wit, and the brilliant language, and you're left with the very lesson the Graveyard poets would preach nearly 150 years later. But though there are shivers to be had from *Hamlet*—the opening scene, with the ghost of the murdered king appearing on the battlements of Elsinore, is good for more than a few—Shakespeare aimed at no such effect when he set a scene in a graveyard and furnished it with moldy skulls. He might have been beyond such cheap tricks, but in any case, his audience would not have responded in the modern way if he had tried to play them. Grim humor, somber moralizing, and an odd mixture of careless-ness and reverence—these marked the premodern attitude toward such places, and the "graveyard scene" displays them all.

That attitude prevailed well into the era of the Graveyard poets, though it was fading by then and would vanish in fifty years or so. But it is prominent in one episode of Henry Fielding's *Tom Jones* (1749). Tom's first love, Molly Seagrim the poacher's daughter, is visibly pregnant by him; unashamed, however, she ventures to church one Sunday, decked out in a fine dress and laced cap, parading her immorality before the outraged eyes of the other local women. Squire Allworthy, Tom's guardian, manages to keep them in order during the service, but when they get outside, a battle breaks loose. At first, Molly cows her foes:

> The whole Army of the Enemy (though near a hundred in Number) . . . gave back many Paces, and retired behind a new-dug Grave; for the Church-yard was the Field of Battle, where there was to be a Funeral that very Evening. *Molly* pursued her Victory, and catching up a Skull which lay on the Side of the Grave, discharged it with such Fury, that having hit a Taylor on the Head, the two Skulls sent equally forth a hollow Sound at their Meeting, and the Taylor took presently measure of his Length on the Ground, where the Skulls lay side by side, and it was doubtful which was the more valuable of the two. *Molly* then taking a Thighbone in her Hand, fell in among the flying Ranks . . .

For a modern reader, the scene is much more amusing in Tony Richardson's 1963 film version of the novel; Fielding's mock-heroic diction was of limited appeal in his own day, and very few will find it funny now.

The point of the rather labored joke, however, is the ludicrous discrepancy between the loftiness of Fielding's language, with its imitations of Homer and Virgil, and the sordid brawl it describes. For both Fielding and his characters, there is nothing chilling about this churchyard; they treat the relics of the dead just as cavalierly as Shakespeare's clowns did. This, too, is a country churchyard, the very kind of place where, only two years later, Gray would indulge his sweetly melancholy fancies. Evidently, not all such places preserved the departed with the hygienic discretion imagined by Gray. Fielding's scene looks positively outlandish, or at least archaic, next to Gray's, both in its incidental details and in Fielding's tongue-in-cheek tone. Modern cemeteries are not maintained in the manner Fielding takes for normal, and modern taste finds it ghoulish even to touch an unearthed skull, let alone fling one.

In many ways, Fielding was old-fashioned for 1749. His down-to-earth wit and pragmatic morality made him appear coarse to those with delicate sensibilities; in the even more delicate Victorian age, *Tom Jones* would be regarded (with some perplexity, because it was also a classic) as a dirty book. The future, strangely enough, would lie with the Graveyard poets, although their works would be forgotten while *Tom Jones* continues to be read. They, at least, were halfway modern—though only halfway—in attributing an unearthly, unnerving aura to the memorials of death and decay. The rough-and-ready attitude that Fielding shared with Shakespeare (and with most of premodern culture) would seem shocking to them, as it does, however faintly, to us.

OUT OF THE CRYPT

By the middle of the eighteenth century, according to Ariès, new ailments were stalking those who came into even remote contact with the relics of the dead. These diseases, which were often fatal, had not been known before. He quotes a document of 1775:

> On April 20, 1773, in Saulieu, in the nave of the Saint-Saturnin church, a grave was being dug for a woman who had died of a putrid fever. . . . The gravediggers uncovered a coffin containing a body that had been buried the previous March 3. As they were lowering the body of the woman into the grave, the coffin opened, the body was uncovered, and there immediately issued from the grave an odor so foul that everyone present was forced to leave. Out of 120 young people of both sexes who were being prepared for their First Communion 114 fell dangerously ill, as did the priest, the gravediggers, and more than 70 other persons, of whom 18 died, including the priest and the vicar, who were the first to be carried away.

This is one case among very many: At about the same time all over Western Europe, the dead were suddenly threatening to kill off the living.

Thirty years earlier, Hervey had appended a footnote on this point to his *Meditations among the Tombs*:

> Some, I know, are offended at our burying corpses within the church; and exclaim against it, as a very great *impropriety* and *indecency*. But this, I imagine, proceeds from an excessive and mistaken delicacy. If proper care be taken to insure from injury the *foundations* of the *building*, and to prevent the exhalation of any *noxious effluvia* from the putrefying flesh, I cannot discover any inconvenience attending this practice.

Perhaps there was none, but the future belonged to mistaken delicacy. Along with the other Graveyarders, Hervey in fact egged on this growing finicky squeamishness. Like them, he entered the time-honored precincts of the dead veiled in a swoony new sensibility that might preach the ancient lessons but also indulged a pleasure that would be the future's sole inheritance.

Such evidence goes to show that, starting at about the middle of the eighteenth century and continuing till our own time, Western people reimagined their relationship with the dead. The ramifications are countless; what interests me, though, is the particular offshoot that leads from the Graveyard poets to today's manufacturers of scary entertainment. I find it intriguing that certain scenes and images have persisted in fiction for more than two hundred years, virtually unchanged, as their reality meanwhile vanished.

The moldering tombs and dank crypts sketched in Graveyard poems have been laid out for us uncountable times in every medium we possess, and each new medium we invent takes them over wholesale. Yet these things have no immediate meaning for us. We do not recognize them as the setting of our future, nor do we connect them with the memory of anyone we've loved. In this, we are the heirs of those squeamish eighteenth-century people who sickened at the sights and smells of old graveyards and who demanded that the noxious dead be moved away from the homes of the living into those tidy zones we know as cemeteries. It has frequently been observed—usually with outrage—that twentieth-century people, Americans in particular, have denied death so fully that we have made it obscene. We no longer die, as people did during the centuries ruled by Ariès's "tame death," in our own beds, surrounded by relatives and friends awaiting our last words. Now we pass away in antiseptic hospital rooms, attended by efficient strangers, or else our lives end suddenly—a fate abhorred by earlier ages but, on the whole, tolerated by ours.

The ghostly double of denial, however, is a weird insistence on remembering death—not in its present form, but the way it looked more than two hundred years ago, at just the time when death started to turn strange and the dead became dangerous. The survival of the premodern landscape of death into late-twentieth-century popular entertainment is an astonishing instance of cultural conservatism. We seem compelled to remind ourselves, over and over, of what in fact we never experienced: the comfortable familiarity with the symptoms of bodily corruption that was apparently felt throughout the West from the Middle Ages to the dawn of the modern age. The scenery of skulls, slime, and putrescence that recurs everywhere in contemporary horror fiction was once a district of everybody's real world; we now know it only from stories, but we probably can list its features as readily as any premodern citizen could.

Of course, we don't immediately feel comfort when we see such scenes, and we certainly don't regard them with the callousness of Shakespeare's gravediggers or Fielding's country women. Instead, we feel a curious thrill, half mental, half physical—a mixture of fascination and revulsion that ranges from the obsessiveness of horror mavens to the equally emphatic recoil of those who wouldn't look at *Night of the Living Dead* if their lives depended on it. The landscape persists, but our responses to it have utterly changed—a bizarre development. It was just starting to happen in the middle of the eighteenth century, which is why I've begun the story of scary entertainment with the Graveyard poets, those uncanny ancestors.

They straddled a gap that was opening as they wrote and that has widened since then to a chasm, into which they fell. The gap came between the two halves of their message: The effects of death are horrific, *but* immortality redeems them. We have forgotten the second half but preserved the first; indeed, we've turned the consolation of immortality into another source of horror. For us, the notion that death is not the end, that the dead live among us in anything but a sentimental sense, is terrifying. If the dead sprout choir robes and white wings, as they do in *New Yorker* cartoons, all is well. But what if their bodies *really* come back?

Our culture's loss of trust in redemption has turned a premodern faith into a nagging modern fear—which helps to explain why the scenes and situations conjured up by the Graveyard poets recur in virtually every work of modern fright, from *Bride of Frankenstein* to all the *Draculas* to Stephen King. "Sometimes dead is better," read the poster for the 1989 film of King's novel *Pet Sematary* (1983): The slogan captured the essence of what the Graveyard poets' message has become in our time. Oddly, at least in its wording, the message is the same; the Graveyard poets, along with the whole prior tradition of funerary art, would only have omitted the "sometimes." For orthodox Christians from the earliest ages to the middle of the eighteenth century, dead was *always* better—provided you had led a blameless life and could rest in peace, awaiting reunion with your flesh on Judgment Day.

Hardly anyone holds that old trust now: If we believe in heaven, we probably expect our souls to be transported there at the moment of death, and we'd prefer that our bodies keep no rendezvous with them. If we deny the afterlife, we get what solace we can from the prospect of oblivion. Yet we're unable, apparently, to give up the confused, illogical, frightening idea of a self-contradictory condition called living death. Vampires, werewolves, zombies, ghouls, men put together from fragments of corpses—in these and innumerable other forms (all of which are better off dead), the twisted memory of lost faith haunts us still.

That doesn't explain, however, why we amuse ourselves with the memory, why we delight in calling it up again and again in the same old guise, like children demanding a favorite story verbatim for the thousandth time. Pundits of all stripes have answered this question in books and articles beyond count. Generally, they apply psychoanalysis, or depth psychology of some sort, to show that horror stories aren't really about animated corpses in cold pursuit of the living; they're about social or sexual anxiety, the pangs of maturation, nostalgia for the womb, fear of incest, anything except what they *say* they're about. The usual assumption among those who analyze such things is that horror stories are fantasy, and fantasy must be a vehicle for some message about reality that, thanks to cultural or personal censorship, can't be conveyed in its literal form.

History tells a different tale. The fear that was new in the middle of the eighteenth century, and that the Graveyard poets began to exploit, was unrealistic perhaps, but it was no fantasy. It certainly wasn't a vehicle: When the Graveyard poets sought to chill their readers' blood with visions of rot, it was rot that chilled, plain and simple. Down in the vault, in 1746, James Hervey treated himself to this bit of speculation:

> Should one of these ghastly figures burst from his confinement, and start up in frightful deformity before me—should the *haggard skeleton* lift a clattering hand, and point it full in my view—should it open the stiffened jaws, and with a hoarse tremendous murmur break this profound silence—should it accost *me* . . .

The imaginary skeleton speaks up in a paraphrase of the Old Testament, with words the prophet Samuel attributes to God: " *'Yet a little while, and* thou *shalt be with me,'*—the *solemn warning*," adds Hervey, "delivered in so striking a manner, must strongly impress my imagination." In the genre that was born from Hervey and his fellows, the real message remains just that.

As usual, though, history tells a tangled tale, and a great deal more had to happen before the legacy of the Graveyard poets turned into *The Evil Dead.* For one thing, along with its estrangement from the old way of death, Western culture grew away from its past altogether, then turned back on it and made it romantic. Alongside the Graveyard poets came a fad for what was called "the Gothic," in poetry, novels, plays, architecture, and interior decor, even in clothing. The entire past became vividly gloomy and compelling. Living people learned to cherish the artifacts of the dead with something like the feeling that now urges us to collect detritus from the fifties and sixties. Feeling became valuable in its own right, and fiction was always eager to profit from feeling. And, eventually, the market for fiction boomed beyond reason or control. Its business was to serve the dire ancestor of what we now call the mass public, scary entertainment's inexhaustible patron.

For adherents of Sensibility, reading could be a stressful business. Engraving by Moreau le Jeune from a French edition of *The Sorrows of Young Werther*. (BETTMANN ARCHIVES)

2

feelings for Sale

THE PLEASURES OF MELANCHOLY

The poets who made up the Graveyard School did most of their characteristic work in the 1740s and 1750s. For some, like Blair and Porteus, it was their only literary activity. Others, like Gray, saw poetry in general as their province; graveyards occupied just one corner of it. Imitators, ranging from merely bad to beyond description, went on mining the vein for decades, evidently failing to notice that it had long since been exhausted.

Like the greeting-card rhymesters of a later century, these late-comers showed no fear of banality. Here, for example, is an excerpt from an "Ode to Melancholy" by Elizabeth Carter (1717–1806), published in 1766:

> Thro' yon dark Grove of mournful Yews
> With solitary Steps I muse,
> By thy Direction led:
> Here, cold to Pleasure's tempting Forms,
> Consociate with my Sister-worms,
> And mingle with the Dead.

And in 1779, Philip Freneau (1752–1832) introduced American readers to *The House of Night* in what should have been a highly familiar fashion:

> Let others draw from smiling skies their theme,
> And tell of climes that boast unfading light,
> I draw a darker scene, replete with gloom,
> I sing the horrors of the *House of Night.*

By and large, however, the trademark motifs of Graveyard poetry—owls, yew trees, skulls, and the like—soon ceased to identify a particular school and became absorbed into the larger vocabulary of Romanticism. They joined such diverse images as crumbling ruins, dim glades, and misty mountain vistas in the cultivation of what the eighteenth century called "melancholy"—a complex state of feeling that even those who sought it out seem hardly to have understood.

Traditionally, melancholy had been defined as a spiritual condition governed by black bile, one of the four humors of premodern medicine. A person might be melancholy by temperament—ruled by that humor and under the special sway of the planet Saturn—but melancholy could also be a temporary state that one might fall into or deliberately seek out. Milton's "Il Penseroso," the fountainhead of Graveyard poetry, is an extended address to this feeling, personified as a goddess; the poem is paired with "L'Allegro," a similar address to Mirth. Taken together, "L'Allegro" and "Il Penseroso" portray the internal drama of a poet endeavoring to choose between mutually exclusive (but equally available) casts of mind. Critics have disagreed for centuries as to Milton's favorite, but, in the judgment of literary posterity, melancholy won hands down.

The primary attributes of Miltonic melancholy are a fondness for silence and dim light, a tendency to drift into introspection, and a rather plaintive yearning for escape from the raucous annoyances of everyday life. The pensive narrators of the Graveyard School and their imitators display the full ensemble; they descend directly from the speaker in "Il Penseroso." From the middle of the eighteenth century onward, however, melancholy underwent some strange

transformations. Not the least was the attachment of this pleasur-
able state of mind to places like graveyards, which ought, by
modern standards, to kill any kind of pleasure. Even stranger was
the way a style of architecture came to be synonymous with a
feeling.

As early as 1726, John Dyer had found the graveyard mood in a
different though equally emotive scene. His poem "Grongar Hill"—
couched in Milton's inevitable tetrameter couplets—spends most
of its time praising the conventional beauties of rural landscape.
Amid the vales and grottoes, however, some unusual features appear: "Old castles on the cliffs arise, / Proudly tow'ring in the
skies!" Upon closer examination, they turn out to be less proud
than creepy; in fact, they look like high-rise graveyards:

> 'Tis now the raven's bleak abode;
> 'Tis now th' apartment of the toad;
> And there the fox securely feeds;
> And there the pois'nous adder breeds,
> Concealed in ruins, moss and weeds;
> While, ever and anon, there falls
> Huge heaps of hoary mouldered walls.

Dyer draws the appropriate moral:

> Yet time has seen, that lifts the low,
> And level lays the lofty brow,
> Has seen this broken pile complete,
> Big with the vanity of state;
> But transient is the smile of fate!

Later in the century, scenes like this would become ubiquitous in
fiction and the visual arts. Like graveyards, they would lose their
overt moral dimension but hold on to the power of arousing melancholy feelings—a power they haven't lost yet.

Late in the twentieth century, we don't customarily think of
architecture in emotive terms. A building may be impressive or
oppressive, gloomy or grand, but on the whole we don't expect
architecture to make us feel anything in particular. The most

interesting of our oldest buildings were long ago rescued from decay and now have been either gutted or restored; in both cases, we see them only under shadowless modern light. We feel something quite different, however, when we come upon a building, especially a house, that somehow has escaped the renovators' sight.

Even an abandoned factory will inspire this modern form of melancholy, but an abandoned home is best. Automatically, it brings thoughts of the people who set their lives there, who pasted up the wallpaper that now peels off in strips, who lived and loved and so on. The litany is familiar. It also slips easily into horror, as innumerable films and books illustrate. We take these melancholy feelings, and their slippage, for granted. But this association of ideas—old houses and fear—is by no means self-evident. When we automatically feel it, we're responding to a lesson our culture learned in the mid-eighteenth century and has been mulling over ever since.

STRAWBERRY HILL

In 1747, Horace Walpole took up residence in a small house called Strawberry Hill, near what was then the distant London suburb of Twickenham. Strawberries did not abound in the vicinity, there was no hill to speak of, and the house was ordinary. But it occupied a lovely site on a bend in the Thames that gave river views from three sides of the property. And the neighborhood, though nouveau riche, was almost fashionable: Expensive villas lined the Twickenham riverbank, and Alexander Pope had lived not far away between 1718 and his death in 1744.

Walpole was thirty-one years old when he bought Strawberry Hill. The third surviving son of Sir Robert Walpole (1676–1745), who became Lord Orford in 1742 (after the deaths of a brother and a nephew, Horace inherited the title in 1791), he possessed none of his father's political ambition and little of his personal power. With a comfortable income, unmarried, Horace devoted himself to the cultivation of friendship. For more than sixty years, he knew everybody who was anybody, in Britain and on the Continent; his published *Correspondence* fills forty-two thick volumes. Yet, like any single, leisured person, he had an intolerable deal of empty time, which he attempted to fill with omnivorous reading, the collection of antiquities, and above all the transformation of Strawberry Hill.

Already by September 1749, he was calling it "Strawberry Castle" and proposing to beg the Duke of Bedford for some neglected stained glass from the duke's ancestral home. By January of the following year, he had begun the project of making "a little Gothic castle" out of the place; work went on till Walpole's death, at age eighty, in 1797. The modest house grew into a mansion of thirty rooms, and the original five acres swelled to nearly forty-seven. For decades it was a tourist attraction. Walpole made his house and grounds freely available to visitors; admission tickets were required, but he gave them away with baronial largess. In 1774, he published *A Description of the Villa of Horace Walpole*, which became, considering its high price and specialized appeal, a bestseller. Strawberry Hill was the remote precursor of the English ancestral homes that now teem with tourists, whose ducal tenants cheerfully plug soft drinks. But Strawberry Hill was fake; everyone knew it, no one better than its owner.

Because Walpole's vision far outstripped his means, stone-colored wallpaper stood in for rugged granite blocks, and painted paper mimicked intricately carved fretwork. Though the artisans Walpole employed copied their originals with great accuracy, there was never any doubt that the results were copies. And though by modern standards the rooms were spacious, they looked cramped next to the cavernous galleries of Walpole's imagination. He was fond of proclaiming the tininess of the place, contrasting it with its imaginary models. "I give myself the airs," he wrote to Henry Seymour Conway in 1755, "in my nutshell, of an old baron." A baron who sits in a nutshell, yet whose airs are as noble as if he owned a real castle: This was Walpole's pose at Strawberry Hill.

Walpole was also an inveterate collector of anything that smacked of antiquity. His letters are crammed with gleeful descriptions of an amazing variety of old *things*. A sixteenth-century suit of armor, a thirteenth-century shrine, "ancient" three-cornered chairs bought up cheap from unsuspecting cottagers—it seems hardly to have mattered what, so long as it wore the delicious patina of age, and so long as those who sold it failed to appreciate the value it had for Horace Walpole.

No criterion beyond oldness governed his collection, though he exhibited a fondness for the funereal, and especially the Catholic. His garden gate, for instance, was copied from that of a thirteenth-century bishop's tomb, and Sir Horace Mann wrote him in 1779 that Lord and Lady Lucan had picked out "a pretty little sarcophagus at Rome . . . with the bones of a child in it. What a treasure for your chapel!" Walpole may never have received this macabre item—it did not appear in the catalogue of the Great Sale of 1842, which auctioned the furnishings of Strawberry Hill—but Mann and the Lucans knew Walpole's taste. As well they might: By 1779, he had been assiduously advertising it for thirty years.

Though Walpole liked to extol the "conventual gloom" of "this *old, old, very old castle*"—he even coined a word, "gloomth," to capture it—there was nothing dismal about Strawberry Hill. On the contrary, its interplay of light and shadow, especially the vivid glow of its painted glass, provided a festive, even jovial air. Walpole didn't intend to frighten either himself or his visitors; tomb gate and tiny skeleton notwithstanding, the horrors of the grave were not on his agenda. He did, however, rejoice when an owl—that favorite bird of his contemporaries, the Graveyard poets—took up residence in his pseudo-medieval Round Tower. And his devotion to things that time had darkened called up inevitable ideas of mortality.

Ideas only, however. Walpole's friend Hannah More neatly phrased the visitor's response to Strawberry Hill in a letter of 1789: Its "Gothic towers and air of elder time," she wrote, "so agreeably keep up the idea of haunted walks and popish spirits." If the place inspired gooseflesh, it was of a distanced, aestheticized order. Treading Strawberry's walks, visitors were moved to contemplate the feelings of those who, in "elder time," might really have believed such spots to be haunted. Strawberry Hill was designed to let them (and Walpole) playact what they would never genuinely feel but desired to imitate: a kind of fear that was outmoded, extinct in their ordinary lives, and as More said, "popish."

The Catholic side of Walpole's artifice was pure titillation: He loved to tease his Protestant correspondents with Strawberry Hill's resemblance to a convent or an abbey, on occasion signing his letters "The Abbot of Strawberry." But for him, Catholicism was merely a tempting mask; though he reached for it frequently, he never put it on. Having installed a "chapel" at Strawberry Hill, he raved to George Montagu about how the sun shone in, through its imitation stained-glass windows, "in all the glory of popery." This "cabinet" was intended to have "all the air of a Catholic chapel—bar consecration!" All the trappings, that is, without their proper meaning or function.

Walpole's pseudo-Catholicism reflected a persistent Anglican fascination with the church from which his nation had split for the rather uninspiring reason that Henry VIII wanted an English divorce. Though there were plenty of living Catholics in Walpole's England, Catholic accoutrements summoned up for him the long-lost days before the 1530s, when Henry gutted the monasteries. Gothicism and Catholicism made a natural pair, because most of the surviving Gothic structures in England had been built in the service of pre-Anglican Christianity, and because decor and religion alike exuded an air of slightly spooky mystery.

For Walpole, everything was decor, even a chapel. Strawberry Hill counts among the first instances in Western history of a man setting up "taste" as the defining trait of his character: In a strangely literal sense, Walpole *was* Strawberry Hill, and vice versa. And that taste was fully self-conscious, even archly so. Walpole dressed himself up and acted himself out in a remarkably modern-seeming way: Although he devoted most of his money and time to improvements at Strawberry Hill, he kept winking at his friends as if to let on that he knew how frivolous the whole thing was, how utterly artificial and uncalled for. Walpole's stance came close to the twentieth-century idea of "camp": a pose that constantly admits to being just a pose but takes itself quite seriously nevertheless.

There was also something outrageous about the taste Walpole chose to make his own. For a century and more before the transformation of Strawberry Hill, Gothic architecture—not to mention the habits of thought associated with it—had been disdained by most cultivated people. They found it crude by comparison with both the Classical style and the Renaissance neo-Classicism that went to ancient Greece and Rome for its models. Walpole was not the first to proclaim the merits of Gothic, nor did he singlehandedly engineer a change in these older, deeply entrenched attitudes. But thanks to his high social position and impeccable connections— also, no doubt, to the sheer gusto with which he publicized his preferences—he lent respectability to a style that had been curious at best, vulgar at worst. Very seldom does an individual achieve such pervasive, long-lasting influence: To a remarkable degree, Walpole can be held responsible for a shift in Western feeling that altered everything from the design of public buildings to the way we fall in love—and scare ourselves.

THE GOTHIC SURPRISE

Properly speaking, "Gothic" refers to a group of Germanic tribes that from the early third century onward encroached upon the northeastern borders of the Roman Empire. In the famous year 410, one of these tribes, the Visigoths, having already devastated Greece, sacked the city of Rome. The Visigoths later migrated into what would become France and Spain, where they converted en masse to Christianity in 589.

That is not, however, what seventeenth- and eighteenth-century people meant by "Gothic." Modern historians often get exasperated with their ancestors on this account: Thanks to an old mistake, "Gothic" now also refers to an architectural style prevalent throughout Europe from the twelfth through the fifteenth centuries. Walpole and his contemporaries, however, regarded as "Gothic" whatever was very old and neither Classical nor neo-Classical. In this idea, they were guided by feeling, not fact. They called "Gothic" anything that gave them a delicious, melancholy little chill.

It's far from clear how an architectural style that produced such masterpieces as the cathedrals of Rheims, Chartres, and Westminster Abbey got saddled with the name of a people chiefly famous for rape and pillage. The main culprit, however, seems to have been Giorgio Vasari, whose *Lives of the Painters*, first published in 1550, is still widely read today. In his introduction, Vasari both stereotypes the style and names it:

> In their buildings, which are so numerous that they have contaminated the whole world, doorways are ornamented with columns

which are slender and twisted like a screw and which cannot have the strength to sustain a weight, however light it may be. And so on all the façades and wherever else there is decoration, they built an abomination of little niches one above the other, with so many pinnacles and points and leaves that they do not look as if they would be able to keep themselves from toppling over. . . . This manner was invented by the Goths, for after they had destroyed the ancient buildings and killed the architects in the wars, those who were left constructed the buildings in this style. They fashioned the vaults with pointed arches of quarter circles, and filled all Italy with these abominable structures, so in order not to have any more of them their style has been totally abandoned. May God protect every country from such ideas and style of buildings!

Vasari did not invent these notions, but he definitively popularized them; they would be repeated endlessly for the next two hundred years, and they formed an important element of the educated opinion Walpole flouted when he gothicized Strawberry Hill.

Twentieth-century visitors to Gothic cathedrals find it almost impossible to imagine that these magnificent buildings could ever have been regarded as barbaric and loathsome. They are so rich, so awe-inspiring, so obviously the products of profound art and consummate craft, that we'd rather side with Walpole, for all his precious airs, than with idiots who griped about such grandeur. Our awe tends to ignore the presence of human remains—dried out by now, but not always so innocuous—beneath the floor and within the walls that enclose us. We're also likely to forget that the awe we feel when sunlight streams through the rose windows of Notre-Dame de Paris, no matter how sincere the feeling is, remains the child of its time.

That time carries the legacy of nearly two hundred years during which Gothic architecture has been venerated far more fiercely than it was despised in the centuries before. We also bear the burden of imitation Gothic, the preferred style for public and many private buildings, and for all churches, in most Western countries from the turn of the nineteenth century till the First World War. The fashion lasted beyond that date on American college campuses, which underwent a construction boom in the 1920s and 1930s that spawned hundreds of pseudo-Gothic courts and quadrangles, all vaguely inspired by the genuine articles at Oxford and Cambridge.

We are both more and less familiar with Gothic architecture than eighteenth-century people were: We know better how to read its language and to appreciate its excellence, but for us it is merely one style among many, huddled together in the urban landscape with a hodgepodge of other styles from baroque to postmodern. Gothic spires, arches, and crenelations have lost the meaning they had for Walpole's time. Then, you might have hated Gothic or adored it, but you couldn't have regarded it as just an option. It came freighted with associations about which you had to feel strongly, because they applied directly to the stature of your own culture and therefore to your stature as a civilized, Western human being.

Though by making Gothic respectable Walpole had a profound effect on fashions in architecture and decor, his most significant achievement was to transform Gothic—and implicitly any mode of design—into what we now call "style." True, he identified himself thoroughly with his minuscule baronial role, but he did so with a giddy air of arbitrariness and in defiance of disapproval. The implication was that he might just as well have gone Chinese as Gothic (there was a fad for chinoiserie at around the same time, especially in gardens, and Walpole dabbled in it, too), that he was neither the slave of his culture's prejudices nor answerable to its dictates. At least in matters of taste, he was an individual, free to choose the style he liked simply because he liked it.

He did not, however, disagree in any important way with those prejudices. Like Oscar Wilde 150 years later, Walpole embraced received wisdom, then reversed its values, turning bad into good. Received wisdom circa 1750 had all been prefigured in Vasari: Gothic architecture was cluttered with ornaments, busy, pointy, and incoherent; in contrast with the stark planes of Classical temples, Gothic buildings gave the eye no place to rest and deceived it with flimsy-looking supports for enormous weights of stone and glass. The anti-Gothic consensus condemned Gothic style for deception and, oddly, a kind of decadence—as if this ancient, aboriginal style had been aged and worn-out at birth.

In 1770, twenty-one-year-old Johann Wolfgang von Goethe arrived in Strasbourg burdened with ideas that by then had long been common currency. As he confessed in his landmark essay "On German Architecture" (1772): "Under the rubric *gothic*, like some entry in a dictionary, I had heaped every synonymous misconception that had ever come into my head concerning what was indefinite, disordered, unnatural, thrown together, patched up, and overloaded." One look at the city's unfinished fourteenth-century cathedral, however, changed all that in an instant:

> With what an unexpected feeling the sight of it surprised me as I came before it! A single grand impression filled my soul—an impression that, because it consisted of a thousand harmonizing particulars, I could certainly taste and enjoy but in no way identify or explain. They say the joys of heaven are like this . . .

Goethe never gushed so about Gothic again, but "On German Architecture" became a hugely influential document in Germany and elsewhere. It helped to launch a long-lasting architectural revival that led to such nineteenth-century achievements as the rebuilding of London's Palace of Westminster (1837–1860) and the completion of Cologne Cathedral (1823–1880), along with such later monuments as New York City's Woolworth Building (1913), the world's first and only Gothic skyscraper.

Many disparate elements fueled the young Goethe's temporary rapture and the enduring movement that followed it: fervent patriotism (hence his insistence that the style of Strasbourg Cathedral was "German" rather than Gothic), the discovery of unity where disorder had seemed to reign, and especially the perception of the designer's spirit suffusing his creation. These themes recurred constantly in the German Romanticism of the late eighteenth century and, with variations, in the parallel revolutions that swept the rest of Europe.

For the history of scary fiction, however, the most significant aspect of "On German Architecture" is not merely that it records a new response to the relics of the once-despised past. Having been surprised by joy, Goethe says, he neither let the feeling pass nor retired to contemplate it. Instead, he returned to the cathedral again and again, glutting himself on his first impression and deepening it:

How often I went back to gaze upon its nobility and glory from
every side, at every distance, in every light of day! . . . How often
the shadows of evening, with their congenial calm, came to soothe
eyes grown dull from searching and gazing! When the innumerable
parts melted into single masses and only they, whole and grand,
stood before my soul and wondrously enfolded my heart, I enjoyed
and knew them at the same time! Then, in gentle intimations, the
genius of the great master revealed itself to me.

Indeed, the very voice of Erwin, the cathedral's designer, "mur-
mured" to the astonished young man, delivering a comprehensive
lesson in the appreciation of Gothic architecture.

Despite its intense seriousness, Goethe's encounter with
Strasbourg Cathedral resembles the sort of effect Walpole produced at Strawberry Hill. In both, the combination of mellow
shadows with the mysterious glory of the past brought on a feeling
of solemnity and amazement in the modern spectator. The chief
difference would seem to be that Goethe's experience was real,
while the thrills of Walpole and his friends had been staged with
self-conscious artifice. Yet by milking his first impression for all
the awe it was worth, deliberately reliving the moment—and
moving it to twilight, when only large, vague shapes could be
seen—Goethe staged his feelings, too. And, unlike Walpole, he
actually got the past to speak.

This affecting scene—a modern visitor struck dumb by the shadowy grandeur of the Middle Ages—is commonplace in the literature and art of the mid-eighteenth century. We have seen a version
of it in the effusions of the Graveyard poets, whose religious intentions did not prevent them from fostering the feelings their scenery
inspired. Those feelings gave a new meaning to the old term "melancholy": They arose from a new sense, pervasive among the
cultivated classes of the age, that the medieval past was both
stranger and more familiar than it had been taken to be, that it
spoke to the present in a voice that was chilling, enthralling, and
delightful, all at once. The realization came as a surprise to those
who, like the young Goethe, felt it for the first time. But surprise was
immediately transformed into a scenario—a predictable, clearly
defined state of emotion that could be reentered whenever one

chose and quite satisfyingly faked, as Walpole did. Gothic melancholy became a feeling to be dabbled in at will, the tastiest dish on the cultural buffet.

FAKING THE PAST

Walpole was not the world's first collector of miscellaneous antiquities, but he led the way both in popularizing the pastime and in suffusing it with new emotional fervor. Since the Renaissance, the relics of Classical civilization had been preserved with care and vastly imitated; even the despised Middle Ages had not been totally neglected. But by and large, the aim of preservation had been to learn from ancient wisdom, and imitation had been a reverent undertaking, not a posture. When the past had no obvious lesson to teach, it could always be moralized, as Dyer and the Graveyard poets did with their crumbling castles and crypts. But Walpole did not build Strawberry Hill in order to advance the world's knowledge of the Middle Ages, and it's doubtful that his guests learned anything in particular from their visits there. They all sought a far different benefit from old things: strong feeling.

Antiquarian scholarship blossomed in the mid-eighteenth century, taking on the rudiments of the specialized, technical forms that characterize it today. But the enthusiasm for ancient relics did not let itself be restricted to what was certified as genuine; it didn't even stop short at reasonable facsimiles like Strawberry Hill. There was, perhaps, not enough of the real thing to go around—or else the real thing failed to satisfy the enthusiasts' expectations of what the romantic past should have been. Whatever the reason, the shortage was evidently most severe in the literary realm. Alongside such real retrievals as Thomas Percy's *Reliques of Ancient English Poetry* (1765) came a remarkable flurry of forgeries, on an unprecedented scale that has never since been rivaled. In at least two cases, forgery had greater cultural impact than any genuine article could have produced.

The best-remembered eighteenth-century literary forger is Thomas Chatterton (1752–1770), whose fame derives mostly from his suicide at the age of seventeen. He became an icon for Romantics all over Europe (none of whom had met him), the archetype of genius snuffed out by a vulgar world. The most famous tribute is William Wordsworth's in his poem "Resolution and Independence" (1807):

> I thought of Chatterton, the marvellous Boy,
> The sleepless Soul that perished in his pride;
> Of Him who walked in glory and in joy
> Following his plough, along the mountain-side:
> By our own spirits we are deified:
> We Poets in our youth begin in gladness;
> But thereof come in the end despondency and madness.

The most interesting thing about Chatterton isn't his early death. It's the way he found to express his premature, undeniable genius.

Nobody would have looked seriously at the poetical flights of a teenager, but there was a market for quaint old poems. And Chatterton himself was deeply imbued with the new romantic feeling for the past. He therefore invented a fifteenth-century "secular priest" named Thomas Rowley and wrote Rowley's poetry for him. Chatterton's father, who died before the boy was born, had been sexton of St. Mary Redcliffe in Bristol, where a quantity of useless parchments was stored; Mrs. Chatterton had been tearing them into strips to hold skeins of thread. Her enterprising son rescued some pieces, made them look still older by rubbing them with dirt, and inscribed on them his own versions of ancient English poetry.

Supposedly, he performed his first such feat in 1764, at the astonishing age of eleven. He succeeded in convincing his schoolmaster, Thomas Phillips, and a few other Bristol worthies that his finds were authentic. He had less luck, however, with Horace Walpole, to whom he wrote in 1769, vainly seeking patronage. Walpole had recently suffered some embarrassment thanks to his support of another, much more artful forger of antiquities; he was not about to be burned a second time. The following spring, undaunted so far, Chatterton set out for London with genuinely ancient visions of fame and fortune. He acquired some hack writing assignments and published one of the Rowley poems in a magazine, but no quick recognition came to him. Evidently crushed by the failure of his dream, he swallowed arsenic; his body was found, in his garret room, on the morning of August 25, 1770.

The myth of Chatterton has had a much longer life than his work, but the work has merits, if only for what it reveals about the fads and fetishes of its age. "Elinoure and Juga," the one Rowley poem published in Chatterton's lifetime, purports to be a dialogue between two "pynynge Maydens" imagining the death of their lovers in the Wars of the Roses (1455–1485). Elinoure proposes the diversion, but Juga speedily gets into the spirit of it:

> Systers in sorrowe, on thys daise-ey'd banke,
> Where melancholych broods, we will lamente;
> Be wette wythe mornynge dewe and evene danke;
> Lyche levynde okes in eche the odher bente,
> Or lyche forlettenn halles of merriemente,
> Whose gastlie mitches holde the traine of fryghte,
> Where lethale ravens bark, and owlets wake the nyghte.

At the end, they find that their imaginary bereavement is all too real. They take immediate action: "Distraughte theie wandered to swollen Rubornes syde, / Yelled theyre leathalle knelle, sonk ynn the waves, and dyde."

Chatterton's artificial superannuation of his language consisted mostly of changing *i*'s to *y*'s and tacking on *e*'s, but he also threw in some real archaisms with which even an eighteenth-century reader would have had trouble. The 1777 edition of his poems provides a great number of footnotes, informing us for instance that *levynde* means "blasted" and *mitches* are "ruins." No contemporary reader, however, would have misunderstood the poem's melancholy. Elinoure and Juga's parting gesture would perhaps be indecorous for an eighteenth-century maiden, but the rest of their antics come strictly from Chatterton's own time; a fifteenth-century person would have been mystified by them. These supposedly ancient maidens are next of kin to Walpole, setting a stage for their feelings and acting on it. And Juga's imagery of forsaken halls, ghastly ruins, and funereal birds isn't very different from the phony-melancholy scenery of Strawberry Hill.

Chatterton attracted few contemporary converts to belief in Thomas Rowley. As usual, Samuel Johnson delivered the wisest verdict. In 1776, he and Boswell went to Bristol to investigate Rowley's reality; they were met by a couple of local zealots, one of whom conducted them up a long flight of stairs into the tower of St. Mary Redcliffe, where they could see the very chest from which Rowley's manuscripts had supposedly been exhumed. Johnson remained good-natured and unconvinced. His judgment was: "This is the most extraordinary young man that has encountered my knowledge. It is wonderful how the whelp has written such things."

Chatterton was a marvelous boy indeed; no inventory of circumstances can account for his precocity. But his brief career suggests how deeply into Western culture's imagination the romantic melancholy of the past had sunk, so deeply that in the 1760s a teenager could know it well enough to manufacture it on his own. He had been preceded in the past-faking game by an older and more successful player, to whom appreciation (and even a share of belief) clung for more than a century. In 1760, James Macpherson, a twenty-four-year-old Scotsman, burst upon the antiquarian scene with *Fragments of Ancient Poetry, Collected in the Highlands of Scotland, and Translated from the Galic or Erse Language*, supposedly containing the outpourings of Ossian, a Scottish (or pre-Scottish) bard, and dating from the dim days of pre-Christian Britain. Bards were extremely popular at the time, though (perhaps because) next to nothing was actually known about them. The Ossianic *Fragments* caused a sensation, particularly among patriotic Scots eager to establish the roots of their own national literature.

An epic would have been especially welcome; Greece, Rome, and even England had them, but so far the Scottish national epic existed only in rumor and desire. A group of enthusiastic Scots, including Boswell, therefore financed Macpherson's return visit to the Highlands, tracking down the rumors. Much to their gratification, the wished-for article soon appeared (in translation): *Fingal, An Ancient Epic Poem, in Six Books* (1762). To their surprise, another one, *Temora*, showed up (in translation) the following year. Whoever Ossian was, he certainly had kept busy: Almost overnight, Scotland had picked up an entire ancient literature—though only Macpherson had seen the original manuscripts.

Ossian had his detractors from the start, but it was not until 1775 that he received a decisive blow. It was delivered by the redoubtable Dr. Johnson, whose *Journey to the Western Islands of Scot-*

land recorded how he and Boswell had done their own research on Ossian's home ground, discovering no evidence that the mysterious manuscripts had ever existed or indeed could exist. Johnson had always disbelieved Macpherson's stories; typically, his reasoning was a model of common sense in action. As he wrote to Boswell, "A nation that cannot write, or a language that was never written, has no manuscripts."

Common sense, however, was not the long suit of most of Ossian's admirers; Macpherson himself seems to have possessed hardly a shred of it. When the *Journey to the Western Islands* was published, he wrote Johnson—the foremost literary authority of the day—a vituperative letter threatening violence. Macpherson's letter is lost, but Johnson had his reply published in newspapers:

> What would you have me retract? I thought your book an imposture; I think it an imposture still. For this opinion I have given my reasons to the publick, which I here dare you to refute. Your rage I defy. Your abilities, since your Homer, are not so formidable; and what I hear of your morals, inclines me to pay regard not to what you shall say, but to what you shall prove.

As for Macpherson's morals, it was about him that, twelve years earlier, Johnson had made the soon-to-be-proverbial remark, "Sir, when he leaves our houses, let us count our spoons."

Johnson armed himself with an oak stick, Macpherson failed to make good on his threat, and the Ossian affair should have sunk into oblivion. It did not. In the teeth of common sense—and despite the continuing nonappearance of the manuscripts—Western Europe went on swooning over the imaginary bard. In 1805, nine years after Macpherson's death, a thickly footnoted edition of *The Poems of Ossian* established that they did contain translations of some "Galic" fragments, though none were nearly as old as Ossian was supposed to be. These fragments lay scattered among fraudulent passages that closely imitated every English poet since Shakespeare, including Macpherson himself. Until then apparently no one, not even Johnson, had caught the echoes. Gray's "Elegy" had been a favorite source, but when Macpherson sent Gray copies of Ossian's "ancient" writings, Gray took them for genuine.

Ossian is virtually unreadable now. If you translate Chatterton's Rowley out of his crazy spelling, you discover some verses with real style and power, but Ossian (who came forth in modern English) is sludge. The predominant mood, however, remains the dolorous melancholy with which the mid-eighteenth century loved to regale itself. This time, the setting is as long ago and far away as it ever got, and the turgidity outdoes even Young's *Night Thoughts*, but the emotional landscape must have seemed familiar. All the evidence shows how appealing it was.

Among the most popular Ossianic outpourings were the "Songs of Selma" in *Fragments of Ancient Poetry*. As far as I can tell, these songs make no sense, common or otherwise. But they certainly are relentless in their apparent expression of feeling and real demand for response. At one point in Macpherson's prose "translation," Colma mourns:

> It is night; I am alone, forlorn on the hill of storms. The wind is heard in the mountain. The torrent pours down the rock. No hut receives me from the rain; forlorn on the hill of winds!
>
> Rise, moon! from behind thy clouds. Stars of the night arise. Lead me, some light, to the place where my love rests from the chace alone! his bow near him, unstrung; his dogs panting around him. But here I must sit alone, by the rock of the mossy stream. The stream and the wind roar aloud. I hear not the voice of my love! Why delays my Salgar, why the chief of the hill, his promise? Here is the rock, and here the tree! here is the roaring stream!

And so on. The ancient past was never like this, anywhere; the eighteenth century acted like this only in print and dreams.

Yet that style was powerful and pervasive; we follow it now, in what seems an utterly different place. We go to a horror movie, or pick up a Stephen King novel, with the intention of putting ourselves through a course of strong emotion that would be horrifying if it were real. Artificial horror might heighten our real feelings; it might counteract them. In either case, we know how to *use* the horror this kind of artifice inspires. Western culture taught itself this odd skill in the middle of the eighteenth century, and the phony poems of Ossian were among its principal vehicles for the lesson.

The correct eighteenth-century way of reading Ossian was not

Dr. Johnson's. We get our best glimpse of the correct or at least socially approved way in the most influential tearjerker of the time, perhaps of all time, Goethe's *Die Leiden des jungen Werther* (The Sorrows of Young Werther), published in 1774. This lachrymose short novel, told largely in letters from Werther to his limitlessly patient friend Wilhelm, founded the young Goethe's reputation, as a mere essay on Gothic architecture could never have done. Principally on its basis, he became the foremost representative of the movement of young German writers and artists called Sturm und Drang (storm and stress); the book also had an immense vogue all over Europe. Werther's yellow waistcoat became de rigueur among rebellious, would-be-poetical young men; and though I've never seen any specific evidence, the legend persists that great numbers of them went beyond haberdashery in their imitation of Goethe's tortured hero. Supposedly they committed suicide, as Werther does at the end of his sad tale.

Young Werther is indeed a stormy, stressful novel, though most of the commotion gets stirred up by Werther himself, in his hopeless passion for Charlotte. She is betrothed, then married, to the rather stodgy Albert, but these inconvenient facts do not prevent Werther from haunting the couple's home, sighing, weeping, and generally acting doomed. His letters to Wilhelm are full of picturesque images portraying his own misery: "All, all is over! Not a hint of that old world, not a pulse-beat of what I used to feel! I am like a ghost who returns to the burnt-out, ruined castle he built when he was a prosperous prince." But the peak (or nadir) comes when Charlotte unwisely invites him to read aloud from his own translation of Ossian.

"He smiled and fetched the songs. A shudder passed through him as he took them in his hands, and his eyes were full of tears as he looked at them. He sat down and read." Several pages of the "Songs of Selma," translated into German, follow, until both Werther and Charlotte lose control.

A stream of tears that burst from Lotte's eyes and relieved her oppressed heart cut short Werther's song. He threw the paper aside, grasped her hand, and cried the bitterest tears. Lotte leaned on her other hand and hid her eyes in a handkerchief. The agitation of both was fearful. They felt their own misery in the fate of those noble men and women; they felt it together, and their tears united them.

Recovering some composure—and evidently believing that things can get no worse—Charlotte begs Werther to go on reading. He does, but Ossian's next bit is a warrior's promise of suicide. Things get worse:

> The full force of these words overcame the unhappy man. He threw himself down before Charlotte in the most complete despair, grasped her hands, pressed them into his eyes, against his forehead; a premonition of his dreadful design seemed to fly through her soul. Her senses grew confused; she pressed his hands, pressed them against her breast; she bent toward him with a woeful motion, and their glowing cheeks touched. The world disappeared. He threw his arms around her, drew her to his breast, and covered her trembling, stammering lips with furious kisses.

Charlotte escapes, and Werther goes home to prepare for death. In the meantime, however, the reader has had an intensive lesson in the proper way to read Macpherson's clever forgeries.

SINCERE ACTING

The nineteenth and twentieth centuries have stereotyped the eighteenth as a coldly rational era marked by deism, mechanism, and rigid formality in all things. Its epitome was Louis XVI's court at Versailles, where the empty, intricate rituals of everyday life aped the mathematical precision of the gardens among which they were carried on. Supposedly, the veneer of enlightened sophistication that characterized the time served merely to gloss over a horrible real world of filth, misery, and brutal injustice toward the poor. The French Revolution stripped off the gloss in a wash of blood, and the Romantic revolution brought Western culture face to face with the irrational depths of human nature that the prior age had attempted to deny.

In defiance of generations of scholarship, this stereotype remains pervasive; you can find it everywhere, from Charles Dickens's novel *A Tale of Two Cities* (1859) through Stanley Kubrick's film *Barry Lyndon* (1975) and beyond. Like most historical myths, it contains a core of truth: Many eighteenth-century cultural authorities did pride themselves on their triumphant rationality, particularly in contrast to the benighted fumbling of earlier ages. And that pride was in large measure a sham, as any such self-congratulation must be, including our own.

But the myth of the rational eighteenth century neglects an important strain in Enlightenment culture that continues to affect us two hundred years later. The gruesome solemnities of the Graveyard poets, Walpole's campy posturing, Goethe's epiphany at Strasbourg, and the rage for an artificial past all reflect what Martin Price has called "the curious self-awareness of the age." Price is chiefly concerned with poets, but his description of the poet as "both actor and audience" applies just as well to those who only read Ossian, or who visited Gothic cathedrals:

> He may, as he tests and studies his feelings, become histrionic—watching with detachment the passions he has worked up in himself. As he celebrates the powers of mind in their superiority to outward and corporeal forms, he may become visionary. As he exercises the creative and evocative power of emotion, he may call into being those personified presences that only passion can animate. Or, as he exemplifies the philosophic eye, he may become at once minutely particular and rapturously transcendent, moving between close attention to the object and a sense of its part in the cosmic order.

Eighteenth-century people who could afford the luxury loved to test and study feelings, gauging their intensity and valuing them on that scale alone, regardless of whether the feelings in question were happy or sad, pleasant or unpleasant. Any emotion, if it was strong enough, could generate pleasure in what Price calls "the theater of mind." It didn't matter whether the circumstances were real, faked, or fictional—a cathedral, an ersatz abbey, or a book. Indeed, fakeness helped, and any real onset of strong feeling fell prey to dramatization intended to make it stronger still.

Two hundred years later, the rhetoric seems merely bombastic, and when we read about eighteenth-century people swooning and weeping, we're likely to suppose that their emotions were as phony as their words. George Eliot felt the same skepticism more than a hundred years ago, when she damned Young for insincerity. Yet Eliot came to realize that there was a third state of feeling, neither genuine nor fake. She called it "sincere acting," and she embodied it in the imposing Princess Halm-Eberstein of *Daniel Deronda* (1876):

> this woman's nature was one in which all feeling—and all the more when it was tragic as well as real—immediately became matter of conscious representation: experience immediately passed into drama, and she acted her own emotions. . . . It would not be true to say that she felt less because of this double consciousness: she felt—that is, her mind went through—all the more, but with a difference: each nucleus of pain or pleasure had a deep atmosphere of the excitement or spiritual intoxication which at once exalts and deadens.

Eliot's pre-Freudian psychology is remarkably acute: She pinpoints the elation that boosts any feeling when it becomes self-conscious, along with the deadness that repetition of such states may eventually bring. She wasn't, apparently, thinking of Young or Goethe when she described the princess, and of course the twentieth-century burgeoning of artificial fear lay in the future. But both eras share a possibly addictive fondness for such paradoxical states of emotion; it makes a strong bond between them, despite all differences in style.

Just as much as it was the Age of Reason, the eighteenth century was Western culture's foremost age of sentiment; fierce rationalism and lachrymose sentimentality went to equal, absurd extremes, sometimes in the same individual. Tears flowed freely from the eyes of both sexes; they served as the infallible sign that feeling had exceeded the power of words to express it and had sought release in an inarticulate but even more eloquent form. For both men and women, stammering, falling silent, slumping over, and fainting outright formed a spectrum of authenticity: The more sensitive you were, the more likely you were to pass out, and you were a better person according to the degree of your sensitive insensibility.

This, at least, is the conclusion one would draw from much

eighteenth-century fiction, in which weeping and slumping occur with a frequency that later generations have found either ludicrous or repellent. Letters and memoirs of the time suggest that real eighteenth-century people possessed somewhat greater staying power than their imaginary counterparts. Yet their fiction persistently offered them images of how they might be at their best, if they should be able to reach it. That best was almost always grounded in a remarkable willingness to overreact. At the same time, because fiction was only images, it required in anyone who modeled himself on it a deliberateness that rendered his reactions immediately insincere, at least from a point of view like George Eliot's. Something similar happens when a twentieth-century moviegoer attends a horror film in order to feel fright: The emotions may be different, and self-improvement is apparently not at issue, but the deliberation, and perhaps the insincerity, are the same.

DEAR SENSIBILITY!

Eighteenth-century fiction, from Samuel Richardson's *Clarissa* (1747–1748) through the Gothic novel that boomed and went bust around the century's end, encouraged a kind of response from its reader that had been rare in prior ages and would gradually disappear from elite entertainment as the nineteenth century progressed. Traces remained in the maudlin stretches of Thackeray and especially Dickens, but by and large the upper stratum of Victorian fiction avoided the blatant appeals to the reader's feelings that offended Eliot in *Night Thoughts* and that marked both Ossian and the early Goethe. Blatancy flourished in such popular entertainments as melodramas and penny dreadfuls, and it enjoyed a powerful resurgence in the new art of film, which ranked even lower than its older rivals. During the latter half of the eighteenth century, however, for the first and only time, the elite of Western society indulged themselves in fictions that promoted immediate, extravagant, and above all irrational responses to virtually any scene or event fiction might portray.

Virtually any—though in real life joy can be as ravishing as sorrow, sorrow won out in fiction. "Sentimental" novels (as they were called, with no pejorative connotations) occasionally sought to milk tears from their characters' happiness, but on the whole they preferred misery, especially when it was suffered in picturesque surroundings. *Werther* was probably the most influential example, but in England, a weepy peak had already been reached with Laurence Sterne's *A Sentimental Journey through France and Italy* (1768) and Henry Mackenzie's *The Man of Feeling* (1771), two very different novels that nevertheless convey similar lessons on how the possessor of a sensitive soul ought to conduct himself.

Sterne (1713–1768) is best known for *The Life and Opinions of Tristram Shandy, Gentleman*, published in nine volumes between 1760 and 1767. *Tristram Shandy* is usually called, for want of a better term, a novel; in fact, it contains snatches of every genre, all stood upside down and made incomparable fun of. *A Sentimental Journey*, which forms a sort of appendix to *Tristram Shandy*, is a much shorter, more unified work—if anything Sterne wrote can be said to display such a dull virtue as unity. It follows the adventures of Parson Yorick, a close friend of the Shandy family, on part of his Continental tour. Except for one brief episode, mentioned in passing, he never gets to the Italian leg of the trip; indeed, he's lucky to make it beyond Calais, his French landing place.

Readers of *Tristram Shandy* already knew Yorick as a thoroughly good if somewhat impractical fellow; in the first volume of that book, they'd even had the opportunity to weep at his deathbed and ponder his tombstone:

> Ten times in a day has *Yorick's* ghost the consolation to hear his monumental inscription read over with such a variety of plaintive tones, as denote a general pity and esteem for him;—a foot-way crossing the church-yard close by the side of his grave,—not a passenger goes by without stopping to cast a look upon it,—and sighing as he walks on,

> Alas, poor YORICK!

Undeterred by death, the sprightly parson sets out in *A Sentimental Journey* to show how, among the various categories of travelers, the sentimental kind goes about the business best. Along the way, he cleverly parodies those of his precursors who ignorantly believed that travel books should describe buildings, scenery, and local customs. There is very little of such mundane stuff in Sterne's novel. Instead, it offers a crash course in the indulgence of feelings.

One of its most revealing yanks at the reader's heartstrings comes at a Parisian hotel, where Yorick finds a caged starling that has been taught to say (in English) "I can't get out—I can't get out." In some danger of imprisonment himself (having barged into France without a passport), Yorick takes the cage to his room and weaves an elaborate fantasy on the theme:

> I was going to begin with the millions of my fellow-creatures born to no inheritance but slavery; but finding, however affecting the picture was, that I could not bring it near me, and that the multitude of sad groups in it did but distract me—
>
> —I took a single captive, and having first shut him up in his dungeon, I then looked through the twilight of his grated door to take his picture.
>
> I beheld his body half wasted away with long expectation and confinement, and felt what kind of sickness of the heart it was which arises from hope deferred. Upon looking nearer I saw him pale and feverish; in thirty years the western breeze had not once fanned his blood—he had seen no sun, no moon in all that time—nor had the voice of friend or kinsman breathed through his lattice—his children—
>
> —But here my heart began to bleed—and I was forced to go on with another part of the portrait.

On he goes for another paragraph, piling up pathetic details and working himself into a frenzy of sympathy: "He gave a deep sigh—I saw the iron enter into his soul—I burst into tears—I could not sustain the picture of confinement which my fancy had drawn . . ."

Pictures of confinement almost exactly like Yorick's were standard features of the Gothic novels that reached their peak of popularity about thirty years after *A Sentimental Journey* appeared. In them, the sentiment is always played straight: The reader is evidently expected to endure just such a course of imaginative agony as Yorick puts himself through (short of total breakdown, however). With Sterne, it's more difficult to gauge the intended effect. Yorick is a sympathetic character in his own right, though he's also shortsighted and occasionally foolish. For a twentieth-century reader, at least, it's difficult to forget that the starling, which launched the fantasy, gets lost sight of from the start and remains caged at the end. And Yorick's quite personal fear of winding up in the Bastille probably has more to do with the intensity of his emotions than any trumped-up feeling for an imaginary prisoner.

Nevertheless, partial parody or not, this scene is a classic enactment of what George Eliot called sincere acting. Yorick needs only the slightest stimulus from reality to prompt tears; for whatever reason, his mind already contains every prop it requires to stage an unbearably affecting little drama. Except for the bird, Yorick is alone under the spotlight: He conjures up a pathetic figure, tricks him out with all the appropriate paraphernalia, watches him suffer, and then—the most sentimental stroke of all—watches himself watching. The experience has practically no cause and no consequences whatever; it's as good as a play, or a movie.

Near the end of *A Sentimental Journey* comes an even more maudlin set piece, this one presented without apparent irony. Here, no hint of self-indulgence detracts from the force of Yorick's emotions. The reader is now in a position analogous to Yorick's when he invented that languishing prisoner: Sterne provides the paraphernalia, but the reader watches just as Yorick does, and both seem intended to feel the same. To a modern eye, the behavior of the characters is only slightly less nauseating than what the reader is supposed to do, but this time the characters are undoubtedly sincere, not acting at all.

On the road from Paris to Lyon, heading for Italy, Yorick passes through Moulins, where he decides to pause for a visit with "poor Maria." Readers of the ninth volume of *Tristram Shandy*, published a few months before *A Sentimental Journey*, would have remembered Maria, whom Tristram encounters there as he follows the same route. Maria is mad, driven so because clerical intrigue prevented her from marrying the man she loves. Ever since the forbidding of her banns, she has sat by the roadside with her pet goat, playing mournful tunes of her own composition on a pipe. Tristram cannot resist her unpremeditated music:

MARIA made a cadence so melancholy, so tender and querulous, that I sprung out of the chaise to help her, and found myself sitting betwixt her and her goat before I relapsed from my enthusiasm.

MARIA look'd wistfully for some time at me, and then at her goat— and then at me—and then at her goat again, and so on, alternately—

Well, *Maria*, said I softly—What resemblance do you find?

Tristram apologizes to the reader for having made a joke in these solemn circumstances, but the rueful humor only enhances the genuine if rather bizarre pathos of the scene.

No such restraint marks Yorick's visit to the newly popular Maria. In the interval, she has lost both her father and her goat; she has gone even madder than before and also picked up—to no one's benefit—the power of speech. Tears bedew her cheeks as Yorick approaches:

I sat down close by her; and Maria let me wipe them away as they fell with my handkerchief—I then steeped it in my own—and then in hers—and then in mine—and then I wiped hers again—and as I did it, I felt such undescribable emotions within me, as I am sure could not be accounted for from any combination of matter and motion.

I am positive I have a soul; nor can all the books with which materialists have pestered the world ever convince me of the contrary.

Maria tells him her sad story, and Yorick makes her several extravagant, empty promises. At which point, the waterworks come on again:

Nature melted within me, as I uttered this; and Maria observing, as I took out my handkerchief, that it was steeped too much already to be of use, would needs go wash it in the stream.—And where will you dry it, Maria? said I—I'll dry it in my bosom, said she—'twill do me good.

And is your heart still so warm, Maria? said I.

I touched upon the string on which hung all her sorrows—she looked with wistful disorder for some time in my face; and then, without saying anything, took her pipe, and played her service to the Virgin.

Yorick has once more shown his knack for working himself up into passions of self-indulgent feeling. In this case, however, the object is a real woman, whose misery he doesn't hesitate to pique for the sake of his own melancholy pleasure.

There seems little doubt that Sterne means his reader to feel along with Yorick and to admire the sensitive parson for the high susceptibility of his nerves. After leaving Maria, Yorick launches into a famous rhapsody on the theme:

> —Dear sensibility! source inexhausted of all that's precious in our joys, or costly in our sorrows! thou chainest thy martyr down upon his bed of straw—and 'tis thou who lifts him up to HEAVEN—eternal fountain of our feelings!—'tis here I trace thee—and this is thy divinity which stirs within me—not that, in some sad and sickening moments, *my soul shrinks back upon herself, and startles at destruction*—mere pomp of words!—but that I feel some generous joys and generous cares beyond myself—all comes from thee, great, great SENSORIUM of the world!

The gloomy excesses of Young's *Night Thoughts* may be an un-named target of this outburst, but the level of shrillness—and of apparent insincerity—is about the same.

A LAUGHABLE DEATH

Eighteenth-century sentimentalism is easy for modern observers to make fun of. It's hard for us to believe that those who indulged in it were anything but frauds or, at best, unconscious comedians. The ending of Mackenzie's *Man of Feeling* is a well-known case in point: It pulls out so many stops that laughter seems the only sane or healthy response. The hero, Harley, has been portrayed throughout the short, fragmented narrative as "a man, sensible to judge, and still more warm to feel"—an admirable character on the whole, whose errors spring only from naïveté and otherworldliness. Having suffered a serious fever, he goes into a decline from which he seems unlikely to recover. Though a young man, he takes his fate philosophically, if long-windedly. As he informs the novel's narrator, "There is a certain dignity in retiring from life at a time, when the infirmities of age have not sapped our faculties."

For a long while, however, Harley has loved Miss Walton, who rumor now says is engaged to Sir Harry Benson. Too shy to declare his feelings—or to question the rumor's accuracy—Harley is ready to die with his secret. But Miss Walton visits his deathbed, and the truth comes out. "It is perhaps the last time we shall ever meet," he tells her.

> "I feel something particularly solemn in the acknowledgment, yet my heart swells to make it, awed as it is by a sense of my presumption, by a sense of your perfections"—He paused again—"Let it not offend you, to know their power over one so unworthy—It will, I believe, soon cease to beat, even with that feeling which it shall lose the latest.—To love Miss Walton could not be a crime;—if to declare it is one—the expiation will be made."—Her tears were now flowing without control.

She admits her reciprocal esteem, and tender pandemonium breaks loose:

> He seized her hand—a languid colour reddened his cheek—a smile brightened faintly in his eye. As he gazed on her, it grew dim, it fixed, it closed—He sighed and fell back on his seat—Miss Walton screamed at the sight—His aunt and the servants rushed into the room—They found them lying motionless together.—His physician happened to call at that instant. Every art was tried to recover them—With Miss Walton they succeeded—But Harley was gone forever!

What is a modern reader to make of this? Eighteenth-century fiction abounds with similar scenes, yet a twentieth-century mind recoils from them, seeking refuge in laughter or disdain. Or psychologizing: Much could be done, in neo-Freudian style, with the postorgasmic stupor into which both the dead Harley and the living Miss Walton fall. Similar clammy eroticism could also be used to dredge up the repressed lust that underlies Sterne's portrayal of mad Maria. Such methods have been employed repeatedly to explain the bizarreries of the Gothic novel, which inherited and heightened the emotionalism of its Sentimental predecessor.

But reading between the lines often uncovers things that, though true, are unimportant compared to what the lines themselves convey. Interlinear sleuthing also fosters a kind of temporal imperialism based on the belief that the present knows better than the past what the past was about; we can give it the meaning it really had, which its inhabitants were too inhibited or undeveloped to see. This error is endemic to the writing of history, for the simple reason that participants in momentous transactions never know what long-range effects their doings will have. And effects proliferate; the history of any past age is ready to be rewritten every generation or so.

In histories that seek to chronicle attitudes rather than events, the error is compounded by a tendency to regard old modes of portrayal and response as inadequate without up-to-date commentary. Twentieth-century commentary usually makes earlier ages look incomplete, as if those who lived then couldn't possibly have filled every twenty-four-hour day. It is perhaps equally distorting—and arrogant—to pick out elements from the past and assign them significance simply because they seem to have present-day descendants. The worst arrogance may lie in supposing that, even if the line of descent exists, we can understand how our ancestors felt by making analogies with how we feel.

Yet in the history I'm sketching here, I think it's at least worth making the imaginative effort—if only because the kinship between eighteenth-century sentimentalism and the genre of modern fright is so surprisingly strong, and because on the surface it seems so unlikely. The connection has less to do with subject matter than with the stance the audience is invited to take toward the spectacle passing before it. The weeping reader of *A Sentimental Journey* or *The Man of Feeling*, with his periwig and ornamental cane, her painted beauty spot and lace mantilla, appears to share nothing whatever with the T-shirted adolescent of either sex who screams and laughs over *Friday the Thirteenth* in any of its incarnations. Yet all have voluntarily entered on a certain scene, where their strongest feelings will be solicited. It hardly matters what the feelings are, so long as they're sad or even repugnant but become delightful when they're witnessed by choice instead of accidentally met.

Eighteenth-century gentlemen and ladies picked out a small variety of scenes where their unwitting successors still agree to undergo strong emotions. First among them is the dismal old graveyard, with its archaic burial arrangements. Next comes the

Gothic building, whether castle or church, real or faked. Then the prison—probably Gothic, looking and smelling much like a medieval crypt—with its languishing inmate, who remains alive amid reminders of death, but just barely. The deathbed, of course. And the poor mad creature deranged by death or other privation, living on and receiving visitors.

We are the heirs of the long-dead people who made these choices. Their legacy, in fact, is much larger than this; it comprises our awe before mountain and ocean vistas, our solicitude for the endangered creatures of the earth, and our belief that a rural life is the only wholesome one, all while we go on tearing down forests to build condominiums. These attitudes, and others like them, are often called Romantic, but they became fashionable long before the Romantic movement had taken hold. So far, we have seen them in scattered, incomplete forms that seem to have little to do with each other. At the end of the eighteenth century, however, the fragments coalesced: The Gothic novel combined them all and passed them on to us, in a shape that has hardly changed for two hundred years.

Real medieval people would have been amazed to see what posterity did to them. Generic "medieval castle," nineteenth-century style. (BETTMANN ARCHIVES)

3

---

feac among
the Ruins

SOMETHING VERY SHOCKING INDEED

Midway through Jane Austen's *Northanger Abbey* (1817) comes a
little conversation that twentieth-century readers are likely to find
as obscure as it is funny. In the fashionable English resort town of
Bath, seventeen-year-old Catherine Morland has recently be-
friended Eleanor and Henry Tilney, brother and sister. The three go
on an excursion to nearby Beechen Cliff, where for a while they
admire and comment on the lovely views. Then Henry mentions
politics, and talk dies. After a general pause, Catherine speaks up in
"a rather solemn tone of voice":

> "I have heard that something very shocking indeed, will soon come
> out in London."
> Miss Tilney, to whom this was chiefly addressed, was startled, and
> hastily replied, "Indeed!—and of what nature?"
> "That I do not know, nor who is the author. I have only heard that it
> is to be more horrible than any thing we have met with yet."
> "Good heaven!—Where could you hear of such a thing?"
> "A particular friend of mine had an account of it in a letter from

67

London yesterday. It is to be uncommonly dreadful. I shall expect
murder and every thing of the kind."

"You speak with astonishing composure!"

Catherine and Eleanor might go on indefinitely with this comedy of
misunderstanding, but Henry interrupts to set them straight.

Eleanor, he says, thought that Catherine's "something" was an
impending riot, to which the militia would be called in. Her other
brother, Frederick, is a captain in the Dragoons and might be sent
into the fray; hence her alarm. But, as Henry explains, Catherine
meant no such real-life horror. Her "something very shocking indeed" was only a book:

> "Miss Morland has been talking of nothing more dreadful than a new
> publication which is shortly to come out, in three duodecimo vol-
> umes, two hundred and seventy-six pages in each, with a fron-
> tispiece to the first, of two tombstones and a lantern—do you
> understand?—And you, Miss Morland—my stupid sister has mis-
> taken all your clearest expressions. You talked of expected horrors
> in London—and instead of instantly conceiving, as any rational
> creature would have done, that such words could relate only to a
> circulating library, she immediately pictured to herself a mob of
> three thousand men assembling in St. George's Fields."

Mistaken references form an ageless source of comedy, but this
instance could not have occurred before about 1795 and became
obscure by 1820. The particulars are topical, and like newspaper
headlines, they grew stale fast.

We know from Austen's sister Cassandra that the first draft of
Northanger Abbey was finished by 1799. The revised manuscript
was sold to a publisher, Crosby and Co., in 1803; when nothing had
been done with it by 1809, one of Austen's brothers negotiated
buying it back for the sum first paid, ten pounds. Another eight
years passed before the novel was published; by then, Austen was
dead. In 1816, however, she had written a brief "advertisement" to
this new-old work: "The public are entreated to bear in mind that
thirteen years have passed since it was finished, many more since it
was begun, and that during that period, places, manners, books,
and opinions have undergone considerable changes."

For most novels, precise dating like this would possess purely biographical interest, if any. In this case, however, the dates 1799 to 1816 bracket, almost exactly, a period when the Western reading public went through a kind of paroxysm it had never surrendered to before. There had been fashions, of course, and enthusiasms that drove their victims wild. But at least in the realm of entertainment—which primarily meant books—there had never been a wave of infatuation like the one that threatens to engulf Catherine Morland. No prior fashion had risen, raged, and sunk out of sight so quickly.

Austen's novels are all, to some degree, contemporary satires, and later readers must stretch their imaginations a little to reach sympathy with characters governed by the manners that prevail in *Pride and Prejudice* or *Emma*. But *Northanger Abbey* is her only work that's stuck so fast to its own time only footnotes can detach it. Evidently, Austen recognized the problem. If the book had been published in 1799, its satire would have been sharply topical; by 1803, the fad it mocked was already on the wane (which is perhaps why Crosby did nothing with Austen's manuscript); by 1816, she needed to apologize for making fun of an outmoded genre. In the century that followed, the books and opinions she satirized were totally forgotten, until modern scholarship disinterred them. Yet only the particulars died, and even they were to rise again.

The "very shocking" story that Catherine awaits with such ghoulish glee is what we would call a Gothic novel. Its usual format looked much as Henry describes—three small, uniform volumes, with a bad engraving at the start of the first, showing a dismal scene. Such books went on sale, of course, but they cost too much for readers of Catherine's limited means. And prices were rising steeply: In 1780, Catherine might have had her three volumes for about seven shillings; by 1810, they would cost her up to a pound. Even if she had the money, however, Catherine is not the book-collecting type; besides, the books she favors are not designed for rereading.

Faddists like Catherine would probably obtain their shocks, as Henry says, through a "circulating library"—a book-lending club that charged its members an annual fee for the privilege of borrowing a specified number of novels per year. From the mid-eighteenth till the end of the nineteenth century, circulating libraries formed the primary channel of book distribution in Britain. During the Gothic fad, some specialized in shocks; the preeminent such specialist (and the likely source of Catherine's expected horror) was the Minerva Public Library, attached to William Lane's Minerva Press. For a while, "Minerva" and "shock" were virtually synonymous—as good (exactly) as a twentieth-century brand name.

Austen's portrayal of Catherine Morland is both timeless and precise in all its details. Like Cervantes's *Don Quixote* (1605–1615), Charlotte Lennox's *The Female Quixote* (1752), and Eaton Stannard Barrett's *The Heroine* (1813), her story belongs to the venerable tradition of fables about the naive reader who learns by hard experience that fiction makes a poor guide to real life. But Catherine's Gothic faddishness marks her indelibly as a child of the late eighteenth century. She typifies a new kind of reader, in whom the Gothic novel found its most fervent audience.

Catherine comes from a moderately well-off clergyman's family. The fourth of ten children, she has been educated, at home, in a young lady's standard accomplishments—principally the piano, drawing, French, and household accounts, for none of which she possesses either aptitude or enthusiasm. She enjoys reading, but her tastes are selective: "provided that nothing like useful knowledge could be gained from them, provided they were all story and no reflection, she had never any objection to books at all."

Catherine knows nothing of the Greek or Latin classics that formed the basis of a gentleman's education, nor has she studied history of any kind. But she has read Shakespeare and some more recent English poetry, including Pope's "To the Memory of an Unfortunate Lady," Gray's "Elegy," and at least part of James Thomson's *Seasons*, a long blank-verse celebration of Nature's splendors. Austen portrays Catherine as a thoroughly ordinary girl of moderate intelligence, average looks, and solid though untested good sense. There have always been people like her, but not until the late eighteenth century was there a kind of book tailor-made for minds innocent of experience and learned only in the art of strong feeling. Not until then did the Catherines of the world constitute a large enough class that a genre of entertainment could flourish by appealing mainly to them.

Not exclusively, of course: Henry Tilney is familiar with the genre, too, and Austen expects some knowledge of it from her own readers (at least, she expected it in 1803). But Catherine and her consorts have made a special game of Gothic horrors, one with distinctly modern rules. Catherine is a novice; she has just begun reading the most famous Gothic of all, Ann Radcliffe's *The Mysteries of Udolpho* (1794), evidently at the recommendation of Isabella Thorpe, another Bath acquaintance. Isabella is a malignant, silly twit, but she keeps up with the latest of everything, including shocks. When Catherine gushes about the joys of *Udolpho*, Isabella subjects her pupil to some gentle instruction. "Dear creature!" she says patronizingly:

> "and when you have finished Udolpho, we will read the Italian together; and I have made out a list of ten or twelve more of the same kind for you."
>
> "Have you, indeed! How glad I am—What are they all?"
>
> "I will read you their names directly; here they are, in my pocket-book. Castle of Wolfenbach, Clermont, Mysterious Warnings, Necromancer of the Black Forest, Midnight Bell, Orphan of the Rhine, and Horrid Mysteries. Those will last us some time."
>
> "Yes, pretty well; but are they all horrid, are you sure they are all horrid?"
>
> "Yes, quite sure; for a particular friend of mine, a Miss Andrews, a sweet girl, one of the sweetest creatures in the world, has read every one of them."

The incongruity is delightful: This "sweet girl" (who is also, Isabella says, "netting herself the sweetest cloak you can conceive") has set up shop as an expert on horrors and a connoisseur of shocks. No doubt she turns from netting her cloak to a horrid book, and back again, without batting an eye.

Today, the incongruity would be still funnier if it hadn't become so familiar. Twentieth-century horror fans are likely to be younger than Catherine, Isabella, and Miss Andrews, and their arcane knowledge more likely concerns videocassettes than books, but the roles of novice and initiate in the horror game have hardly changed. Nor has the total lack of connection between fictional horrors and any aspect of the devotees' real lives. *Northanger Abbey* pokes fun at some particular foibles of late-eighteenth-century society that were already passé by 1816, but in many ways, only the details have changed over the last two hundred years.

Novice though she is, Catherine has a clear idea of what she wants from these books: They must be "horrid." And though she knows no Latin, she uses that word in something like its Latinate sense. The Latin adjective *horridus* means "rough" or "bristly" as well as "horrible"; until late in the eighteenth century, "horrid" might describe a beard or a patch of weeds as well as a frightening sight. Catherine's meaning is not unrelated; she wants to read books that make her hair stand on end, that turn her skin "horrid" with gooseflesh. Of course, she ascribes to the books a quality that really belongs not to them but to the response she hopes they'll elicit. Isabella and the authoritative Miss Andrews agree: The novels on Isabella's list have nothing necessarily in common beyond the feeling they inspire. They do have other similarities— indeed, in many ways they're virtual copies of one another—but that's not how their first readers knew them. Miss Andrews and her acolytes wanted gooseflesh; the novelists' only mandate was to supply it.

All the titles Isabella mentions are genuine, though except for Catherine's starter set, *The Mysteries of Udolpho*, and Ann Radcliffe's *The Italian* (1797), they were well sunk in obscurity by 1816. All nine were first published in English between 1794 and 1798 (Isabella is nothing if not up-to-date), and six have some German connection, either setting or putative source—an accident that has led many twentieth-century critics to imagine a larger German influence on the Gothic novel than in fact existed. Like Graveyard poetry, which it resembles in many of its effects, the Gothic novel was an English invention. It was usually set, however, in France, Spain, or Italy. When Continental imitators followed the fad, they often returned the favor by locating their horrors in remote, foggy England.

Twentieth-century critics of the Gothic novel have analyzed its few acknowledged masterpieces dozens of times—isolating themes, psychologizing their meanings, finding surprising social relevance in these apparently escapist fictions. Critics have occasionally been troubled by the failure of what they call Gothic to fit any convenient mold. It had no clear-cut beginning, it spilled out on all sides, and it ended like the Wicked Witch of the West, by melting. As is often the case with generic labels, "Gothic" can cast more shadows than light, if it's applied prescriptively or if one goes searching for the mysterious essence at its heart. I prefer to side with Catherine Morland, who used "Gothic" to name spooky old buildings; when it came to novels, she expected them to be not Gothic but simply "horrid."

THE REAL STRAWBERRY HILL

Historians of the Gothic novel commonly trace the fad back to the self-elected Abbot of Strawberry, Horace Walpole. His little book *The Castle of Otranto*, published on Christmas Eve, 1764, usually gets credit (or blame) for having founded the genre and established its link to the architectural style that shares its name. This "Gothic Story," as Walpole subtitled it, originated in the same baronial fantasies that were remodeling Strawberry Hill; *Otranto* sprang from a dream, as he wrote in a famous 1765 letter to William Cole:

> Shall I even confess to you, what was the origin of this romance? I waked one morning, in the beginning of last June, from a dream, of which, all I could recover, was, that I had thought myself in an ancient castle (a very natural dream for a head like mine filled with Gothic story), and that on the uppermost banister of a great staircase I saw a gigantic hand in armour. In the evening I sat down, and began to write, without knowing in the least what I intended to say or relate.

The Castle of Otranto is, in a way, the real Strawberry Hill, granite instead of paper; the novel, however, is just as fake as the house was.

The first edition pretended to be the translation, by a certain William Marshal, of a sixteenth-century Italian volume by "Onuphrio Muralto, Canon of the Church of St. Nicholas at Otranto." A copy had supposedly been found "in the library of an ancient Catholic family in the north of England," and Marshal offered it to the English public "as a matter of entertainment." The offer was so gladly received that the small first printing—probably 250 copies or fewer—soon sold out. A second edition, of 500 copies, appeared in April 1765. Walpole attached a new preface, admitting authorship and claiming, rather grandiosely, to have taken as his models first "nature" and then the "great master of nature, SHAKESPEARE." *Otranto* had reached a seventh English edition by 1793; it was translated more than once into French and Italian, and in over two hundred years it has never gone out of print.

When it first appeared, *Otranto* had the powerful attraction of not looking quite like any other book. Today, we can see it as a harbinger, if not the fountainhead, of all the frightening fictions that have succeeded it. Walpole was distinctly ahead of his time: Horrid novels became a full-fledged craze only in the mid-1790s, thirty years after *Otranto*, and few of them resembled their supposed ancestor except in incidental details. But for *Otranto* and its progeny, details are usually the most important things, far outweighing such critics' choices as style, structure, tone, and even coherence. The majority of scary entertainments fall short on all these points; they tend to neglect the critical virtues in favor of momentary effects. Often, the book, play, or film that aims to frighten makes no internal sense, because the would-be frighteners have ignored logic in favor of minute-to-minute impact. This preference was as characteristic of the eighteenth-century Gothic novel as it is of twentieth-century horror movies.

The Castle of Otranto didn't really found a genre; it established the rudiments of an emotive repertoire that the next generation of horrid novelists—many of whom weren't yet born when *Otranto* was published—would imitate and extend. Walpole's novel relates the fulfillment of an "ancient prophecy": "that *the Castle and Lordship of Otranto should pass from the present family whenever the real owner should be grown too large to inhabit it.*" The idea for the prophecy apparently came from Walpole's dream of "a gigantic hand in armour," which makes an appearance later in the novel. There is also a gigantic helmet, and at the end the murdered Alfonso arises ("dilated to an immense magnitude"), knocks down the castle walls, and ascends into heaven.

Gigantism did not fare well as a trigger of shocks. So far as I know, no other horrid novelist made much use of it before Mary Shelley in *Frankenstein* (1818), and there the Monster's eight-foot stature is among his less frightening attributes. Only in the 1950s did gigantism belatedly come into its own, with films featuring all sorts of immensely dilated animals and insects as well as human beings. The ancient curse fared better: In one form or another, the vengeful return of the past became a staple of the horrid fad, and it has remained popular in scary fictions of all sorts, from ghost stories to detective novels.

There may be something inherently ludicrous about oversized creatures; they inspire a certain awe, perhaps, but mostly they suggest wholesale property damage. The avenging past, however, especially the past that is dead or thought to be, retains the frightening power it had for Walpole's time. Even then, the device was far from new; Walpole might have found it in *Hamlet*, *Macbeth*, or, more benignly, *A Winter's Tale*. Or he might have consulted any number of Jacobean tragedies, in which revenge frequently motivates the plot. *Otranto*, however, despite its woodenness, manages to convey a subtle mixture of dread and fascination that was new to the mid-eighteenth century and that we have inherited.

This is all the more curious because the novel is set, as Walpole's first preface says, sometime between 1095 and 1243—a much earlier, supposedly more primitive time, yet one that seems overburdened by the accumulation of its own history. The castle is of great age and evidently much too large for the needs of those who now inhabit it. Below, it is "hollowed into several intricate cloisters," through which even the residents have difficulty finding their way. The cloisters are connected to a "subterraneous passage" leading to the vaults of St. Nicholas's church. And nearby, along the seacoast, is "a chain of rocks, hollowed into a labyrinth of caverns." No mention is made of what purpose, if any, these complicated structures once had. Now, they evidently have none, though they remain parts of what Walpole's characters uneasily call home.

Otranto's castle is a dream, but a remarkably durable one. The vast majority of horrid eighteenth-century novels contain at least one building like it, and it survives in every spooky house and haunted basement the tradition of horrid fiction turns out. *Otranto* contains an array of other machinery that scary entertainments continue to recycle, including a cowled figure that turns slowly to reveal "the fleshless jaws and empty sockets of a skeleton." The gloomy tyrant Manfred, whose designs set the story moving and

whose abdication ends it, can also be seen as the crude precursor
of villains from Mrs. Radcliffe's Montoni and Schedoni down to
Dracula and Freddy Kruger. But nothing has been more influential
than the castle itself—the inspiration for the novel, and its foremost
legacy.

Like Strawberry Hill, *The Castle of Otranto* is short on historical
accuracy but very long on the cultivated feeling of pastness. Its
characters live in an era that sent shivers down eighteenth-century
spines, yet they feel those shivers, too, as no twelfth-century
person would have done. Walpole's princes, knights, and friars
are also both superstitious and Catholic, which for Walpole and
his Anglican readers meant approximately the same thing. In his
first preface, he apologized, on historical grounds, for the "preternatural events" that stud the tale: "Belief in every kind of prodigy
was so established in those dark ages, that an author would not
be faithful to the manners of the times, who should omit all
mention of them." In fact, when Walpole's characters flee along
labyrinthine passages or recoil from talking skeletons, they are
standing in for eighteenth-century readers, who gladly underwent
such terrors in the modern safety of a book or the painted galleries of an artificial abbey.

Otranto offers a potent brew of Graveyard School gloom, Gothic
melancholy, and pseudo-Shakespearean histrionics. It had no immediate successors, however; another generation would pass before the genre it seemed to found became a craze. The history of
scary entertainment is full of such intermissions: Trends get de-
toured, dwindle, and die, only to burst into life again decades later.
In this case, the gap had two principal causes. For all its carrying
on, *Otranto* is in many ways a rather austere book, whose characters do not indulge their feelings in the Sentimental style. Sentimental fiction came into vogue mainly after *Otranto* appeared, and the
novel contains only one foreshadowing of it—a brief interlude
when the hero, Theodore, enters a forest and seeks out "the gloomiest shades, as best suited to the pleasing melancholy that reigned
in his mind." This sort of self-indulgence, the forte of Sterne,
Mackenzie, and the young Goethe, became a standard feature of
the late-century Gothic novel and seems to have been necessary to
produce its full range of effects.

Otranto also failed to found a school for a second, more important reason: Ignorant, sensitive readers like Catherine Morland and Isabella Thorpe (not to mention the learned Miss Andrews) did not yet exist in sufficient numbers, nor had circulating libraries expanded far enough to support a book fad. *Otranto* enjoyed its initial success on the basis of only a few hundred copies; even at the end of the century, initial printings of novels would seldom be much larger, but each library copy would be lent out many times, reaching readers whose imaginations were far better stocked than their pocketbooks. By then, a fair profit could be turned by imitating horrid successes, grinding out scores of flimsy fictions whose chief selling point was that they could barely be told apart. What we know as a genre comes fully into being when publishers (or movie studios) can count on a predictable demand for a more or less uniform product—one that rings only slight changes on a proven, familiar formula. When these factors united, as they did in the 1790s, the genre of horrid fiction was born.

OLD DARK HOUSES

There is no way of estimating how many horrid novels were published during the genre's first heyday. In *A Gothic Bibliography* (1941), Montague Summers lists nearly two thousand titles published in the United States and Western Europe between 1790 and 1820, not counting reprints and new editions. But Summers's understanding of "Gothic" was remarkably broad. It's difficult to imagine what horrors could have lurked in an anonymous novel called *The Clergyman's Widow and Her Young Family* (1811), except perhaps its style. Yet it bore the Minerva Press imprint, which may be why Summers roped it in.

Often, one has to take Summers's word for it that the books he lists were ever published. If they failed to catch on in their own time, and if later generations failed to enjoy or find merit in them, they vanished. Few gentlemen—the only class then equipped or inclined to accumulate private libraries—would have deigned to notice such stuff. University libraries disdained all novels, and public libraries of the twentieth-century sort did not yet exist. Besides, the circulating system guaranteed that a book of even modest popularity would pass through so many hands it eventually fell apart into waste paper.

Until the 1920s, even scholars believed that the titles on Isabella's agenda of horrors were fictitious: They seemed too appropriately silly to be anything except Austen's satirical inventions. *The Midnight Bell* and its companions were real enough, but they were almost totally derivative, fodder for readers who consumed such books by the dozen. When that appetite faded, so did the books. Posterity preserved some of the more original contributions to the horrid craze—like *Otranto*, *Udolpho*, and Matthew G. Lewis's *The Monk*—but it was left to modern scholarship to disinter the opportunists, many of which now can be read in limited library editions. I know of only one twentieth-century reader, Summers, who demonstrated something like the voraciously indiscriminate taste that animated Miss Andrews and her fellow horror fans.

Summers remarks on the frequency with which buzzwords like "castle," "abbey," and "priory" appear in the titles of novels now called Gothic; he takes this as evidence of the "congenital and indigenous" connection between horrid fiction and Gothic architecture. Titles also served—in an age of minimal, rudimentary advertising—as a signal to the would-be reader that the special chills he expected from both buildings and books were to be found between these covers. *Northanger Abbey* satirizes both such titles and the expectations they played upon. When Catherine gets invited to visit the Tilneys at the "Northanger" she has often heard them mention, she is delighted to find that their home is an "abbey."

> With all the chances against her of house, hall, place, park, court, and cottage, Northanger turned up an abbey, and she was to be its inhabitant. Its long, damp passages, its narrow cells and ruined chapel, were to be within her daily reach, and she could not entirely subdue the hope of some traditional legends, some awful memorials of an injured and ill-fated nun.

On the way there, Catherine excitedly remarks to Henry that she looks forward to "a fine old place, just like what one reads about"— which launches him into an ironic horrid novel in miniature:

> [Y]ou must be aware that when a young lady is (by whatever means) introduced into a dwelling of this kind, she is always lodged apart

from the rest of the family. While they snugly repair to their own end of the house, she is formally conducted by Dorothy the ancient housekeeper up a different staircase, and along many gloomy passages, into an apartment never used since some cousin or kin died in it about twenty years before. . . . Will not your mind misgive you, when you find yourself in this gloomy chamber—too lofty and extensive for you, with only the feeble rays of a single lamp to take in its size—its walls hung with tapestry exhibiting figures as large as life, and the bed, of dark green stuff or purple velvet, presenting even a funereal appearance. Will not your heart sink within you?

On he goes for two more pages, providing a perfect inventory of Gothic horrors: a mysterious chest, an unaccountably fascinating portrait, strange hints from the housekeeper, a door that will not lock, a thunderstorm, a secret vault, a secret passage, a dagger, a pool of blood, an ancient manuscript, and a lamp that "suddenly expires in the socket, and leaves you in total darkness."

With this preparation, Catherine can hardly help getting in trouble at the real Northanger—a thoroughly modernized house where the only dark secret is General Tilney's thoroughly traditional greed. But what's most interesting about Henry's catalogue is its accuracy: Both he and Jane Austen seem far better versed than poor Catherine in the full range of horrid clichés. Catherine has read only *The Mysteries of Udolpho*, in which many of them appear, but Henry must have plowed through more than Miss Andrews's short list to arrive at his handy digest. Evidently, not only young women went mad for horrors: Fashionable young men supped full of them, too, if only to demonstrate their immunity.

Every item on Henry's list was a cliché in 1799 and remains one, repeated constantly, with slight variations, in twentieth-century horror stories and films. Though *The Castle of Otranto* came first, it was Ann Radcliffe's *Udolpho*, thirty years later, that distilled Walpole's tentative mixture of phony history and artificial fear into a form that could easily be copied by the hundreds of imitators who immediately sprang up. Radcliffe added a heavy dollop of what *Otranto* had lacked—Sensibility. The result intoxicated its first readers and left them thirsting for more, which a legion of opportunists was ready to provide.

Next to nothing is known of Ann Radcliffe except that she was born Ann Ward in 1764 (the year *Otranto* was published), married

William Radcliffe in 1787, and died in 1823. During a scant eight
years, 1789 to 1797, she published five novels that helped to set the
course of Western cultural history; a sixth, *Gaston de Blondeville*,
appeared posthumously in 1826. She lived to see the fad for copying her explode, fade, and nearly die, but we have no record of her
thoughts on the matter. She was as good as anonymous; her books
bear an individual stamp, but they also crystallized the cultural
commonplaces of her time, and they succumbed to such wholesale mimicking that it soon became impossible to tell the real thing
from the copy.

In *The Mysteries of Udolpho*, Radcliffe's fourth novel, young
Emily St. Aubert travels from the south of France to the Apennines
and Count Montoni's ancient castle. Her first view of it set a long-
lasting pattern:

> "There," said Montoni, speaking for the first time in several hours,
> "is Udolpho."
> Emily gazed with melancholy awe upon the castle, which she
> understood to be Montoni's; for, though it was now lighted up by the
> setting sun, the gothic greatness of its features, and its mouldering
> walls of dark grey stone, rendered it a gloomy and sublime object. As
> she gazed, the light died away on its walls, leaving a melancholy
> purple tint, which spread deeper and deeper, as the thin vapour
> crept up the mountain, while the battlements above were still tipped
> with splendour.

More than a century later, Jonathan Harker arrives at Castle
Dracula:

> Suddenly I became conscious of the fact that the driver was in the act
> of pulling up the horses in the courtyard of a vast ruined castle, from
> whose tall black windows came no ray of light, and whose broken
> battlements showed a jagged line against the moonlit sky.

Seventy-eight years later yet, in Stephen King's *'Salem's Lot*
(1975), Ben Mears surveys the Marsten house:

> It was huge and rambling and sagging, its windows haphazardly
> boarded shut, giving it that sinister look of all old houses that have
> been empty for a long time. The paint had been weathered away,

giving the house a uniform gray look. Windstorms had ripped many of the shingles off, and a heavy snowfall had punched in the west corner of the main roof, giving it a slumped, hunched look.

Stoker was no doubt aware of Castle Dracula's Radcliffean precedents; King suggests that Shirley Jackson's *The Haunting of Hill House* (1959) was the inspiration for Hubie Marsten's evil home. Jackson, at least, knew that her novel belonged to a much older tradition. Already by the early twentieth century, the spooky house had become the kind of cultural artifact known as a cliché: The audience's intimacy with it was presumably so close that spoofs, takeoffs, and parodies automatically made sense. There was also pleasure (and money) to be gained from repeating scary clichés with a spin that made them funny. The popularity of spooky-house comedies on the early-twentieth-century stage, and in films from the twenties through the forties, testifies to the appeal of laughing at old dark houses.

Even the silliest spooky-house comedy, however, clung to the vestiges of Gothic awe. The best films of the kind, like *The Cat and the Canary* (1927) and, incongruously, *Topper Returns* (1941), trod a razor-thin line between fright and fun, lurching crazily from a scene meant for screams to one played for laughs. After World War II, spooky-house farces went out of fashion, though the house itself endured. In recent years, especially in films, that cliché has grown progressively shiftier as well as more self-conscious.

When, for instance, *'Salem's Lot* became a TV movie in 1979, director Tobe Hooper gave the Marsten house an interior that recalled the domestic abattoir in Hooper's *The Texas Chainsaw Massacre* (1974), while its exterior resembled the horrible Bates house in *Psycho* (1960). Hitchcock's film had followed Robert Bloch's 1959 novel, reversing inherited values to make intactness even eerier than ruin. Mary Crane (Marion in the movie) peers through the house's parlor window:

At first glance she couldn't quite believe what she saw; she hadn't dreamed that such places still existed in this day and age.

Usually, even when a house is old, there are some signs of alteration and improvement in the interior. But the parlor she peered at had never been "modernized"; the floral wallpaper, the dark, heavy, ornately scrolled mahogany woodwork, the turkey-red carpet, the high-backed, overstuffed furnitiure [sic] and the paneled fireplace were straight out of the Gay Nineties.

The permutations are evidently endless; at least, the purveyors of scary entertainment haven't run out yet and seem unlikely to do so soon. *The Texas Chainsaw Massacre* gives the venerable tradition a wicked little twist by providing two houses: the rotted, crumbling one is innocuous, while the well-kept white one with the neat picket fence turns out to be a pit of bloody horror. And in George Romero's *Night of the Living Dead* (1968), horror lurks everywhere outside the house and spends most of the film clumsily trying to break in.

Haunted houses had been known long before the eighteenth century; the Roman writer Pliny the Younger (ca. 61–ca. 112) described one in the second century A.D. Perhaps, as King says, there has always been something "sinister" about empty old houses. But they haven't always been a staple of fiction, so well known that a momentary glimpse or a few sketchy sentences can be counted on to call up a complex tangle of emotional associations. That convention began with the Gothic novel, which drew on the new uncanniness of death, the new strangeness of the past, and Western culture's new love affair with the Middle Ages to forge an image that blended them all.

Mrs. Radcliffe's sinister buildings are not haunted; only her garrulous, gullible servants believe that ghosts really pace their dank corridors. By and large, imitative eighteenth-century Gothic followed her example (and neglected Walpole's) by confining the supernatural to backstairs rumor; like Mrs. Radcliffe, her followers reaped the rewards of ghostly effects while avoiding the low-class taint of superstition. Curiously, superstition—usually Catholic—was the chief satirical target of the whole early Gothic genre, while it sought to raise the very gooseflesh it condemned as a symptom of ignorant belief.

Like the sentimental fiction from which it grew, the Gothic novel reflected a deep doublemindedness in its culture's attitude toward the countryside and those who dwelt there. On the one hand, rural scenes refreshed the city-dulled spirit and brought the visitor close to nature's invigorating source. On the other, permanent country dwellers were crude, ignorant, and lousy with degrading superstitions. The Gothic remained faithful to Walpole's precedent at least in this: The chills it solicited were genteel, self-induced, and untroubled by either commitment or belief. Gothic novels might be aimed at a relatively unsophisticated audience, but their intended readers were no bumpkins. They were, like Catherine Morland, the children of the urban or suburban middle class; they had no desire really to dwell among the untrodden ways, only to go there on an occasional excursion.

Besides, Mrs. Radcliffe and her followers didn't need to summon up real ghosts in order to induce horrid feelings. Scenes of noble, neglected architecture could bring on gooseflesh without supernatural help. In the Gothic novel, Walpole's artifice and Goethe's awe congealed into a repertoire of staple effects that could be deployed again and again with guaranteed results. The most schematic instance in Radcliffe's work comes early in her third novel, *The Romance of the Forest.* Pierre de la Motte has fled from Paris with his entourage (lately joined by the interesting orphan Adeline). Just after sunset, he spots "some dark towers" silhouetted against the western sky. Hoping to find a place to spend the night, La Motte investigates.

> He approached, and perceived the Gothic remains of an abbey: it stood on a kind of rude lawn, overshadowed by high and spreading trees, which seemed coeval with the building, and diffused a romantic gloom around. The greater part of the pile appeared to be sinking into ruins, and that, which had withstood the ravages of time, shewed the remaining features of the fabric more awful in decay.

His knocks at the "Gothic gate" producing only "hollow sounds," he goes through into the abbey chapel, where he has an epiphany:

> La Motte paused a moment, for he felt a sensation of sublimity rising into terror—a suspension of mingled astonishment and awe! He surveyed the vastness of the place, and as he contemplated its ruins, fancy bore him back to past ages. "And these walls," said he, "where once superstition lurked, and austerity anticipated an earthly purgatory, now tremble over the mortal remains of the beings who reared them!"

It's hardly plausible that a man in La Motte's desperate situation, with his wife, his servant, and a mysterious teenage girl waiting anxiously nearby, would linger to indulge such moonshiny reflections. But for Radcliffe, as for her successors, plausibility mattered less than the impact of the moment, and this moment is a rich one. It mixes all the ingredients of early horrid fiction: Hervey's meditations on the dead beneath the floor, Walpole's arch Gothicness at Strawberry Hill and in *Otranto*, Goethe's spontaneous awe before Strasbourg Cathedral, and the self-regarding sensitivity of Sterne and Mackenzie. It does so without attempting to understand the ingredients or the effect of their blending; Radcliffe is strong on effects, very weak on causes. She is like her reader, like Catherine Morland, ignorant but sensitive. And that remains the source of her power.

INTRICATE DESOLATION

The Mysteries of Udolpho takes place late in the sixteenth century, but Udolpho, like Otranto, is immensely older than even its own old time. It has been uninhabited for two years (except by the decrepit Carlo and his wife), and the roof of the great hall has fallen in. It's also "such a strange rambling place," as Annette, Madame Montoni's servant, says, that one easily gets lost there. Which Annette and Emily proceed at once to do, on their way to Emily's room "at the other end of the castle."

Their route is like memories from a weary dream: Armed against the dark with only a single lamp, they go up a staircase and down a corridor, around a corner, down a winding passage, and into a gallery, while the gabby servant (a type borrowed from Walpole, who claimed he found it in Shakespeare) chatters on about apparitions. Finally,

> Annette, perceiving that she had missed her way, while she had been so eloquently haranguing on ghosts and fairies, wandered about through other passages and galleries, till, at length frightened by their intricacies and desolation, she called aloud for assistance: but they were beyond the hearing of the servants, who were on the other side of the castle, and Emily now opened the door of a chamber on the left.

Two centuries later, this is still an eerie moment, heightened by the curious detail "on the left." Perhaps Radcliffe supplied it in order to emphasize that, at this point, neither Annette nor Emily nor the reader can tell left from right in the dreary labyrinth of Udolpho.

The door opens into "a suite of spacious and ancient apartments" in which the furniture is "covered with dust, and dropping to pieces with the damps, and with age"; no one has lived there, reports Annette, "for many, many years, they say." Undaunted, Emily pushes on through an unspecified number of rooms till she comes to one "hung with pictures," where a painting of a triumphant soldier makes her shudder and turn away. His face seems to resemble that of the sinister Montoni! But in the same room hangs another picture that has the reverse effect on Emily: It fixes her attention, because it is "concealed by a veil of black silk."

"Have you gone on with Udolpho?" Isabella asks Catherine in *Northanger Abbey*.

> "Yes, I have been reading it ever since I woke; and I am got to the black veil."
> "Are you, indeed? How delightful! Oh! I would not tell you what is behind the black veil for the world! Are you not wild to know?"
> "Oh! yes, quite; what can it be?—But do not tell me—I would not be told upon any account. . . . Oh! I am delighted with the book! I should like to spend my whole life in reading it."

The intrigue of the black veil was and is the most famous feature of *Udolpho*; it spans two thirds of the book, and it has often been taken as typical of the techniques pioneered by both Radcliffe and the horrid novel in general.

Thanks to Annette's discouragement, Emily does not lift the veil on her first visit to the damp suite. The next night, however—having meanwhile discovered a secret staircase leading down from her bedroom (through a door that will not lock), listened to more ghost stories from Annette, and admired the "proud irregularity" of Udolpho's architecture—she yields to the "ancient grandeur" of the place and returns to the mysterious picture. Annette's reported rumors have inspired Emily with "a faint degree of terror," yet, setting a pattern that generations of lantern- and flashlight-bearing

maidens will follow, she feels irresistibly drawn to the thing that
scares her most. Her reward is appropriate:

> Emily passed on with faltering steps, and having paused a moment at
> the door, before she attempted to open it, she then hastily entered
> the chamber, and went toward the picture, which appeared to be
> enclosed in a frame of uncommon size, that hung in a dark part of
> the room. She paused again, and then, with a timid hand, lifted the
> veil; but instantly let it fall—perceiving that what it had concealed
> was no picture, and, before she could leave the chamber, she
> dropped senseless on the floor.

This must be the point Catherine has reached when she begs not
to be told the secret: midway through the second of *Udolpho*'s four
volumes. *Northanger Abbey* never reveals her feelings about what
the veil conceals; as far as Austen is concerned, Catherine never
finishes *Udolpho*.

Which is just as well, because the revelation is a worse letdown
than that of the mundane evil inhabiting Northanger Abbey. Practically at the end of the fourth volume—more than four hundred
pages later in a modern paperback, about six hundred in an
eighteenth-century edition—after innumerable intrigues that
seems to have no connection with the black veil, the reader discovers that, indeed, they have none:

> It may be remembered, that, in a chamber of Udolpho, hung a
> black veil, whose singular situation had excited Emily's curiosity,
> and which afterwards disclosed an object, that had overwhelmed
> her with horror; for, on lifting it, there appeared, instead of the
> picture she had expected, within a recess of the wall, a human
> figure of ghastly paleness, stretched at its length, and dressed in the
> habiliments of the grave. What added to the horror of the spectacle,
> was, that the face appeared partly decayed and disfigured by
> worms, which were visible on the features and hands. On such an
> object, it will be readily believed, that no person could endure to
> look twice.

Fifty years earlier, Blair, Porteus, and company would have had
their readers dwell on exactly such an object; but Emily, despite the
sixteenth-century setting of her adventures, is the child of a later
sensibility. She faints.

This three-dimensional Graveyard poem, however, turns out to be made of wax: Long ago, when "monkish superstition" ruled the land, a former marquis of Udolpho had been commanded to contemplate it daily as a reproof to his pride and penance for his sins. His descendants, though they skipped the penance, preserved the image. The veil has no other function in *Udolpho* than to keep the reader turning hundreds of pages; it is unconnected to the rest of the plot, and no character but Emily is even slightly affected by it. A century and a half later, when the detective novel had developed its own generic rules, this kind of false clue would be known as a red herring. But few latter-day novelists would dare to plant such a rank one.

At a long stretch, the clue-planting techniques of the twentieth-century detective novel may be said to derive from tricks like *Udolpho*'s black veil. As a way to build suspense, whether the anticipated horrors turn out real or fake, the device of the veil that must not be lifted (or the door that must not be opened, the words that must not be spoken) has been imitated in hundreds of guises. But in *Udolpho*, the veiled picture merely serves to test Emily's mettle, and perhaps to confirm the narrator's assertion that "a terror of this nature, as it occupies and expands the mind, and elevates it to high expectation . . . leads us, by a kind of fascination, to seek even the object from which we appear to shrink."

Mrs. Radcliffe's contemporary imitators ignored the device entirely. It may have been beyond their abilities (they were a feeble lot) to sustain interest in a single problem over so many pages. For whatever reason, Henry Tilney's otherwise exhaustive catalogue of quasi-Radcliffean clichés makes no mention of black veils or anything like them. And Henry is right: Though it later became standard, the long postponement of promised horrors did not form part of the original horrid repertoire.

At first glance, the omission seems odd, especially since the horrid novel obsessively followed Walpole and Radcliffe in basing its plots on old crimes that come back to haunt the present. Often the crimes were committed by fathers, and vengeance falls upon their daughters—which has led several twentieth-century commentators to expatiate upon the incestuous subtext of the genre, along with its subtle social subversiveness. On the whole, however, the evil father or father figure was merely a convenience for horrid

novels, like the impossibly noble heroine and hero who intermina-
bly reprised their ancient roles. Sinister barons, counts, and monks
bore an air of pastness, of history, and therefore of death, that was
chilling in itself: Like Gothic castles, they were old, weathered,
and—psychologically, at least—intricate. They hardly needed sex
to make them scary.

Even so, the horrid novel never developed the large-scale technique of clue dropping adumbrated by *Udolpho*'s black veil; it
would be refined to precision only in the twentieth century. Instead
of planting clues early and explaining them late, forming a bridge
across the whole narrative, horrid novels tended to plant a clue,
explain it after a few chapters, plant another, explain it fairly soon,
and so on. The result was boxcar fiction, a string of mysteries
interspersed with solutions. Those who complain about the minuscule attention span supposedly induced by saturation with
television should read a few eighteenth-century Gothics.

It's tempting to imagine that Mrs. Radcliffe and her imitators
would have become a horde of Agatha Christies if they'd been
granted the skill. Skill was certainly in short supply among the
imitators, but the evidence of their books suggests that they failed
to write whodunits because neither they nor their audience would
have known how to enjoy such mental exercises. Indeed, intricacy
of any kind seems to have frightened them, whether it came in the
form of architecture, psychology, or the construction of a story.
Horrid villains are the most convoluted characters in their books;
for them, mental complexity is torture, and the fact that they suffer it
suffices to brand them evil. When horrid novelists ventured into
clue planting, they tended to solve all mysteries as soon as possible
and to apologize for the delay.

An illuminating example is *Manfroné; or, The One-Handed Monk*
(1809) by Mary-Anne Radcliffe, whose name, though no doubt
genuine, was even more opportunistic than her fiction. (No relation
of the famous Mrs. Radcliffe, she profited from the coincidence.)
This eminently run-of-the-mill horror starts off with a bang, as the
pensive Rosalina, dozing in a remote apartment of Colredo, her
ancestral Italian castle, is startled awake by "a tall figure in a sable
mantle, advancing towards her with a noiseless pace." Rosalina's
screams rouse her father, who rushes in, duels with the interloper,
and drives him away. Only later does Rosalina's servant, Carletta,

spy a grisly object on the floor: "a human hand, blood-stained, and apparently but lately severed from its limb." Carletta faints, and Rosalina sickens. When the feisty castellan Lupo arrives, he matter-of-factly picks up the hand, examines it, and tosses it out the window into Lake Abruzzo.

The novel's pace slackens considerably after the frantic opening chapter. Numerous subsidiary mysteries spring up in the first volume; all but one are solved in the second, an achievement that seems to please the ersatz Mrs. Radcliffe. "In our next chapter," she writes just before the end of Volume 2, "we shall present our readers with the development of certain mysterious events which were related in the first volume." When she has done so, by means of a long, awkward flashback, she ungrammatically crows: "And thus have we accounted for the many mysterious occurrences which had taken place as related in the first volume."

These declarations were probably as ingenuous as they seem, but they omit one thing: that severed hand. After Lupo ditches it, the hand goes unmentioned till Volume 4, when it reappears under even grislier circumstances:

> The breathless body of the duca [Rosalina's father] lay stretched on his couch; the bosom was bare; a dagger was deeply planted in the breast, the hilt of which was encircled by the ghastly fingers of a skeleton hand, and the clothes of the bed were dyed with the blood of the unfortunate Rodolpho.

This is striking enough, but like most striking moments in horrid fiction, it remains just that: a moment. Like the other Mrs. Radcliffe's black veil, the lost-and-found hand has nothing to do with the novel's main intrigues, and no discernible strategy links its two appearances.

Mary-Anne Radcliffe also makes no effort to exploit the coincidence that Rodolpho cuts off a living hand in Volume 1 and is apparently stabbed by a skeletal one some 750 pages later. No one in *Manfroné*, not even Rosalina, notices a connection. Sixty pages later yet, it is revealed that the sinister monk Grimaldi and the menacing prince di Manfroné (who supposedly drowns late in Volume 1) are the same person. Only an extremely inattentive reader could have failed to guess their identity long before, but nothing (except the novel's subtitle) has suggested that either villain might be one-handed. This neglected mystery is solved very late, midway through Volume 4, when, struggling with Grimaldi, Rosalina makes the confusing observation that "he had but one hand, and that his other arm was shorn at the wrist!"

Eventually, Manfroné-Grimaldi explains that though "the waves of Abruzzo rolled over my form," he was saved from drowning and lingered in the neighborhood to recuperate.

> While pondering in my mind how I should effect an entrance into Colredo, I one day strayed on the margin of the lake which was beneath the western front, when as my eyes were cast to the ground, I saw my lost hand rotting in the blast: I snatched up the bones, and, having carried them to my cell, solemnly swore that they should grasp the dagger whose point should be buried in Rodolpho's heart.

All questions answered, *Manfroné* limps to its end, where the poor man's Mrs. Radcliffe tacks on her moral: *"To be good is to be happy."*

Manfroné is an utterly nondescript novel by a writer whose highest flights fail to achieve mediocrity. It can no longer be read for pleasure, but it illustrates which aspects of their sentimental-Gothic inheritance Mrs. Radcliffe's imitators picked out for exploitation and which they ignored or treated lightly. By 1809, when *Manfroné* appeared, the conventions of the horrid novel were solidly established, and its vogue was already on the wane. The lesser Radcliffe might have been a poor writer, but she knew what buttons to press to raise gooseflesh on her later generation of Catherine Morlands.

Intricate plotting evidently possessed little horror value. Unlike *The Mysteries of Udolpho* (or for that matter Ann Radcliffe's other novels), *Manfroné* demands no stretch of memory, hardly even of attention, on the reader's part. It is a series of set pieces—some sentimental, some violent, all more or less detachable from what precedes and follows them. Intricacy of character or motivation also gets short shrift. Mary-Anne Radcliffe's good characters— principally Rosalina and her lover, the long-suffering Montalto— must strive, endure, and struggle with conflicting allegiances. But their hearts remain single and simple, which in *Manfroné*'s morality exhausts the definition of goodness. The characters who experience inner turmoil—Rodolpho and Grimaldi-Manfroné—are bad, it seems, purely on that account. In the long run, however, no character's motivation, intricate or not, makes any difference. Good and bad do battle so that striking scenes may be arranged. That was Mary-Anne Radcliffe's only good: Scenes made her readers' hair stand on end, which was all she aimed at. Nearly two hundred years later, her successors have the same plain goal.

HORRID FURNITURE

Scenes consist of props, backdrops, and action. When the staging of scenes is of primary interest, plot and character dwindle to excuses for the performance of certain deeds in certain settings. An excellent case can be made for Ann Radcliffe's having had larger interests in mind: Both *The Romance of the Forest* and *The Mysteries of Udolpho* purvey courses of instruction for the young feminine mind, and *The Italian* adds a nuanced portrait of a tortured middle-aged man. But Mrs. Radcliffe's first imitators—along with their descendants down to the present day—went after none of that. Instead, they borrowed her furniture.

It wasn't originally hers, of course. She had borrowed it from Walpole, from Giambattista Piranesi's engravings of imaginary prisons, and from seventeenth-century landscape painters like her favorite Claude Lorrain and Salvator Rosa. Especially in her early career, she tossed in a heavy rhetorical dose of Edmund Burke's *Philosophical Enquiry into the Origin of Our Ideas of the Sublime and the Beautiful* (1757), which served her as an emotional training manual. If Mrs. Radcliffe's imitators were aware of those precedents, they copied them according to her recipe. They also boiled their borrowings down to a minimum, turning Mrs. Radcliffe's often lavish descriptions into a sort of shorthand. That is, they took whatever was most striking in Mrs. Radcliffe's novels and transformed it into a set of clichés. No doubt they didn't do so consciously; they merely responded to what their market demanded. Their repertoire was, however, remarkably uniform and consistent. A host of more or less incompetent scribblers seemed to know, as if by instinct, that a large class of readers had acquired a bottomless appetite for certain scenes and situations. Wretchedly though they wrote, there was nothing incompetent about their salesmanship.

Their characters had been clichés long before Mrs. Radcliffe laid hands on them: the incessantly distressed young heroine; the bloody but unbowed young hero; the erring father; the chatty, supposedly amusing servant; the skulking, gliding villain à la Shakespeare's Richard III or Iago. The horrid novelists' methods of intrigue and suspense also had long prior histories; some dated further back than even the remote Middle Ages, in which their books were commonly set. The only thing new about the horrid novelists was their relentless concentration on a handful of stock characters and plots, along with the special air of melancholy mystery they sought to evoke by means of an equally limited stock of scenery.

Manfroné is typical. In the opening chapter, Rosalina's own bedroom has thoroughly spooked her before any assailant arrives. It is "spacious and lofty," with wainscoting of "dark cedar," and her flickering lamp "scarcely shed its faint lumen farther than the table on which it was placed."

> An almost nameless sensation, but in which terror held a share, disturbed Rosalina; for, as she gazed around, she almost fancied the distant shades as the shrouds of spectral forms, gliding along with noiseless pace; and fancy made her listen in idea to the hollow tones of their sepulchral voices.

Servants arrive to pursue the unhanded villain; they follow a trail of blood through an open panel in the wall and down a flight of steps, hoping to trace his flight.

> In this, however, they did not succeed; for after descending them, they found that they led into the subterraneous apartments of the castello, whose intricate turnings and windings they for a long time paced, till at last, satisfied that the object of their pursuit must have left the precincts of the castello by some concealed entrances to the vaults, they returned to Rosalina's chamber.

This is, of course, the same peculiar architecture that confuses Emily and Annette at Udolpho. It was repeated, with hardly a variation, throughout Radcliffe's followers' work, and by 1809 it had become formulaic, along with the sentiments it supposedly in-spired. Accompanying every castle (or castello) is a monastery, with its own familiar battery of built-in sensations:

> Rosalino [*sic*] felt a melancholy pleasure in pacing the long and lofty aisles of its chapel, and in viewing the monuments of departed worth. The tombs of her ancestors here rose in proud magnificence, adorned with all that human art could bestow, while their inmates had long since returned to their original earth, as in a few revolving years would the time-worn marble that served to record their virtues to their posterity.

Rosalina's sex change is no doubt a typo; the cliché remains intact.

It is the Graveyard poets' favorite lesson again, trimmed to within an inch of meaninglessness. Mrs. Radcliffe's elaborate descriptive set pieces have been cut down to phrases like "proud magnifi-cence" and "all that human art could bestow"; trusting an informed audience, the second Mrs. Radcliffe felt no need to stretch for a chord when a single note would serve her purpose. Her readers knew (and she knew that they knew) what feelings they wanted; there was no need to whip them up each time from scratch. Like her fellow imitators, Mary-Anne Radcliffe tamed the Graveyard cliché by gelding it. Ann Radcliffe had not done that. In *The Romance of the Forest*, when La Motte visits a similar scene, he carries the cliché to its proper conclusion: " 'A few years,' said he, 'and I shall become like the mortals on whose reliques I now gaze.' "

Eighteen years later, in *Manfroné*, Rosalina gets no farther than the decay of marble, which will prove a good deal slower than her own. Perhaps she stands in for the vigorous young Catherine Mor-lands and Henry Tilneys, the potential readers of such books. If so, they were the first generation in Western history who needed shield-ing from both the effects of mortality and its inevitable applicability to themselves. Sixty years earlier, the Graveyard poets had begun to sentimentalize the evidences of human decay, though they had still worked in the interest of an ancient, chastening moral. Ann Rad-cliffe transmitted the moral clearly enough, but she swathed it in raptures that mystified its source and dulled its chastening effect. For Radcliffe's imitators, the source had sunk into utter mystery and the effect had become a chill with nothing to teach.

Manfroné is typical, but the quintessential horrid novel is T. J. Horsley Curties's *The Monk of Udolpho*, published in 1807 and reprinted for the first time only in 1977. During those 170 years, hardly anyone saw the novel; at least, no one mentioned it in print except the indefatigable Summers, who praised it for representing "in their most flamboyant colouring all the features of the Gothic novel." Impenetrable obscurity also engulfs Curties. Summers reports that he lived in London and published six novels between 1799 and 1807, *The Monk of Udolpho* being his last; so far as I can discover, posterity knows nothing more of him. He was an unmitigated hack who lacked any trace of originality and never strove for any.

The title of *The Monk of Udolpho* is so baldly imitative it barely exists on its own: Take M. G. Lewis's *The Monk* and Ann Radcliffe's *The Mysteries of Udolpho*, squeeze them together, and there you have it. In fairness to Curties, it should be said that the title wasn't his idea. In a preface, he declares that a "more legitimate appellation" would have been *Filial Piety*; the publisher, however, had already advertised a novel called *The Monk Udolpho* when the "intended composer" died, and Curties took on the assignment. Somewhere along the line, an "of" found its way onto the title page, transforming "Udolpho" from a bastardized surname back into the name of a place—a place, however, that does not appear in the novel.

By 1807, at least at Curties's level of ambition, such absurdities didn't matter much. In the imagination of horror fans like Austen's Isabella Thorpe and of those who catered to them, "monk" and "Udolpho" (like "abbey," "castle," and "mystery") had been worn down to buzzwords, signals rather than signs. They didn't mean anything; they simply announced gooseflesh. Throughout its four volumes, *The Monk of Udolpho* operates in just the same way, seeking only to trigger prepared responses that Curties's precursors, especially Ann Radcliffe and Lewis, had taught their readers to expect. There's not a trace of originality or invention in all 973 pages of Curties's leaden prose—but then originality would have violated the rules of the game.

The Monk of Udolpho opens at midnight in the castle of the duke of Placenza, as "the youthful illustrious heiress," Hersilia, is startled awake by "the loud echoes of repeated knocking, sounding

hollowly through the domes and silent corridors of the palace."
The duke, her father, rushes into Hersilia's bedroom, apparently
dying, with a dire confession to make: He has pledged his estate,
his daughter's inheritance, to a "gamester." Before long, "the Father Confessor of the palace" noiselessly slinks in; this is the
creepy Udolpho, whose looks (as soon as she notices his presence) arouse in Hersilia "a nameless sensation of alarm and dark-
ling conjecture." Which is hardly surprising:

> His stature was tall, and even gigantic, inclined rather to the robust
> than meagre! he wore a full hood, which was generally drawn over his
> whole face and fastened under the chin, so that the real expression of
> his saturnine features could never be distinguished; across his eye-
> brows was bound a white linen forehead cloth, upon which was
> displayed in the centre the ghastly grinning ensign of a Death's head,
> said to be the emblem of an order of monks founded by Udolpho, and
> delineated in his own person with such pertinaceous [sic] exactitude
> as to render its first sight too horrible for a repetition . . .

One might wonder how Udolpho can see where he's gliding. But no
matter: The game, as Sherlock Holmes would say a century later, is
afoot.

It hardly lets up; Curties's pace is vigorous, at least. Extreme
repetitiousness, however, quickly turns the novel's would-be thrilling scenes into something close to parody. Hersilia spends most of
her time lurching between passionate melancholy and desperate
confusion; during the interludes, Udolpho invariably slithers up,
inspiring automatic surges of "nameless horror." Heroine and villain, indeed, come to resemble each other in the extremity of their
agitation. Udolpho's face may turn black "with an expression of
every baleful passion that could deform the human character; it
was dreadful, it was terrific, and even horrible; as was the tremendous oath of revenge which . . . issued from his gnashed teeth!"
But meanwhile, Hersilia "shuddered, a faint sickness chilled her
blood, her eyes alternately closed and opened, memory tortured
her inmost spirit; for all within was anarchy, confusion, and hope-
lessness."

The motives for such paroxysms are both convoluted and irrelevant; they interest Curties far less than the symptoms they produce.

Virtually everyone in *The Monk of Udolpho* (including the peerless young hero, Lorenzo) vibrates fiercely all the time—as the reader, evidently, is also supposed to do. Like Mary-Anne Radcliffe and other horrid latecomers, Curties wastes no ink justifying extremes of emotion: Whether such responses spring from evil or good, they are good for the reader, because the reader bought or borrowed *The Monk of Udolpho* exclusively for their sake. Filed down to kneejerk level, the sentimental self-indulgence of Sterne, Mackenzie, and Goethe led to this.

Eventually, a second villain arrives to plague the illustrious Hersilia: Sanguedoni, to whom the duke has gambled away both his estate and his daughter. Sanguedoni, too, suffers from chronic agitation—"here Sanguedoni grinned a ghastly horrible smile of alternate dread and pallid exultation"—but, perhaps because his head isn't tied up in a bag, no one observes his resemblance to Udolpho, who has meanwhile glided out of sight. When the monk reappears, he and Sanguedoni take turns menacing Hersilia; neither she nor any other character notices that the two men are never seen on the same rampart at the same time. Early in Volume 3, Udolpho makes approximately his dozenth unexpected appearance, during a thunderstorm:

> He seemed at that moment a being more than super-human, like nothing earthly, surrounded by the awful horrors of the tempest, enmazed in the sulphureous lightnings' flames. His gigantic black outline looked like the spirit of the storm, hurling its devastating thunders on the prostrate earth. . . . His voice now sounded, whose hollow low sepulchral tones were distinctly heard by Hersilia, tones which, like the raven's fearful screams, boding evil, ever vibrated harsh discord on her ear, and ever excited emotions of alarm and disgust.

This is one of Curties's grandest stylistic flights. It owes its peculiar lifelessness, in part, to his stilted eighteenth-century rhetoric, but also to the utter lack of conviction that infects even his strongest bids for gooseflesh. The storm, the sepulchre, and the raven—which, sixty years earlier, were among the Graveyard poets' most harrowing effects—have shrunk to feeble clumps of metaphors. Curties was a virtuoso in the deployment of horrid-novel clichés, but he lacked the smallest clue about how to make them work. Perhaps the fault wasn't entirely his: After hundreds of knock-offs in less than two decades, Mrs. Radcliffe's formula had run a bit thin by 1807. Two years later, however, even the dimly talented Mary-Anne Radcliffe was able to do far better in *Manfroné*, and of course these same clichés have enjoyed a vigorous career for nearly two more centuries. Curties's blatant cynicism defeated him: Unable to believe in his props, he could only rearrange them, not give them power.

Udolpho offers to rescue Hersilia from Sanguedoni's clutches. Improbably enough, she accepts, and after many hours on mule-back, the maiden and the monk arrive at the Castello di Ubaldi, a bargain-basement version of the villain's namesake: "On a lofty eminence was [*sic*] seen some bold gigantic towers, whose broken moss-clad battlements and walls displayed at once the ravages of time and long neglect." This "fearful abode" possesses all the requisite spooky-house features, in cartoon form: "shattered gate," "heavy chains," "unsocial glooms," "grass-grown court," and "gothic grandeur." There is even a "middle aged woman, of very unprepossessing demeanour," who informs the new arrivals that the place is about to fall into ruins, thanks to last night's "hurri-cane."

Curties has barely bothered to describe Hersilia's home castle—or any other locale, for that matter—but he lavishes attention on Ubaldi, repeatedly stressing how large, dark, intricate, and above all rotten it is. On the way to her distant sleeping quarters, Hersilia

> ascended a once noble but decayed flight of broken steps, which led under a gloomy vaulted porch into a large pillared hall of vast circumference and dreary comfortless aspect; for the ceiling was in many places so dilapidated, as to admit the damps and chilling blasts of the keen mountain winds, which swept in hollow gusts through the extended vistas of this immense fabric, whose darkened aisles now filling the misty twilight of fast approaching night, ren-dered half its recesses indistinguishable, and wrapt in vapoury glooms.

When a cynical writer starts making greater efforts than his contract stipulates, sympathy has waylaid him. Curties wastes no energy on

Hersilia, Lorenzo, or even Udolpho-Sanguedoni; the banal intrigues that set them moving get minimal treatment at best; scenery
is hardly mentioned. But when, after five hundred weary pages, *The
Monk of Udolpho* reaches this dank ruin-in-progress, Curties suddenly becomes descriptive and emotive at once. For the first time,
he has left off merely manipulating his readers. Now he's spooking
himself.

Hersilia's designated apartment lies, of course, an immense
distance from the castle gate. As the ill-favored Beatrice leads her
away, they enact a parody of Emily and Annette's trek through
Udolpho. Contrary to his custom, however, Curties elaborates this
cliché instead of trimming it. He goes on for pages as they cross a
hall, climb crumbling marble steps, traverse a vaulted corridor, and
catch sight of "the remains of innumerable doors and low-vaulted
openings." Curties's topography is as vague and dreamlike as Mrs.
Radcliffe's, but he puts more emphasis on rot: The castle's air is
"moist and unwholesome," its "wholly deserted" rooms both "old"
and "frightful." The building is like a vast charnel house, or a
gigantic rotting corpse.

When the tour is done, automatic writing resumes, and the last
four hundred pages of *The Monk of Udolpho* drag their weary
length along. Virtually every cliché on Henry Tilney's list makes its
appearance: the isolated chamber (whose last occupant died
there), the rumors of ghosts, the mysterious chest in a dark corner,
the lamp that won't stay lit. It's almost as if Curties had read
Northanger Abbey, failed to notice the satire, and used it as his
blueprint. In the end, Udolpho-Sanguedoni's identity is revealed,
Lorenzo reappears, Hersilia is rescued, and just deserts get univer-
sally distributed. Curties lays down his pen after the novel's lame
lesson: "Heaven may afflict, but man must not complain."

The Monk of Udolpho, in contrast, provides plenty to complain
about. It is wretchedly written, poorly constructed, shrill and dull at
the same time. Perhaps hack work in any age shares these qualities, but this hack novel also illustrates the degree of debasement
that had overtaken the horrid formula in the remarkably short span
of thirteen years between *The Mysteries of Udolpho* in 1794 and
Curties's pale simulacrum in 1807. No wonder Austen's publisher
gladly returned the manuscript of *Northanger Abbey*. By the end of
the nineteenth century's first decade, the repertoire of thrills that

had slowly evolved through Graveyard poetry, ersatz Gothicism, and Sentimental swooning had become so banal even a child could play it. Indeed, a virtual child did just that, when seventeen-year-old Percy Bysshe Shelley published his first horror, *Zastrozzi*, in 1810 (a second, *St. Irvyne; or, The Rosicrucian*, followed later that year, but Shelley had turned eighteen by then).

Horrid fiction did not die, of course; it flourishes among us still. But the oddest aspect of its history is that, having taken Western culture by storm, the horrid novel proceeded to blow itself out almost as fast. To some degree, it merely went underground, slipping from the level of respectable middle-class entertainment to that of magazine stories and penny dreadfuls, where it straggled on through the middle of the nineteenth century. Even there, however, its appeal was limited and intermittent. The Victorian age, which twentieth-century popular wisdom makes out to have been the heyday of ghoulies and ghosties, was in fact a time of virtual famine compared to the ages that preceded and followed it.

The phenomenon is mysterious, but some clues may be found in the other arena where fictional horror enjoyed an early triumph, the theater. From the moldering ruin to the flickering lamp, the whole roster of horrid clichés was fundamentally visual; it begged for stage adaptation, and playwrights and managers eagerly complied. For the same few years when the Catherine Morlands of the world trembled over the pages of horrid novels, theatergoers gasped at horrid plays. Then the theater, too, woke up—or dozed off, depending on your point of view—into the uneasy domesticity of the Victorian age.

Over-the-top melodrama style: the Wolf's Glen scene from Weber's *Der Freischütz*. (BETTMANN ARCHIVES)

4

Stages of fear

EXPLICITNESS

On the whole, the horrid novel was a genteel genre, tailored to the sensibilities of the middle-class young men and women who formed its chief readership. Few horrid novelists invoked the supernatural without a rational explanation; belief in ghosts was usually confined to comical peasants and servants. Even fewer writers dwelt on sex, bloodshed, or rot. They hinted at such matters constantly, but on the brink of explicitness they drew back. *Manfroné*, with its severed hand, is something of an exception, but it came late in the horrid-novel fad, when the tenderest reader may have been yearning for a dose of stronger medicine.

There was, however, no visible trend in that direction. At its sputtering end, in the 1820s, the genre remained as polite as it had been in the 1790s. Even the last great English Gothic, Charles Robert Maturin's *Melmoth the Wanderer* (1820)—which is exceptional for both its convoluted structure and its unashamed reliance on the supernatural—evokes far more thunder than blood. Six years later, when the horrid novel's condition was terminal, Maturin's admirer William Child Green furnished a "beautifully bossed and speckled" demon and a whole pondful of gore in his *Abbot of Montserrat; or, The Pool of Blood.* The demon is real, but the sanguinary pond turns out to be fake—disappointing every recorded twentieth-century reader of that lame novel.

In the twentieth century, especially its latter half, sympathy with the original horrid novelists has become difficult to achieve. Their aim is clear—to give a delightful chill—but the means they employ seem feeble and foolishly dainty. The clinical displays of body parts, both intact and severed, that characterize today's horror fictions possess a raw power utterly lacking in the stylized, sanitized scenes those old novels conjure up. Yet there is, I think, a direct line of descent from *Manfroné* to, for instance, George A. Romero's full-color blood feast *Day of the Dead* (1985), with its close-ups of spilling guts. The differences between the novel and the film are more of degree than of kind. Both plunge their audiences into a universe reeking of death, where the past will not stay dead but rises to plague the living; both demonstrate that life and death have more in common than the living like to suppose.

Between the 1740s and the 1790s, the ancient, somber lesson of the Graveyard poets was transformed into a commercial article. Stripped of religious connotations, pushed back into a fanciful, impossible past, the lesson lost its original point and became a vague, half-remembered horror. As Western culture drew away from intimacy with death, the Graveyard poets' crypts and charnels turned into haunted places, remote yet uncannily familiar, whose convoluted innards decayed like corpses and resembled them in their wet, secret intricacy. The rise of a reading public that had never seen a real charnel house, for whom the aftereffects of death grew steadily stranger as delicacy hid them away, led to the fearful mystification of rot. Only rarely did the horrid novel admonish its readers to consider their own inevitable death, prefigured in the relics of the past. Instead, death and decay became unaccountably scary old things. In these old books—which now have become what they once portrayed—decay belongs far away, beyond the edge of life. When youth and beauty go over the edge, the result is horror. And, of course, youth and beauty must eventually return, so that life can carry on.

Just one eighteenth-century novelist sent his people over and left them there. Matthew Gregory Lewis's *The Monk*, first published in March 1796 (when Lewis was four months short of turning twenty-one), broke all the horrid genre's rules before they had well been formed. Not only does the novel revel in the supernatural without apology or excuse; it also provides graphic portrayals of sex and violence that can raise eyebrows even two centuries later. For better or worse, Lewis's explicitness seems surprisingly ahead of its time. Eighteenth-century readers were surprised, too: *The Monk* raised a chorus of moral outrage, and Lewis obligingly expurgated it, especially in the fourth edition (1798). According to Montague Summers, even late in the nineteenth century the novel "was spoken of as a lewd book and still regarded with sternest disapproval"; booksellers commonly listed it "with pornography." Grove Press, which in the 1950s and 1960s prided itself on reissuing suppressed sexy shockers, published what it billed as the first unexpurgated American edition in 1952. As Summers also comments, however, it would be impossible to exaggerate the "success and scandal" of *The Monk* in its own day. Everybody read it, and everybody with literary pretensions had something to say about it.

Modern critics have emphasized *The Monk*'s far-ranging influence: Nathaniel Hawthorne, Mary Shelley, and E. T. A. Hoffmann, along with many others, certainly knew the book, and perhaps they were inspired by it to some of their stronger bids for gooseflesh. But the writers on whom modern critics have concentrated belonged to a self-conscious elite; they had little in common with the employees of the nascent entertainment industry that churned out horrid diversions for Catherine Morland and her friends. Literary artists such as Samuel Taylor Coleridge, Percy Shelley, and Thomas Lovell Beddoes made a quite different use of Gothic materials from the horde of imitators who scurried after Ann Radcliffe.

Among other things, those artists psychologized Gothic horrors, bending them into nightmares of the waking mind. That fashion swept the fear industry only after the middle of the nineteenth century. And artists were not content merely to copy their precursors, introducing just enough variation to please an easily jaded taste that nevertheless shrank from any challenge to familiarity. Instead, they probed clichés till they screamed. When Coleridge, for example, went after horrors in "Christabel" (1816), he produced a work so deeply disturbing he could not bear his own conception and left the poem unfinished.

Understandably, seeing profundity there rather than drudging imitativeness, modern critics have foraged through the artistic past to assemble a tradition of "Gothic" fiction that looks brash, brave, and adventurous. That tradition, however, is also somewhat patchy, since it is confined to those rare works that succeed in both raising chills and pleasing critics. Studies that leapfrog from *The Monk* to *Frankenstein*, from Edgar Allan Poe to Bram Stoker, usually cast bored or disdainful glances across the vast plains of mediocrity that stretch away from such peaks. But it is there, down among the rip-offs, that culture makes its choices of what to let live and what to embalm.

Run-of-the-mill horrid novelists did not batten on *The Monk*. And genteel devotees of the horrid left it alone—at least if you trust Jane Austen, which is generally a safe bet. *The Monk* does not appear on Isabella's list of delicious horrors; it is mentioned only once in *Northanger Abbey*, and in a context that clearly indicates Austen's opinion of Lewis's masterwork. On first meeting Isabella's crass, blustery brother John, Catherine asks him her favorite question: "Have you ever read Udolpho, Mr. Thorpe?"

> Udolpho! Oh, Lord! not I; I never read novels; I have something else to do. . . . Novels are all so full of nonsense and stuff; there has not been a tolerably decent one come out since Tom Jones, except the Monk; I read that t'other day; but as for all the others, they are the stupidest things in creation.

As if Thorpe's vulgarity didn't sufficiently damn his judgment, he goes on to reveal his ignorance that *Udolpho* was written by Mrs. Radcliffe.

Thorpe probably hasn't read *The Monk*—it would take a busy "t'other day" to get through its three stout volumes—but Lewis's dose of horrors was just coarse enough to suit florid young bucks with reputations to uphold. It was the ideal horrid novel for those who never read horrid novels—and so it has remained. Anomalous though it was, however, *The Monk* stands apart from the norm of horrid fiction chiefly because it makes explicit what Radcliffean writers left implied. Lewis's repertoire of castles, monasteries, and crypts, trembling heroines, stalwart heroes, and evil Catholic clerics did not differ markedly from the Radcliffean formula that inspired him and that Radcliffe's followers would run into the ground. The chief difference is that Lewis pursued the implications of these clichés-in-the-making further than any other English novelist dared or was able to do.

The Monk consists of two linked but easily separable plots: the corruption and eventual damnation of the monk Ambrosio at the hands of the demonic Matilda; and the trials of Raymond and Agnes, whose love must surmount gruesome obstacles before its happy ending. The Raymond-and-Agnes plot also features a long flashback, about a fifth of the novel's length, in which Raymond recounts his adventures in Germany, where he first met his sweetheart. These include a hairsbreadth escape from brigands, an encounter with the Wandering Jew, and a run-in with the ghostly Bleeding Nun of Lindenberg. For purposes of recycling—the hallmark of horrid fiction, then as now—*The Monk* offered three rich sources, though they were of unequal usefulness.

The least useful was Lewis's main plot, which gave *The Monk* its title. The prominence of gliding monks in later horrid novels can be ultimately traced to Ambrosio, but the immediate source was Ann Radcliffe's Schedoni in *The Italian*, published the year after Lewis's novel. Her monk was probably intended, as several modern critics have suggested, to show how sinister clerics *should* be portrayed. Schedoni is far more subtly drawn than sweaty Ambrosio, but he's also tidied up; Schedoni lusts for power, not orgasm. By contrast, once Matilda has awakened Ambrosio to sexual pleasure, the famously chaste monk can think of nothing else; driven inexorably from each transgression to a worse one, he ends by raping and murdering his sister and murdering his mother.

Along the way, Ambrosio engages in bouts of voluptuous excess that the nineteenth century found pornographic; the twentieth might pause before rejecting that opinion. There remains something titillating about a young woman (Matilda) disguising herself as a novice monk (Rosario) in order to entrap a paragon of chastity—especially since, at the very end of the novel, (s)he turns out to have been a male demon all along. Ambrosio dallies warmly with Rosario, but when Rosario becomes Matilda, all hell breaks loose:

> He sat upon her bed; his hand rested upon her bosom; her head reclined voluptuously upon his breast. Who then can wonder if he yielded to the temptation? Drunk with desire, he pressed his lips to those which sought them; his kisses vied with Matilda's in warmth and passion: he clasped her rapturously in his arms; he forgot his vows, his sanctity, and his fame; he remembered nothing but the pleasure and opportunity.

In the Radcliffean version, villains are already evil when they arrive; the story of how they got that way is usually saved until quite late, when it is told briefly, by way of accounting for their dirty deeds. Lewis filled in that gap with a vengeance and a difference. Not only did he make Ambrosio's corruption graphically sexual; he also made it the centerpiece of his novel.

The Raymond-and-Agnes plot of *The Monk*, with its digression on the Bleeding Nun, concentrates on gruesomeness rather than sex; it therefore proved much more adaptable for recycling, as Lewis himself discovered. Agnes's woes derive from her premarital pregnancy by Raymond, but Lewis doesn't linger on that. Inducted against her will into the convent of St. Clare, Agnes falls victim to the fanatical prioress, Mother St. Agatha, who desires for her women the same chaste reputation that attaches (falsely) to Ambrosio's men. When Agnes's pregnancy is revealed, the prioress orders her mock burial, with worse to follow. This story—told near the end of the novel, by Agnes herself—gives Lewis the chance to dwell upon decay as no one had done since the Graveyard poets, though with a purpose they would never have recognized.

Awakening from drugged sleep, Agnes finds herself in the convent crypt:

> I was oppressed by a noisome suffocating smell; and perceiving that the grated door was unfastened, I thought that I might possibly effect my escape. As I raised myself with this design, my hand rested upon something soft: I grasped it, and advanced it towards the light. Almighty God! what was my disgust! my consternation! In spite of its putridity, and the worms which preyed upon it, I perceived a cor-

rupted human head, and recognised the features of a nun who had died some months before.

This is bad enough, but soon Agnes is conveyed to a secret cell, still deeper underground and crawling with "reptiles of every description." There, in darkness and solitude, she gives birth to Raymond's child, which dies after a few hours.

Camilla, the nun who brings her food each day, begs her to surrender the little corpse for burial, but Agnes refuses.

> I vowed, not to part with it while I had life: its presence was my only comfort, and no persuasion could induce me to give it up. It soon became a mass of putridity, and to every eye was a loathsome and disgusting object, to every eye but a mother's. . . . Sometimes I felt the bloated toad, hideous and pampered with the poisonous vapours of the dungeon, dragging his loathsome length along my bosom. Sometimes the quick cold lizard roused me, leaving his slimy track upon my face, and entangling itself in the tresses of my wild and matted hair. Often have I at waking found my fingers ringed with the long worms which bred in the corrupted flesh of my infant.

The reader's prior knowledge that Agnes has survived these horrors may blunt the effect of their telling, but she reels them off with such perky matter-of-factness that she becomes rather horrible herself.

Or perhaps she's merely childish: Lewis finished the first draft of *The Monk* when he was nineteen, and it betrays both an adolescent's guesswork at biology and his Chattertonian lust for rapture. It also shows how deeply versed in the romance of rot any reader could become in the late eighteenth century. Though literary historians seldom place Lewis in their company, he belongs (with Chatterton, Wordsworth, Byron, and Shelley) among the marvelous crop of poetical boys England produced in the era we now call pre-Romantic. Most died young—Chatterton at 17, Shelley at 29, Byron at a comparatively hoary 36. Wordsworth lived to be 80, an achievement that embarrassed everyone but him. Moderate in this if nothing else, Lewis died in 1818, aged 42, on the return journey from a family plantation in Jamaica; he was buried at sea.

As far as the horrid novel was concerned, he might as well have died in 1796. Shocking and bestselling though *The Monk* was, Lewis never wrote another novel. Perhaps he realized that he had already shoved that genre as far as it went; the only surviving son of a very wealthy father, he had no need to crank out copycat horrors. He continued writing, however, for more than a decade after *The Monk*, producing poems, stories, and above all plays, fifteen of which were staged between 1798 and 1812. Though his novel's success had permanently dubbed him "Monk" Lewis, his dramatic efforts sought no extremes of sex or violence. They were wholly of their time, or just slightly ahead of it, setting short-lived trends. They were also remarkably various, ranging from *The Castle Spectre* (1798) to *The East Indian* (1800), a highly popular comedy, and *Timour the Tartar* (1811), an exotic "equestrian" melodrama that capitalized on the new fad for real, live horses galloping across the stage.

Even when he shocked no sensibilities, Lewis always aimed to surprise. *The Monk* still does that, but Lewis's theatrical works have sunk from sight in the slough of drivel spewed out by European and American theaters during most of the nineteenth century. Until recently, historians of English drama tended to sprint from Richard Brinsley Sheridan's comedies of the 1770s to Oscar Wilde's of the 1890s, nodding briefly at such midcentury playwrights as Dion Boucicault and Tom Taylor but otherwise dismissing the period as a vulgar aberration. Even Allardyce Nicoll, the English theater's most assiduous twentieth-century scholar, who strains for generosity till it hurts, admits that early nineteenth-century plays were no better than their audiences, which were horrid:

> [T]he auditorium of an early nineteenth century playhouse was a place lacking both in taste and in good manners, a place where vulgarity abounded, where true appreciation of the drama was subordinated, not to witty if somewhat improper badinage as in the Restoration theatre, but to rude and foolish practical jokes, to the roaring of a drunken bully, to the besotted solicitations of a prostitute.

Nicoll wrote in the 1930s; recent historians have often reversed his values, idealizing such scenes—especially the American ones—as carnivals of cultural democracy. The period from the late eighteenth century to about the middle of the nineteenth seems in fact to have been a rare interval in the history of Western theater when the playhouse was neither middle-class nor aristocratic but genuinely popular. And though their value judgments differ, all authorities agree that by the middle of the nineteenth century, across Western Europe and in the United States, the performing arts were well launched on a process of sorting into the categories of highbrow and lowbrow, elite and popular, polite and vulgar, that we now take for granted.

It was the rowdy theater of the nineteenth century into which Lewis moved after shocking the polite world with *The Monk*. Not a highly genteel place, it would soon get less so, thanks in part to Lewis's efforts. The early-nineteenth-century theater, however, was the true heir of the horrid novel, quickly latching on to its favorite effects, intensifying them to a degree that the printed word was incapable of, and maintaining its delight in horrors long after written fiction had grown tired of them. Eventually, the stage, too, would fall out of love with old-style fear—a signal that a new style, far scarier than the old, was about to be born. In the meantime— carnival.

A NIGHT AT THE THEATER

Going to the theater in the early nineteenth century was no casual undertaking. If you went, for example, to Astley's Amphitheatre in London on June 10, 1833, your evening's entertainment began at about 6:30 with a performance of *The Siege of Troy; or, Giant Horse of Sinon*, a quasi-historical extravaganza ending with a "grand tableau" of the Greek and Trojan armies, while the "Castle and City blazes [*sic*]" in the background. Next, you marveled at the ersatz-Oriental splendors of *Chinese Wonders; or, The Five Days Fête of Pekin*. This gave way to a "Rustic Tale of Love and Harvest Home" called *The Reaper*, which highlighted "the Execution of some Equestrian Feats"—a rather modest way of describing Astley's specialty, daredevil horses and riders. Finally, you thrilled to *The Hag of the Storm; or, The Doomed Knight*, an anonymous adaptation of Lewis's 1811 spine-tingler, *One O'Clock! or, The Knight and the Wood Demon*.

The management reserved its best for last. In typical early-nineteenth-century style, Astley's playbill gave an immodest inventory of the finale:

> sudden Convulsion of Nature and Awful Darkness of the earth, preparatory to the Fiery Appearance of the Sorceress demanding her Victim. Sleeping Chamber of Mystery, and the Fathom Deep Cell of Sorcery. Ropey Altar of Human Bones—The Dark Powers of Evil Fall, and the Rightful Heir is Re-enstated in the honour of the Domains of Holstein, whilst the Doomed Knight is borne off by the Dragon Daemon.

And so to bed, after midnight—having had, to say the least, your money's worth.

Three thousand five hundred miles to the southwest, and six years later, your evening at the American Theater, Philadelphia, would be just as long and various, though more homespun. First, *As You Like It*; then "Il Diavolo Antonio and His Sons," presenting "a most magnificent display of position in the Science of Gymnastics"; then Mr. Quayle singing "The Swiss Drover Boy"; then La Petite Celeste in "A New Grand Pas Seul," followed by Miss Lee dancing "La Cachuca"; then Mr. Quayle returning for "The Haunted Spring," followed by Mr. Bowman telling "a Yankee Story"; then the evening wound up with a full-scale performance of James Kenney's 1807 melodrama *Ella Rosenberg*.

All over Western Europe and the Americas, for fifty years, evenings at the theater took this promiscuous, miscellaneous form. Persons who valued decorum stayed home or visited such sanctuaries as Paris's Comédie Française, where a chaster seventeenth-century tradition lived on. Ballet and opera also attracted more fastidious souls—though even these entertainments, which the twentieth century has crowned the soporific monarchs of elite culture, behaved rather rudely in their youth. Persons who valued coherence stayed home as well; some whiled away the time they saved by writing plays, some of which were published, very few of which ever made it to the stage.

Especially in England and the United States, the early years of the nineteenth century saw a sharp, almost total rift between poetry and drama, between elite writing intended for private perusal and popular writing intended for performance. Most of the great English Romantics wrote plays; Coleridge's *Remorse* and Byron's *Marino Faliero* even made it to the stage, though their success was slight. In the next generation, Robert Browning went through a brief phase of playwriting during the 1840s, but just two of his verse dramas were staged, both for brief runs. Not until the end of the century, with Arthur Wing Pinero, Oscar Wilde, and especially George Bernard Shaw, did the highest quality of writing (though prose, not poetry) return to the English-speaking stage.

The rift healed sooner in France, where Victor Hugo's *Hernani* scored a simultaneous literary and popular success as early as 1830. In Germany and Scandinavia, the naturalism of Gerhart Hauptmann, Henrik Ibsen, and August Strindberg demonstrated by 1880 that artistic integrity need not be incompatible with stage-worthiness. But at least in the first decades of the century, almost everywhere in the West, literary worth seemed to preclude performability, and vice versa. Scholars have cited many reasons for the dilemma: the coarseness of theatrical audiences, the low pay available to playwrights, the insatiable demand for new plays, which relentlessly sacrificed quality to quantity. Another important reason, however, was an attitude problem on the part of those writers who, if they'd been willing to dirty their hands, might have raised the artistic level of the debased and degenerate stage.

Blaming the audience was a favorite pastime. An amusing example, which mocks the attitude even while embodying it, is the "Children's Fairy Tale" *Der gestiefelte Kater* (Puss in Boots), by the German poet, novelist, and translator Ludwig Tieck (1773–1853). Tieck's satire—which was published in 1798, though not performed until 1844—presents a wretched play called *Puss in Boots* being watched by an unruly audience whose demands the incompetent "poet" labors in vain to satisfy. His play is a mess to begin with, jumbling together shards of Charles Perrault's old fairy tale and such irrelevancies as a princess who has read Young's *Night Thoughts* and yearns to write "a horrid ghost story," an idiotic king with an inordinate fondness for rabbits, and a pair of generic lovers, known as He and She, who come out of nowhere and go back there.

Tieck's play within a play makes splendid fun of all the incommensurate diversions a night at a turn-of-the-century theater might

offer. The hodgepodge is made yet crazier by the fractious spectators, who hiss, pound, and chatter whenever something displeases
them, a frequent occurrence. Sometimes they also ask insightful
questions, like "What on earth was the point of that last scene?"
and "In what time period is the piece supposed to be set?" After the
lovers' first appearance, the question of unity comes up, only to get
slapped down:

> FISCHER: Ah, but that was something for the heart. It does you
>   good to see stuff like that.
> LEUTNER: Really fine diction in that scene.
> MÜLLER: But I wonder if it's necessary to the whole play.
> SCHLOSSER: I don't care about the whole play. When I cry, I cry,
>   and that's good enough for me. It was a heavenly scene.

Müller's voice is a lonely one. The other spectators, like the readers
of horrid novels, want only to be amused from moment to moment.

Tieck's poor poet is doomed to fail. He tries everything: dancing
apes and bears, trained birds, elephants and lions, a ballet, Harle-
quin, a coach drawn by eight real horses. Some spectators like
this, others that, but the general mood grows steadily more hostile. Finally, near the end of the third act, all the stops get pulled
out:

> The pit begins to applaud as the stage changes. The fire and water
> from The Magic Flute begin to play. Above, the open Temple of the
> Sun appears; the sky is open, and Jupiter sits in it. Below, hell with
> Tercaleon, goblins, and witches on the stage, many lights, etc. The
> public claps immoderately; all is in an uproar.

Even this, however, cannot save the poet. In an epilogue, he issues
a (versified) plea for mutual understanding—only to get pelted
with "rotten pears and apples and rolled-up paper." This evening at
a theater within a theater ends in a rout.

Puss in Boots attacks several contemporary German targets—
especially Mozart, whose *Magic Flute* (first performed in 1791)
seems to have been Tieck's bête noire. But his satire also provides
a double-edged portrait of the theatrical conditions that prevailed

throughout Western Europe from the end of the eighteenth century until the middle of the nineteenth, and in some places still later. Tieck's playwright may be a fool, yet the silliest thing he does is attempt to reconcile high artistic ambitions with a campaign for approval from an opinionated, disrespectful public. Only bursts of crude, strong feeling, no matter how preposterous, can please them, and then only while each feeling lasts; as soon as one burst fades, they yelp for another. How can any self-respecting artist hope to quench a thirst like that?

An impossible task, of course. Yet the flight of art from the early-nineteenth-century theater did nothing to dim its raucous, garish, brilliant vitality. Reading those old plays—those that made it into print, as most did not—amounts to sifting dust and ashes. Much of the language bears no relation to human speech; the plots don't even nod at credibility; the characters barely deserve that name, since they either plunge from action to action incoherently or adhere to vice or virtue with lunatic singlemindedness. The plays hardly differ from the horrid novels that preceded them, accompanied them for a while, then faded away. But the theater had one decisive advantage over the novel: When words failed, as they often did, spectacular stage devices and stirring music could take their place.

As playbills of the time attest, the early-nineteenth-century theater was a wonderland of impressive visual and aural effects. Plot, character, language, meaning—all that a Tieckish "poet" revered—took second place to coaxing oohs and aahs. Stage machinery, of course, was primitive by twentieth-century standards. Most London theaters, for example, employed candles and oil lamps till the 1850s, when gaslight was installed. Until the middle of the century, in most theaters the auditorium and the stage remained equally, though dimly, lit throughout the performance, except for a "fierce glare" from the footlights that made "deep upward shadows on the countenances of the performers," whether they wished to look villainous or not.

These and many other obstacles to convincingness were gradually disposed of during the course of the century, until by the 1890s the electrically illuminated, picture-frame stage had become standard, as it still is. Reading the playbills and printed texts for earlier plays, with their breathless invocations of battles, thunderstorms, burning cities, and specters wreathed in blue fire, one finds it hard to imagine how such effects were produced at all. To a late-twentieth-century eye, accustomed to the utmost verisimilitude, they would probably look naive. Yet that late-twentieth-century eye gazes upon a flat glass surface about two feet wide, where faded colors blur and flicker, and believes it sees the real world there.

Captious though early-nineteenth-century theatrical audiences could be, freehanded with rotten fruit on occasion, they seem to have suspended disbelief enthusiastically. They never mistook illusion for reality—only late in the century would plays even start to ask for that strange feat—but they took eager part in the make-believe, gleefully riding the waves of emotion that playwrights, actors, and stage technicians set surging. Virtually any emotion would do, so long as it came sharp and clear, trimmed of tedious nuances. Across that spectrum, artificial fear traced a fiery blue stripe.

ENEMIES OF THE STATELY

The theater has always recycled the culture it lives in: Aeschylus and Sophocles drew many of their tragedies from familiar myths, and Shakespeare plundered every book he laid his hands on. Parasitical as ever, the late-eighteenth-century theater saw a hot property in the horrid novel and moved in—abetted, as it would be for decades, by the absence of copyright laws. Yet at first, playwrights shied away from exploiting the very qualities that made the horrid novel popular: Gothic awe, supernatural terror, and a general swooniness in regard to landscape and love. Instead, the early adapters of horrid novels jammed their sprawling hot properties into the narrow, frigid mold of Restoration and Augustan tragedy, purifying but denaturing them.

Robert Jephson's *The Count of Narbonne*, the earliest would-be horrid play in any language, premiered at Covent Garden, London, on November 17, 1781. It was inspired in part by *The Castle of Otranto*, though it changed the locale to France and altered every character's name but Theodore's. According to actress, novelist, and playwright Elizabeth Inchbald, who wrote introductory "Remarks" for an 1807 edition of the play, the elderly Horace Walpole attended some rehearsals and gave his imprimatur to Jephson's "close imitation" of his novel. He could hardly have objected to this five-act blank-verse "tragedy" on grounds of decorum. It dispenses entirely with *Otranto*'s gigantic claptrap, which was a good idea. But, instead of using the theater's scenic resources to instill a Gothic mood (as Walpole had been doing for thirty years at Strawberry Hill), Jephson relied on pseudo-Shakespearean rhetoric:

> The owl mistakes his season, in broad day
> Screaming his hideous omens; spectres glide,
> Gibbering and pointing as we pass along;
> While the deep earth's unorganized caves
> Send forth wild sounds, and clamours terrible . . .

Thus the unhappy countess in Act I; she carries on like this for much of the play.

The Count of Narbonne, of course, predated Mrs. Radcliffe's horrid formula by more than a decade. Her theatrical adapters and imitators, however, shared Jephson's determination to swaddle strong feeling in robes of stateliness. James Boaden's *Fontainville Forest* (1794), for example, pulled whatever tiny fangs Radcliffe's *Romance of the Forest* possessed. Boaden then outdid himself by taming *The Monk*. His *Aurelio and Miranda* (1798) not only avoided all "recourse to supernatural agency"; it also puffed up Ambrosio (Aurelio) and Matilda (Miranda) into speechifying lovers who spend most of Act IV debating whether chastity is the best policy and deciding at last that it is. Boaden's play no doubt gave John Philip Kemble and Sarah Siddons, the foremost English actors of their day, ample occasion for fine poses. But it emasculated Lewis's novel even more thoroughly than Lewis had done.

Aurelio and Miranda also introduced a troupe of musical gypsies; their role is minor, but their presence in the play shows that even the high-minded Boaden wasn't deaf to the siren song of spectacle. Some dramatists had harkened sooner, including Miles Peter Andrews, who with Frederick Reynolds and others had fabricated *The Mysteries of the Castle: A Dramatic Tale*, first staged in 1795. Vaguely inspired by *The Mysteries of Udolpho*, this semiopera (one hardly knows what to call it) offered its viewers a tasty mixture, as the prologue promised:

> Our Bard, long known to you, this night makes up,
> Of various beverages—a kind of *cup*;
> Of Music, Pantomime, and graver scenes,
> Perhaps a dash of terror intervenes . . .

Terror is in short supply, despite "an old Castle" with "an appearance of great antiquity and ruins." There are, however, plenty of songs, including an opening chorus by "SICILIAN GIRLS coming from the Hills," who would not have seemed out of place, more than a century later, in a Rudolf Friml operetta:

> Gaily tripping to and fro'
> We village maids to market go,
> And with jest and jocund lay,
> Oft beguile the tedious way . . .

Like Boaden's gypsies, Andrews's happy peasants provided a refreshing change of mood from the high-toned gloom that pervaded the rest of *The Mysteries of the Castle*. But this "cup" of alternating frivolity and rant also foreshadowed the truly miscellaneous, even incoherent entertainments that crowded the stage during the first half of the nineteenth century.

Boaden and Andrews did their chief work for London's "major" theaters, Drury Lane and Covent Garden. Thanks to the Licensing Act of 1737, only these two houses (and after 1766 the Theatre Royal, Haymarket, during the summer) were permitted to show plays of a "legitimate" kind. All other theaters had to confine themselves to "illegitimate" drama, a vaguely defined category that included pantomimes, animal spectacles like Astley's horse extravaganzas, sung shows like operas, and anything that relied on music. This enforced distinction between high and low—which endured, officially at least, until 1843—helps to account for the numbingly stately quality of the earliest horrid adaptations in England.

Already by the late 1790s, however, stateliness had gone into full flight from even the major theaters. Monk Lewis's first horrid play,

The Castle Spectre, which premiered at Drury Lane late in 1797, marks a turning point. This "most typical specimen of all Gothic melodramas," as Summers calls it, dished up, along with several songs, a banquet of horrid clichés: Osmond, the usurping earl; Reginald, the rightful earl, thought to be dead but actually hidden in a secret cell; Angela, the lost heiress; yet a third earl, Percy, disguised as a peasant; comical, superstitious servants; and, of course, the Spectre, Evelina, Reginald's wife, whom Osmond murdered sixteen years ago.

She doesn't appear till the end of Act II, but she's worth waiting for:

The folding-doors unclose, and the Oratory is seen illuminated. In its centre stands a tall female figure, her white and flowing garments spotted with blood; her veil is thrown back, and discovers a pale and melancholy countenance: her eyes are lifted upwards, her arms extended towards heaven, and a large wound appears upon her bosom.

Evelina comes back at the denouement to rescue Reginald and to allow Angela to stab the vile usurper; in the end, "REGINALD *kneels to* EVELINA *as the* GHOST *slowly ascends. Tableau and* CURTAIN."

Lewis has it both ways with his Castle Spectre. For the first two acts, he uses rumors of her presence (conveyed by servants) to build expectations of something horrid to come. At the end of Act II, these expectations are brilliantly satisfied, without a word being spoken, in a purely visual coup de théâtre. But Evelina looks more like a Catholic martyr than a creature from beyond the grave; her intentions are honorable, and her final ascent no doubt takes her among the angels. Like the Bleeding Nun in *The Monk*—who haunts the earth because her remains "lie still unburied"—the Castle Spectre evokes a graveyard chill only to warm it over: The dead do walk, but with benevolent designs.

This cop-out, which became an enduring cliché, resembles *Udolpho*'s trick of explaining away the supernatural after a few hundred pages of suspense. Although Evelina is real, *The Castle Spectre* more closely follows Radcliffe's precedent than Lewis's own. There is no lust in the play, and the only invocation of rot comes early in Act II, when Osmond describes his dream of a visit from long-dead Evelina:

> "We meet again this night!" murmured her hollow voice! "Now rush to my arms—but first see what you have made me! Embrace me, my bridegroom! We must never part again!" While speaking her form withered away: the flesh fell from her bones; her eyes burst from their sockets; a skeleton, loathsome and meagre, clasped me in her mouldering arms!

No doubt William Barrymore, who played Osmond in the 1797 Drury Lane production, made the most of the footlights' deep shadows as he delivered these words. But they are only words, and they describe a dream.

The Castle Spectre's visual effects temper horror with awe; the same is true of the play's music, which it uses sparingly but with strong dramatic impact. When the Spectre bids farewell to terrified Angela, *"Instantly the organ's swell is heard; a full chorus of female voices chant 'Jubilate!' A blaze of light flashes through the Oratory, and* ANGELA *falls motionless on the floor."* The burst of sudden light and sound seems calculated to frighten at first, then to soothe and uplift as its heavenly nature becomes clear. It must have been a thrilling moment for the audience, though of course, for the undevout Lewis, a cynical one. He understood that what theatergoers wanted was not a long dose of any single emotion but a rapid, varied series of breathing exercises—from tensely held breath to shrieks to gasps to chuckles to hisses, then around the course again. Just as much for the spectators as for the actors, a play was first of all a physical experience. And Lewis provided exactly that.

The sustained stateliness of legitimate tragedy—which Jephson, Andrews, and Boaden sought to preserve even in their Gothic adaptations—could not hold up long in such a climate of demand, especially while shrewder playwrights like Lewis eagerly pandered to these new, illegitimate tastes. And so legitimacy faltered. Perhaps its nadir came in 1811, when Lewis premiered two plays: *One O'Clock!*, a reworking of his 1807 showpiece *The Wood Daemon; or, "The Clock Has Struck"* (both had music by the ubiquitous

Michael Kelly), and *Timour the Tartar,* with its galloping horses. Lewis wrote *Timour,* which opened on April 29, at the request of Covent Garden's manager, Thomas Harris. Two months earlier, Harris had revived George Colman's 1798 *Blue Beard; or, Female Curiosity!* (music by Kelly, of course), borrowing illegitimate Astley's stud. *Blue Beard* had scored an enormous success; Harris wanted equestrianism; with some reluctance, evidently, Lewis complied.

When borrowed horses caracoled (or whatever they did) on Covent Garden's stage, especially when a long-established novelist and playwright agreed to crank out horsey antics almost overnight, the entertainment industry had entered a phase that we, late in the twentieth century, can recognize. Indeed, it had become an industry, in the modern sense, for the first time. Slavishly imitative though they were, writers who catered to the horrid-novel fad look like village artisans compared to the endlessly resourceful, grossly overworked minions of early-nineteenth-century theater. They grabbed anything that would sell, copied it till it stopped selling, then moved on.

Many playwrights were incredibly prolific. George Dibdin Pitt, for instance, is credited with producing some 140 dramas, melodramas, farces, burlesques, and pantomimes between 1831 and 1857; the phenomenal James Robinson Planché, who specialized in farces and "extravaganzas," turned out well over 200 pieces in his fifty-year career. Though playwrights worked hard for their money, productivity gained a boost from the absence of any need for originality. In the English-speaking theater, novels both horrid and mild provided a rich source for royalty-free adaptations. But there was also the Continent, especially France, whose stages English adapters plundered with a remarkable voraciousness and an utter lack of conscience. Nicoll estimates that at least half the English plays written between 1800 and 1850 "must have been suggested by Parisian models" if not wholly copied from them.

Germany contributed its share, too, especially the numerous productions of August Friedrich Ferdinand von Kotzebue. His 1796 spectacle *Die Spanier in Peru oder Rollas Tod* (The Spaniards in Peru; or, Rolla's Death) enjoyed probably the greatest success of any play, all over Europe, around the turn of the nineteenth century. It was adapted into English several times, most notably by Richard Brinsley Sheridan as *Pizarro* (1799). Guilbert de Pixerécourt's 1802 French version, *Pizarre ou la conquête de Pérou* (Pizarro; or, The Conquest of Peru), seems to have been derived from both Kotzebue and Sheridan, but in the theatrical world, credit seldom went where it was due, and the frantic pace of back-and-forth copying makes the hunt for influences a rather pointless business.

German playwrights also churned out a spate of "robber" or "bandit" dramas, from Friedrich Schiller's *Die Räuber* (The Robbers) in 1781 through Karl Friedrich Hensler's *Rinaldo Rinaldini, der Räuberhauptmann* (Rinaldo Rinaldini, the Robber Captain) in 1798. The later fad for horses on stage can probably be traced to the Germans, as can the robber gangs that barge into many horrid novels (though, following Mrs. Radcliffe, English novelists always called them "banditti," even when they popped up in France). On the whole, however, despite Germany's reputation as a haunted land, German playwrights did not go in for chills. Their specialty was spectacle of the heroic kind, along with extravagant weepiness in regard to domestic virtues. And by the third decade of the nineteenth century, as horrid drama reached its peak in England and France, Germany's influence had faded.

In a sense it is appropriate that the English-speaking stage should have been engulfed in French adaptations, because at least in the realm of the frightful, England was only getting back what it had exported to France a few years earlier. Before and during the Revolution, works like Hervey's *Meditations* and Young's *Night Thoughts* were highly popular there; by the late 1790s, Ann Radcliffe, Monk Lewis, and other horrid English writers had been translated, imitated, and of course dramatized. Shipped back to England after the turn of the nineteenth century, frightening theater had taken a form that would survive, in one way or another, until the advent of film, which would adapt it yet again and bring it down to us. When nervous violins rise to accompany a potential victim through the gloom of any latter-day horror movie, they echo across nearly two hundred years, to the French innovation that stripped the last shreds of stateliness from the European stage— melodrama.

MUSIC, MAESTRO!

The word *"mélodrame"* was evidently coined by Jean-Jacques Rousseau, who defined it in 1766 as "a kind of drama in which words and music, instead of proceeding together, are heard in succession, and in which spoken phrases are to some degree announced and prepared for by musical phrases." Etymologically, the word simply means "music-drama," and so it was understood (though it remained uncommon) till late in the eighteenth century. No clear line divided operas with interludes of dialogue, like *The Magic Flute*, from plays with musical interruptions, like *The Mysteries of the Castle* and other early Gothics.

Credit for inventing melodrama in the modern sense usually gets assigned to Guilbert de Pixerécourt (1773–1844), whose career nicely illustrates what it took to be a playwright in those years. By his own account, Pixerécourt wrote or collaborated on 120 shows between 1798 and 1834; they included tragedies, comic operas, "fairy pieces," and pantomimes, along with such specialty items as *Le Chien de Montargis, ou la forêt de Bondy* (The Dog of Montargis; or, The Forest of Bondy, 1814), which spotlighted canine derring-do. With tireless rapacity, he foraged among German plays and novels, English novels (both *Udolpho* and *The Monk*), and anything French that struck him as exploitable. He had a fondness for the novels of François-Guillaume Ducray-Duminil, several of which he dramatized. One of them, *Coelina, ou L'Enfant du mystère* (Coelina; or, The Child of Mystery, 1798), gave Pixerécourt his first hit; it also helped to set the course of European drama, and scary entertainment, for the next fifty years.

Adapted under Ducray-Duminil's title, *Coelina* premiered in 1800 at the Ambigu Comique, the foremost playhouse along the "Boulevard du Crime," the Parisian equivalent of London's more dispersed "illegitimate" theater. *Coelina*'s immediate and lasting success guaranteed foreign imitation, which in England came late in 1802 with *A Tale of Mystery; A Melodrame* by Thomas Holcroft. To complicate matters—but once you venture into the subterraneous vaults of Western culture, everything becomes complicated—in the following year, Mrs. Mary Meeke published an English version of the novel, *A Tale of Mystery; or, Celina.*

Pixerécourt's *Coelina* is often called the first melodrama (though he did not label it so), and Holcroft's *Tale of Mystery* wins dubious credit for having introduced melodrama to the English stage. Holcroft's plot and characters, at least, do not differ markedly from those of a thousand earlier horrid novels and plays. There is the heroine, here named Selina, under pressure to marry the son of the evil Count Romaldi, though she loves her cousin, Stephano. There are the usual comical servants, along with Francisco, a kindly old man who was nearly killed by brigands eight years before and who remains dumb on account of the drubbing they gave him.

At the start of Act II, it appears that youth and beauty will prematurely triumph, as Selina and Stephano are about to marry and the audience is treated to *"the humorous dancing of the Italian peasants"* (in Radcliffean fashion, the play is set in Italy around the turn of the seventeenth century). But joy turns to sorrow when Romaldi produces a birth certificate proving that Selina is illegitimate. Not to be outdone, the well-meaning but oddly reticent Montano reveals that Selina is actually Francisco's child, and quite legitimate; that Romaldi is Francisco's brother; and that it was Romaldi who led the attack on Francisco eight years before, hoping to kill him and marry his wife, whom Romaldi vilely lusted for.

Exposed as a double-dyed villain, Romaldi flees into a romantic landscape, as a thunderstorm comes up, and delivers a desperate speech that will be imitated hundreds of times:

Whither fly? Where shield me from pursuit, and death, and ignominy? My hour is come! The fiends that tempted, now tear me. (*Dreadful thunder.*) The heavens shoot their fires at me! Save! spare! Oh, spare me!

The good guys arrive and capture Romaldi, Selina and Stephano are united, and all ends happily.

Most of *A Tale of Mystery* was already conventional by 1802. It offers the same remote, picturesque setting, the same impacted family relationships (spiced with potential incest), the same return of the past to haunt the present that had been cramming bookshelves and stocking stages for a decade at least. It foreshadows the future chiefly in its neglect of the supernatural—the "fiends" Romaldi complains of are mental monsters—and in the prepackaged nature of its villain. Romaldi boils down Gothic villainy, with its heritage all the way back to Milton's Satan and Shakespeare's Iago, to a literal cliché: a ready-made bundle of attributes that can be dropped into position wherever needed without inventing anything at all. Crowds of Romaldis peopled the nineteenth-century stage; eventually, remorse left them and they turned into villains, pure, simple, and just about unmotivated, reaching apotheosis in Bram Stoker's Dracula. Romaldi is the melodramatic stage villain almost complete, the original Snidely Whiplash.

Romaldi, however, was not Pixerécourt's and Holcroft's most important contribution to the frightful repertoire. A Tale of Mystery also used music in an innovative way that would soon become standard and is with us yet. Earlier plays of all kinds had featured musical interludes, and some horrid ones, like Lewis's Castle Spectre, had sought to intensify strong moments with organ peals and choruses. But in the first act of A Tale of Mystery alone, music is called upon to express "discontent and alarm," "chattering contention," "pain and disorder," along with a dozen other emotions. Music plays under spoken words as well as before and after them; sometimes, it does the talking while the actors pose:

> Music loud and discordant at the moment the eye of Montano catches the figure of Romaldi; at which Montano starts with terror and indignation. He then assumes the eye and attitude of menace, which Romaldi returns. The music ceases.

These stage directions demonstrate the modular quality of turn-of-the-nineteenth-century acting: One movement meant "terror," another "indignation," while a certain stance and cast of eye meant "menace." Actors could learn these techniques by rote, out of all context, and plug them in whenever they were called for, without a thought of motive, situation, background, or any of the other things the twentieth-century theater holds dear. We don't know what tunes played as A Tale of Mystery wheezed along; perhaps, unlike the actors' gestures, music had to be composed from scratch for the occasion. But by the middle of the nineteenth century, if not earlier, stage music had grown modular, too. It had curdled into a couple of dozen indefinitely repeatable phrases known as "melos," each identified with a distinct emotion being expressed on stage and, presumably, felt in the audience.

Composing scores for melodramas became mosaic work:

> Much as a maker of mosaic pictures fashions his individual scenes out of a stock of similar-size variously coloured tiles, the *chef* [*d'orchestre*] from his folio selected appropriate melos and arranged these in a sequence which suited the needs of the melodrama in preparation. . . . [T]he *chef* then gave to each musician a schedule listing the sequence of melos to be performed in order that the musician, from his desk and with his own folio of numbered melos, could follow his conductor.

The huge demand for stage pieces that were new yet familiar, ringing slight changes on well-known themes, led to modular playwriting: the forging of a clichéd cast—hero, heroine, nice old man, comical servant, villain—that could be made to fill any borrowed or stolen plot. Modular acting followed: Hard-pressed actors had no time to learn each part anew, even if the part merited fresh study, which was unlikely. And modular music supplemented the rest, because theater musicians were underpaid and overworked, too.

To call these activities "modular" is anachronistic, of course. But their participants were industrial in a fully modern sense, churning out indistinguishable products for an anonymous audience, and they had geared themselves to mass production a century before Henry Ford set up his assembly lines. Prose fiction, the only other large-scale entertainment medium of the time, remained comparatively a cottage industry until at least the 1860s. The typical early-nineteenth-century theater product was a heterogeneous article compounded of low comedy, high sentiment, suspense, catchy tunes, perhaps a few dances, and in many cases a graveyard chill or two. Little effort was made to force these diverse, even contradictory elements into any sort of coherence. One piece might emphasize comedy, another thrills, but each took its place in evening-long barrages of entertainment designed to pluck every string of the spectators' hearts, as strongly and often as possible.

The horrid novel exhibited some of this same scattershot strategy; twentieth-century readers, accustomed to more concentrated horrors, are often disappointed to find that Mrs. Radcliffe spends more time on alpine sublimities than on the creepiness of Gothic ruins. But just as horrid plays dispensed their chills in sharper doses, so too they mixed them more thoroughly with other effects intended to raise different though equally powerful emotions. I know of no early-nineteenth-century play that could be called strictly horrid—or strictly anything else, for that matter. Fear was one of many tones on the melodramatic scale, and melodrama aimed to sound them all.

In the horrid novel, Gothic awe grew quickly into Gothic fear; the two were inseparable, and melodrama deepened their kinship. Cheery sentiments could be instilled from a simply set stage—all it took was a dewy-eyed heroine, or perhaps a few happy peasants—but fright put a heavy burden on the theater's technical resources. Indeed, it was partly on account of the demand for awesome-frightening effects that stagecraft made its most notable advances. From the time of the Graveyard poets until our own day, artificial fear has relied on contrasts of light and dark, sunshine and "gloomth," as Walpole called it. The uniform dimness of eighteenth-century theaters was ill suited to contrasts, but when the demand arose, technicians accomplished remarkable things with blue and red fire, fairly often burning theaters down as a side effect. No doubt gas would have eventually been laid on and, later, electricity installed in theaters, as they were in private homes. But the theater, like the home, had provided scenes for such technology decades before it existed. In both places, desire came first.

At least four sets of trapdoors pierced the narrow, brightly footlighted stage that nineteenth-century theaters inherited virtually unchanged from the Renaissance. When playwrights meant to be scary, they made use mostly of two: the "grave trap" (named for the graveyard scene in *Hamlet*) and the "cauldron trap" (for the witches in *Macbeth*), through which spectral visitors rose and sank. The need for subtler chills added two more traps to the roster.

In 1820, J. R. Planché adapted into English Charles Nodier and Achille Jouffroy's smash-hit melodrama *Le Vampire* (based on Polidori's "Vampyre") as *The Vampire; or, The Bride of the Isles.* The first production, at London's English Opera House, introduced the "vamp trap," a pair of spring-controlled doors cut into the scenery, which allowed the fiendish Ruthven to disappear through apparently solid walls.

In 1852, when the fad for ghostliness had considerably faded, Dion Boucicault's *The Corsican Brothers* brought in the most elaborate trap yet. The play was another French borrowing, from Alexandre Dumas's novel *Les Frères corses*, and there had been several French stage versions; at least five English ones were licensed during 1852 alone. For the Boucicault version, technicians at the Princess's Theatre, London, managed to satisfy the requirements of Louis's ghost, which *"glides across the stage— ascending gradually at the same time."* An extraordinary apparatus of platforms, pulleys, and brushes went into action to produce this effect, which had never been attempted before and never would be again, except in the frequent revivals of *The Corsican Brothers.*

The "Corsican trap" is an extreme example of the lengths to which stagecraft was pushed by the desire for horrid effects. Nearly every night, however, technicians had to make ghosts rise, demons appear, wounds drip blood, ghastly fires burn—all with the most rudimentary equipment. That they triumphantly achieved these illusions is a tribute to their genius, which today's finest theater designers share. Paradoxically, however, the brilliant inventiveness of early-nineteenth-century stagecraft worked toward the decline of the very emotions that had spawned it.

By 1840, a strong trend toward naturalism had shown itself in all aspects of the theater business—in playwriting and acting as well as stage effects. Horrid plays continued to be written and performed, but they tended to appear at the lowest-class houses, and with decreasing frequency. Even the most blood-and-thundery melodramas now preferred mills with real running water, like the one in *A Tale of Mystery*, to the crypts and vaults of *The Castle Spectre.* That "old crusted grizzly skeleton melodrama," as H. Chance Newton called it, had already dropped out of the regular repertoire; it was last performed in 1880, as a curious relic of dead fashions. The very sophistication of nineteenth-century stage technology, its burgeoning ability to make the stage resemble the world outside its doors, hastened the public's loss of interest in old-style, fantastical horrors.

A similar development had begun much earlier in the novel, which was largely done with gooseflesh of all sorts by 1820. Sir Walter Scott's immensely popular romances (which were also widely adapted to the stage) helped to tame the long ago and far away by treating it as history. After Scott's death, in 1832, the novel took a realistic, domestic turn, as drama would do a decade or so later. This is not to say that fear vanished from libraries and theaters; domesticity bred its own nightmares, and even the old style of scariness would rise again in new trappings. But midcentury horrors looked so different that their ancestors were forgotten, or glanced at with patronizing smiles. Before it faded, however, old-style fear enjoyed one final, splendid fling.

SWANSHRIEK

The voracious appetite of early-nineteenth-century theater meant that any large hit, wherever it began, stood a good chance of turning overnight into a hemispheric phenomenon. For a while, Kotzebue dominated the French, English, and American stage; then Pixerécourt sent the tide back across Germany, while England and the United States plundered them both—without, of course, financial benefit to either writer. The higher-class genres of opera and ballet seldom suffered such depredation, though two spooky artworks of the 1840s, Richard Wagner's opera *Der fliegende Holländer* (The Flying Dutchman) and the ballet *Giselle* (music by Adolphe Adam, choreography by Jean Coralli and Jules Perrot), were ground into plentiful fodder by melodramatists.

Their success was certainly impressive, but nothing in the century, not even the later troops of *Corsican Brothers*, matched the fad for Carl Maria von Weber's opera *Der Freischütz*, which premiered at the Berlin Schauspielhaus on June 18, 1821. Eight-year-old Wagner saw it performed in Dresden the following January; decades later, Weber's foremost successor would recall its unprecedented impact: "The most divergent political alignments met here at a common point: from one end of Germany to the other, *Der Freischütz* was heard, sung, and danced." To mention politics in connection with an opera might strike a twentieth-century reader as bizarre, but Wagner merely followed Goethe, who in the 1770s had found (or fabricated) politics in Gothic architecture when he called it "German."

Wagner's later operas were political, too, at least insofar as they invoked a myth that transcended the petty grand duchies and dukedoms into which Germany was divided. *Der Freischütz*, though hardly so grandiose, was intensely Germanic in source, language, and spirit. It won praise for rescuing German opera from effete Italian influences, returning to the path of Mozart's *Magic Flute*, which in some ways it resembles. Johann Friedrich Kind's libretto derives from a supposedly native legend first published in 1810; it is set in the same mountainous woodland where the brothers Grimm had placed many of their *Kinder- und Hausmärchen* (Children's and Household Fables, 1812–1815); and its characters are the simple, hearty forest folk with whom even cosmopolitan Germans liked, at times, to identify themselves.

These quasi-political qualities no doubt contributed to the opera's vast success in a splintered Germany still recovering from the Napoleonic wars. They may also account for its relative unpopularity in France, where it never joined the standard repertoire. But *Der Freischütz* took England by storm. A loose translation was performed at the English Opera House early in 1824, and by the end of that year five melodramas had been spun off it, along with three burlesques. Kind's libretto didn't reach London till 1832, but by that time English audiences on all levels were thoroughly familiar with some version of the show, though few had seen what Weber and Kind wrote. The craze was all the more remarkable because most Englishmen could neither understand the title nor pronounce it, yet all adaptations went by that name (usually without the umlaut, which no doubt seemed merely decorative). "Der Freischutz" became synonymous with the strongest possible deployment of stage effects intended to instill awe and fear.

English theatergoers cared nothing for German patriotism, but they responded enthusiastically to deep woods and brave hunters, types they already knew well from hundreds of horrid plays and novels. The plot was pure cliché as well, with just enough innovation to make it appealing. The hero, Max, must win a rifle-shooting contest in order to gain the hand of the heroine, Agathe, the head forester's daughter. Max's marksmanship is hardly up to the challenge, so he makes a deal with the villain, Kaspar, who agrees to cast seven magic bullets, which will fly wherever the shooter wishes. Little does Max know that Kaspar is in thrall to the demon Samiel, who will claim Kaspar's soul unless he can pass the cursed magic on. In the end (and the nick of time), Kaspar falls victim to his own evil scheme. Max's treachery is exposed, but thanks to a kindly hermit's intervention, he is forgiven and united with Agathe. The curtain falls on a chorus of blissful thanksgiving.

Good triumphs in *Der Freischütz*, but evil was its main selling point. The high point of evil came in Act II, Scene 4, the famous "Wolf's Glen" scene, which called upon every ghastly cliché stagecraft had devised, threw them all together, and even doubled a few:

Frightful forest glen, mostly overgrown with firs, surrounded by high mountains, from one of which a waterfall plummets. The full moon shines pallidly. Two thunderstorms are coming up from opposite directions. Farther forward, a lightning-shattered, withered tree, rotten within so that it seems to glow. On the other side, on a gnarled branch, sits a large owl with fiery, rolling eyes. On other trees, ravens and other forest birds.

A chorus of "Invisible Spirits" sings some of the eeriest music ever composed. Gloomy male voices chant dire nonsense ("Moon's milk fell on the weed . . . Spider's web is bedewed with blood"); between verses, alarming females cry "Uhui! Uhui!"

That may not look scary in print, but the vocal contrast is unsettling for even a twentieth-century listener. It must have been much more so for audiences of the 1820s, who were unaccustomed to assaults by music. In good melodramatic fashion, the spirit chorus sets the mood for the scene that follows, an exhaustive cavalcade of horrors. As a distant bell tolls twelve, Kaspar comes on and sets up his bullet-casting apparatus, centered on a skull surrounded by black stones. Demonic Samiel appears, along with assorted apparitions; the skull turns into a casting oven; Max, fearfully approaching, sees both his mother's ghost and a vision of Agathe, got up like Ophelia and about to throw herself under the waterfall. The moon grows dark, the forest birds flap their wings, and the theater's technical resources seem stretched to the limit. But that's only the beginning.

As Kaspar casts each magic bullet, he calls out its number; as the numbers climb, effects escalate. At "One!" the birds come down from their perches and hop about; "Two!" brings a black boar dashing across the stage; "Three!" summons up a storm that *"bends and breaks the treetops."* Ghostly wheels and ghostly horses at "Four!"; phantom hunters, dogs, and deer at "Five!"; at "Six! Woe is me!"—pandemonium:

> *The whole sky turns to black night; the thunderstorms, which have been battling each other till now, come together and let loose frightful lightning and thunder. Torrential rain falls; dark-blue flames burst from the earth; will-o'-the-wisps show on the mountains; trees, clattering, are torn up by the roots; the waterfall foams and roars. Pieces of rock plummet down; din of the elements from all sides; the earth seems to sway.*

Nothing before had equaled this, and nothing since has topped it. In less expert hands, Kaspar's despairing "Seven!" might have brought on an attempt to exceed excess, but though it summons the horrible Samiel (who appears where the withered tree was), the final, fatal bullet also brings an end to the tumult. Max makes the sign of the cross, and the distant bell tolls one.

Small wonder that audiences went mad for *Der Freischütz*: It gave them everything they already knew, but in higher doses. When English melodramatists laid hold of this hot property, they followed the same principle; lacking the brilliance of Weber and Kind, however, they pushed it over the edge into absurdity. John Kerr's version, *Der Freischutz; or Zamiel the Spirit of the Forest, and the Seventh Bullet*, which opened at the Lyceum on July 22, 1824, exemplifies what imitators did to Weber and Kind, as they had done to Mrs. Radcliffe a generation before. Weber's music is gone, of course. Though the outline of the plot remains, the characters' names are all changed, and the setting has been moved to a never-never land that mingles qualities of Germany, Spain, and Ireland. But the Wolf's Glen is more itself than ever: a *"dreary site,"* with *"scattered yews and blighted shrubs,"* where bats as well as owls *"are seen on the precipices."*

Ganstrom (Kerr's Kaspar) fumbles with a charnel's worth of bones, not just a skull. He also wields a bloodstained *"mistic sword"* and uses a bat's wings to fan his fire. And when he casts the magic bullets,

> *adders—toads, and other noxious reptiles creep from out their holes. . . . Bats descend, and hideous snakes crawl around the circle. . . . a burning carriage encircles the ring. . . . Skeletons rise from the earth; fiends and fearful shapes hover round the glen, and hideous yells rend the air. . . . The moon, as well as the waterfall, are now transformed to blood; the trees are torn up with their roots. . . . The rocks suddenly burst asunder; huge precipices fall with a fearful crash; the waterfall disappears, and Zamiel is discovered seated on a fiery horse entwined by fearful shakes [sic]; from whose horrid jaws issue volumes of flame.*

Had they seen this, Weber and Kind might have wept. Whatever good taste their *Freischütz* possessed was bludgeoned to death in Kerr's *Freischutz*. Even their fine diminuendo goes: Kerr peaks at the seventh bullet; then he just stops.

Yet, as in the case of *The Monk*, the difference between tastefulness and vulgarity was principally one of degree. Like any popular dramatist of the time, Kerr tried to give his audience what it wanted, and what it wanted, he evidently thought, was more and more of everything. With his bats and reptiles, Kerr reverted to the old-style horrors of the Graveyard School, which Kind's libretto largely avoided. Kerr also laid them on as thick as they went, hoping perhaps to make up in quantity what quality could not provide. He faced many competitors in that busy 1824 season, each determined to top the others. Excess was the only weapon they had.

In the long run, it failed them—though, of course, the only long run they cared about was 1824's. Weariness among readers had already driven Gothic horrors down and out of the novel; a glut of overblown, maniacally repetitive productions like Kerr's *Freischutz* cast the same pall over theatergoers. By the middle of the century, as the theater started to turn genteel again, such blatancy came to seem both vulgar and a little naive. When midcentury playwrights sought to make their viewers' flesh creep, they employed new methods that shunned noxious reptiles in favor of creatures that slithered closer to home. Like contemporary novelists, they latched on to the domestic and psychological, finding darker abysses in the mind of the man next door than any Montoni, Ambrosio, or Kaspar could show.

Thanks to the efforts of novelists, playwrights, composers, choreographers, designers, musicians, actors, dancers, singers, painters, carpenters, publishers, printers, booksellers, assistants and slaveys of all kinds, and urchins who went down the block for beer, by the middle of the nineteenth century the West had established an industry whose sole product was entertainment. It was an urban industry, though its product reached the remotest hinterlands; it came from anonymous cities, where differences of race, religion, and heritage, like proverbial country girls, lost their virtue. It sucked up difference and spewed out sameness: haunted forests from Germany, dark monasteries from Spain, banditti from Italy, demons from the mysterious East, ghost stories from every nation's peasants, singing gypsies, thieving gypsies, second-sighted gypsies, whatever the occasion demanded.

Artificial fear counted as only one among the entertainment industry's many flavors of emotion; at no time did it rank first in popularity, and it was seldom dispensed unaccompanied by laughter, sentimental tears, and widemouthed awe. It blended easily into all these emotions and others besides, sometimes vanishing altogether in the mix. It came into favor, lost it, took new forms, wore them out, devised newer ones, and then disinterred the old, which seemed newest of all until they wore out again. Scary entertainment possesses no clear-cut, linear history, no series of landmark works that developed from one to the next. It better resembles a poorly managed warehouse where nothing gets junked and nobody ever takes inventory.

Most of the stock was on hand by the first quarter of the

nineteenth century; nearly two hundred years later, it still sells. A few shelves, however, remained to be filled. So far, the urban, deracinated, homogenized audience for modern fright had failed to include itself among the available sources of horror. That discovery was coming and, as the twentieth century knows, it's the scariest of all.

TERRIBLE DISCOVERY·OF·A·SKELETON

Victorian fear lived right next door—or in the next room. (ILLUSTRATION FROM *'Orrible Murder* BY LEONARD DEVRIES, TAPLINGER PRESS, 1971.)

5

feac Comes home

REAL-LIFE HORRORS

On the night of October 24, 1823, John Thurtell drove a hired gig into a gloomy Hertfordshire lane, where he murdered his companion, William Weare. Thurtell bashed in Weare's skull with the butt of a pistol, shoved the muzzle into the wound, and mashed his brains. He severed Weare's jugular vein, shot him in the head, and knocked his upper teeth out. Thurtell then joined his accomplice, Joseph Hunt, at the nearby cottage of William and Elizabeth Probert. After a drink or two, the men returned to Gill's Hill Lane and concealed Weare's corpse under a hedge. Back at the cottage, all but Thurtell, who felt unwell (perhaps because Weare's blood had spurted into his mouth and up his nose), ate pork chops; later, they went to the lane again to fetch the corpse, which they dumped into the Proberts' pond.

This clumsy crime had an obvious motive (gambling debts) and such dull-witted perpetrators that the crude detection methods of the time snared them at once. Thurtell was hanged on January 9, 1824. Hunt's evidence for the Crown won him transportation; he died under respectable circumstances, in New South Wales, nearly forty years later. Similar service gained immunity for William

Probert, but he was hanged in 1825 on a charge of horse theft. The last we hear of Elizabeth Probert is that she appeared "distraught" on the eve of her husband's execution. In the eyes of a sentimental observer, she might achieve some pathos; the other participants, however, were brutes—even the victim, who played the same game as his killers and merely lost.

Yet the Thurtell-Hunt case became a sensation: Newspapers all over England thrived on it for months, every writer worth his salt had to find an angle, and references to it blotched English fiction for decades. Twentieth-century commentators unanimously express puzzlement at this phenomenon. Most side with Richard D. Altick, who concludes that the case granted enthralling glimpses into "the life and characters of the world of Regency fast-buck operators," among whom Thurtell was famous long before the celebrated crime. Following Altick's lead, Albert Borowitz's book-length study tries to build the case up into a *Dark Mirror to Regency England*, as his subtitle calls it.

Desperate doings make a perennial source of interest for more timid souls—the majority—whose careers never drive them into corners from which murder is the only way out. Such stories inspire wonder and fear, exactly like tales of outlaws, banditti, and false earls. The Thurtell-Hunt story belongs in the venerable tradition of popular crime that leads back to Robin Hood; it was modern chiefly because of the overheated attention the media lavished on it. To speak of "media" in the 1820s is anachronistic, of course. Yet Thomas Boyle has seen in newspaper coverage of the case several features—insistence on the hot currency of the news, claims for the unique ferocity of the murder, the reportage of gruesome details— that look forward to the unbridled sensationalism of the 1860s; these features also anticipate the *Weekly World News* of a much later age. Boyle also notes that Thurtell was no outlandish villain but "*one of us*"—that is, a gentleman, hardly different in most ways from those who read about his dreadful deed.

Ghastly as it was, the Thurtell case did not occur in a crumbling Italian castle two centuries ago; it happened just last week, in peaceable, familiar Hertfordshire. The culprits were tacky, but that made them familiar, too. The fear they elicited was of a new kind— rudimentary so far, but soon to burgeon. It came from the sense that, in the modern world of 1823 (which seemed to have been torn from the past without a link to hold it fast), familiarity did not mean safety. Behind any ordinary door, unimaginable horrors might lurk; behind any commonplace pair of eyes, abysses might gape. As cities grew and urban anonymity spread its mixed blessings, this sense became ubiquitous; today, it inhabits cities, suburbs, and countryside about equally. Today's frightening entertainment routinely exploits it, but the entertainment industry had discovered that market as early as 1823.

Thurtell and Hunt were arrested on October 29, five days after Weare's murder. Hearings began the following day, and on the 31st the London *Times* printed its first article on the case. Less than three weeks later, on November 17, *The Gamblers, a new Melo-drama* opened at London's New Surrey Theatre. According to the playbill, audiences gazed upon

The Identical Horse and Gig,
Alluded to by the Daily Press in the Accounts of
THE LATE MURDER,
TOGETHER WITH THE
TABLE AT WHICH THE PARTY SUPPED,
The SOFA as DESCRIBED to having been SLEPT on,
WITH
Other Household Furniture,
AS PURCHASED AT THE LATE AUCTION.

The Surrey's enterprising manager, Llewellyn Williams, capitalized brilliantly on public fascination with the commonplace accoutrements of the crime. He fared less well, however, with the play he commissioned to inhabit them.

By any standard, *The Gamblers* is a wretched piece of work, baldly reflecting both the haste of its composition and the limited skill of its contriver. Yet it's a fascinating document, for those very reasons. Even if the anonymous author had it in him to write a good play, there was no time for care and no reason for it. Plentiful materials lay ready to hand: the facts as newspapers were reporting them, the auctioned articles Williams had snapped up, and the hand-me-down clichés of melodrama. The playwright needed only to fling them together— which he clumsily did, producing a weird farrago of total realism and the most outlandish carrying-on. *The Gamblers* closely follows the outline of the case, so far as it was then known. It keeps reality's constellation of characters but gives them theatrical names: The Proberts become William and Amelia Mordaunt, Thurtell becomes Thomas Woodville, and Hunt is Joseph Bradshaw. The play irons out all confusions of motive and ambiguities of guilt. Woodville is a double-dyed villain in the Romaldi mold; Amelia is a cartoon version of her long-suffering namesake in Fielding's 1751 novel, *Amelia*; Bradshaw is a conscience-plagued villain à la Mrs. Radcliffe and her imitators. Good or bad, they spout the same dialect, spoken nowhere on earth except behind footlights:

> WOODVILLE: The night is dark and horrid as my purpose. . . . O
> could I but win the ruined Mordaunt to my will, and urge him
> to conspire my victims [*sic*] fall; then might I say, security,
> thou art mine, and laugh at all to come. But, hark! I hear
> footsteps . . .
>
> AMELIA: Oh, what a world of ruin has one vice, detested gam-
> ing, brought upon us all! Mordaunt, so honest, tender, mild
> by nature, has that propensity made almost wicked! . . .
> Hark! footsteps! . . .
>
> BRADSHAW: [T]he awful silence that breaks through earth and
> air contracts such horrors that, villain as I am, my con-
> science starts and makes me shudder at this damning deed.
> But hark! I hear the horse's tramp.

The arrival of anything real in the midst of such flapdoodle was bound to make a jolt, but *The Gamblers* featured the very gig in which Weare's blood had gushed, the very horse that, if it could speak, might name his murderer.

These engaging artifacts appear twice in Act II, which ends with the murder of Weare (William Frankly in the play). Following ancient rules of decorum that Shakespeare had freely broken, *The Gamblers* puts the crime offstage; no ghastly details are specified. But the playwright expected his audience to know them well, and by wheeling out the actual scene of the crime, the management encouraged spectators to envision such things as imperfectly scoured bloodstains. Extremes of realism and stage cliché meet in *The Gamblers* and madly switch places: Reality gets hammered into melodramatic convention, which is then invaded by props that aren't props at all. No doubt the process is more amusing to speculate on than it would be to watch.

The first production of *The Gamblers* pitched reality against fiction in yet another way. Thurtell's trial had hardly gotten started when the play opened; after the play's second night, November 19, his counsel entered a plea at the Court of King's Bench that the Surrey be enjoined from further performances until the trial was over. *The Gamblers* went into brief hibernation, only to emerge on January 15, 1824, six days after Thurtell's hanging, for a new run. Newspapers had been far from reticent about their judgments of guilt and innocence, but the play was categorical—not because the playwright had weighed the evidence, but because he'd stuffed reality into melodramatic molds. Ironically, his hierarchy of guilt corresponded closely to the court's: in descending order from Thurtell (Woodville) to Hunt (Bradshaw) to Probert (Mordaunt). That, however, was an accident.

The Gamblers wasn't the first English play to recycle a recent crime. *The Tragedy of Mr. Arden of Feversham* (1592) and *A Yorkshire Tragedy* (1608), both sometimes attributed to Shakespeare, had drawn on such material more than two centuries earlier; the latter even focuses on the deadly consequences of "detested gaming." In 1818, five years before *The Gamblers*, a certain "S. N. E." had published at Warwick *The Murdered Maid; or, The Clock Struck Four!!!*, based on the quite recent, local murder of Mary Ashford by Abraham Thornton. This "drama"—not, as the preface declares, a low-class *"Melo Drama"*—seems to have been intended for reading only, though it was evidently staged at Norwich in 1820. In many ways, it is an interesting play, mingling Gothic specters, up-to-date news, and at least a rudimentary notion of psychology. It flickered, however, on the margin of the margin, and hardly anyone then or since seems to have noticed it.

A century later, H. Chance Newton recalled working on productions of *The Gamblers* "in after-years" (possibly the 1870s), though without the famous gig and, naturally, the horse. The play's basis in a real-life case lent it a cachet that made up for hamstrung dialogue, even when Thurtell and company had long been forgotten. Other, similar plays fared even better, surviving well into the twentieth century. The anonymous *Maria Martin; or, The Murder in the Red*

Barn, for example, was produced as early as 1840; Newton granted it the honor of "freezing my young blood" in the 1860s; six decades later, he gloated over the "horrifying shrieks" a 1927 revival was coaxing from its audiences. Tod Slaughter, who played the villain in that production, went on eight years later to star in a film version, *Murder in the Red Barn.*

Maria Martin (also spelled "Marten") was killed by William Corder in May 1827; he buried her body in the soon-to-be-infamous red barn, owned by his family, and for nearly a year he kept up the fiction that he and Maria had run off to London to be married. But her stepmother started having dream visions of Maria's true fate, and in the spring of 1828 the young woman's badly decomposed corpse was unearthed. Corder was hanged on August 11. As in the Thurtell-Hunt case, the scene of the crime became a tourist attraction; by the end of the year, the unlucky barn had been nearly torn to pieces by souvenir hunters. The case spawned several theatrical adaptations, along with a long-lived marionette show that Altick calls the "most popular of all" such entertainments in the last third of the nineteenth century.

Though the various *Red Barns* preserved the principals' names, like *The Gamblers* they polished rough facts into the slick stereotypes of melodrama. The real-life Maria had already borne Corder an illegitimate child before he lured her to her death; on stage, she became a paragon of rustic virtue. Corder was a farmer's son, but playwrights made him a sneering aristocrat in the tried-and-true Romaldi style; Slaughter's Corder is even called "squire" and "lord of the manor." And in all versions he speaks standard villainese:

> How well this pent-up soul assumes the garb of smiling love to give my fiend-like thoughts the prospect of success! . . . The deed were bloody, sure; but I will do it, and rid me of this hated plague. Her very shadow moves a scorpion in my path. I loathe the banquet I have fed upon. By heaven! be still my heart.

All versions, however, preserve real life's most theatrical elements: the atmospheric murder site, the stepmother's visions, and the villain's anguish in the condemned cell.

By the 1860s, newspaper coverage of murders and other domestic mayhem had grown so thorough that playwrights and novelists could rely on their audiences' awareness that a tidy bourgeois surface might easily conceal the most appalling extremes of depravity. Boyle, who has extensively studied these developments, inclines toward a dire view. Readers of such reports obtained scary glimpses into the "universe of death" they inhabited:

> A pattern common to the police reports emerges: A private tragedy is made public in the courtroom. Melodrama ensues. Morbidity and sexuality overlap. The God of the establishment, though mentioned in the obligatory manner, seems ridiculously far away. Surface notions of respectability are implicitly challenged. There is a kind of black humor which, while happily attacking surface piety, also manages to communicate a sense of unease.

This is a bit melodramatic in its own right, but accurate enough as far as it goes. Boyle overlooks, however, one significant aspect of the Victorian fondness for tales of murder next door: When nineteenth-century readers felt their blood run cold, they *enjoyed* the feeling. It was, before all else, a form of entertainment.

DREADFUL BUTCHER'S BUSINESS

Boyle's own principal source testifies to this. He relies heavily on five thick volumes of newspaper clippings, carefully cut out and pasted up by William Bell Macdonald, a Scottish naval surgeon who devoted more than twenty years to his hobby, between 1840 and 1861. The collection is huge—an estimated nine million words—and thoroughly indexed; Bell Macdonald evidently suffered from the same mania for categorizing that afflicted that other unsavory Victorian indexer, the anonymous author of *My Secret Life.* But Bell Macdonald's obsession with violent crime, though perhaps he carried it too far, was quite respectable. His *Various Trials Cut from Newspapers* represents only an overdone instance of a common nineteenth-century household amusement.

Its most enthusiastic early advocate was Thomas De Quincey (1785–1859), famous as the English Opium-Eater, who explored the entertainment value of violent death in his essay "On Murder Considered as One of the Fine Arts," published in three parts between 1827 and 1854. Already in 1823, however, his "On the Knocking at

the Gate in *Macbeth*" proposed that murder was a fit matter for
aesthetic appreciation and, indeed, that a coterie of gentlemen had
already grown jaded on the subject. They had been spoiled by the
Ratcliffe Highway murders of December 1811: seven people bludgeoned to bloody death, supposedly by John Williams, a seaman.
De Quincey remarked:

> On which murders, by the way, I must observe that in one respect they
> have had an ill effect by making the connoisseur in murder very
> fastidious in his taste and dissatisfied by anything that has been since
> done in that line. All other murders look pale by the deep crimson of
> his; and, as an amateur once said to me in a querulous tone, "There
> has been absolutely nothing *doing* since his time, or nothing that's
> worth speaking of."

De Quincey's intent may have been satirical in 1823, but by 1854, in
the third part of "On Murder," he turned serious. That brief "Post-
script," often reprinted as an essay in its own right, contains as much
thrilling interest as any melodramatist (or moviemaker) could wish.

Instead of merely relishing the Ratcliffe Highway murders, De
Quincey imaginatively reconstructs them, riding roughshod over
facts but brilliantly sustaining a tone of breathless dread. Mary, servant of a hosier named Marr, returns to his shop from a fruitless
errand in search of oysters for supper. She rings the bell and taps
lightly at the door (it is after 1:00 AM, and she fears to wake the Marrs'
baby): "To her astonishment—but with the astonishment came
creeping over her an icy horror—no stir nor murmur was heard ascending from the kitchen." Now comes "an incident of killing fear
that to her dying day would never cease to renew its echoes
in her ear":

> Yes, now beyond a doubt there is coming an answer to her summons.
> What was it? On the stairs—not on the stairs that led downwards to
> the kitchen, but the stairs that led upwards to the single story of
> bedchambers above—was heard a creaking sound. Next was heard
> most distinctly a footfall: one, two, three, four, five stairs were slowly
> and distinctly descended. Then the dreadful footsteps were heard
> advancing along the little narrow passage to the door. The steps—oh,
> heavens! *whose* steps?—have paused at the door. The very breathing

can be heard of that dreadful being who has silenced all breathing except his own in the house.

Dreadful footsteps were solidly clichéd by 1854, though that hasn't stopped scary entertainers from using them ten thousand times since then. Few, however, have equaled De Quincey's skill at raising gooseflesh.

Trembling Mary's real name was Margaret Jewell; the Marrs' Christian names were Timothy and Celia; the baby was Timothy Jr., three and a half months old. De Quincey either omits these facts or gets them, among many others, wrong. For accuracy on the Ratcliffe Highway murders, you have to consult P. D. James and T. A. Critchley's *The Maul and the Pear Tree* (1971), a typical twentieth-century true-crime study that, along with its hundreds of counterparts, demonstrates the enduring fascination of real-life atrocities. Faithful to their genre, James and Critchley seek to strip away the romantic gloss laid on the case by prior writers like De Quincey. But they also want to re-create De Quincey's air of thickening dread. At real life's most melodramatic points, they can't help imitating him.

In James and Critchley's version, Margaret doesn't knock at the Marrs' door; she rings once, twice, a third time,

and this time heard a sound which, to the end of her life, she would never recall without a *frisson* of horror. . . . There was a soft tread of footsteps on the stairs. Someone—surely her master?—was coming down to open the door.

No doubt this is exactly what happened, yet for both Victorian and modern chroniclers it becomes a moment of special intensity because its effect is fortified by the conventions of horrid fiction. The approach of unidentified footsteps had been such a Gothic cliché that even the talentless author of *The Gamblers* attempted to exploit it. De Quincey pulled out all the stops in an effort to chill his readers' blood; mere accuracy didn't worry him. Accuracy is the watchword of such latter-day ventures as James and Critchley's, but the tradition of scary entertainment has taught them how to make fact as chilling as fiction.

From the 1820s to our own day, the purveying of real-life horrors has grown into a substantial industry. It has thrived in every medium, and especially horrid cases have enjoyed remarkable longevity. In the autumn of 1888, for example, the murderer known as Jack the Ripper slaughtered at least five women in London's Whitechapel district, and newspapers gloried in the murders, with illustrations. In 1988, Jack's centenary, his crimes became the subject of several books and at least three television specials, one of which invited viewers to phone in votes on the killer's identity. In August 1892, someone took an axe to Mr. and Mrs. Andrew J. Borden of Fall River, Massachusetts; that more domestic mayhem also spawned international reportage. Books and articles followed, along with a ballet by Agnes de Mille, an opera by Jack Beeson, and a remarkable TV movie (1975) starring Elizabeth Montgomery as the probable murderer, Lizzie Borden.

Both cases remain officially unsolved, a fact often called on to explain their enduring interest. That explanation also exonerates the interest by making it intellectual, as the enthusiasm inspired by fictional murder mysteries is also taken to be. True-crime stories, however, characteristically focus on the gruesome details of their cases—how many times the razor slashed or the axe came down, and especially on how much blood was spilled and where it splashed. Edward D. Radin's 1961 treatment of the Borden murders describes the discovery of Andrew's corpse:

> Dr. Bowen found Borden stretched out on the sofa, his head on a pillow, his long legs resting on the floor. . . . Fresh blood was still oozing from the massive skull wounds and the severed eye was hanging down out of its socket. Dr. Bowen had to clean the face before he was able to recognize Borden.

Frank Spiering's considerably trashier version, published in 1984, puts it this way:

> There was blood everywhere, on the flowered carpet, on the wall over the sofa and even splattered on a picture hanging from the wall. Andrew's head was bent slightly to the right, but his face was unrecognizable as human. There were eleven distinct cuts across the forehead between the ears and above the mouth, slicing the flesh into a grotesque, seething patchwork. Fresh blood still seeped from the

wounds. One eye had been cut in half and dangled from its socket. The nose had been severed, lopped loose from the upper jaw.

Whatever interest may be on call here, it's not intellectual. Yet, of course, the second, lurid version comes closer to the goal of any "true" narrative—a full inventory of facts.

It is tempting to see these two passages as symptomatic of the revolution in explicitness that occurred between 1961 and 1984, especially in scary entertainments. For Radin, one ghastly physical detail sufficed; Spiering had to supply half a dozen, along with gouts of overheated prose. The revolution did happen, but real-life horror stories had been indulging in explicit ghastliness a century earlier. In 1854, for instance, De Quincey waxed typically florid as he described a neighbor's discovery of the slaughtered Marrs:

> Rapidly the brave man passed onwards to the shop and there beheld the carnage of the night stretched out on the floor, and the narrow premises so floated with gore that it was hardly possible to escape the pollution of blood in picking out a path to the front door.

This is reticent, perhaps, even by the standards of 1961; yet the focus of interest, the source of real-life fright, is the same spectacle of ruined human flesh that Spiering would dwell upon in 1984 and that contemporary horror films exploit to the uttermost.

In the mid-nineteenth century, there were few true-crime writers like De Quincey, who produced substantial, thoughtful essays. Most such stories could be found only in newspapers and pamphlets, which meant to shock if they did nothing else. The sharply stratified society of Victorian England came together in its fascination with these grim things. In 1861, the indefatigable Henry Mayhew reported that no fewer than 1,650,000 copies of a broadsheet on the Red Barn case had been sold; taken together with other screeds on similar horrors, Mayhew's total came to ten million over a span of about twenty years. Most estimates put the total population of England at under seventeen million during the same period.

No statistics are available on who bought and read such publications, but plentiful evidence suggests that the taste for real-life horrors crossed class boundaries that neither novels nor plays could breach. A famous scene in Dickens's *Great Expectations* (1861) illustrates the perhaps predictable popularity of horrid journalism among illiterate or semiliterate provincials. At the Three Jolly Bargemen public house, in a southeastern seaside village, Mr. Wopsle, the parish clerk, reads aloud from a newspaper for the delectation of his less educated neighbors:

A highly popular murder had been committed, and Mr. Wopsle was imbrued in blood to the eyebrows. He gloated over every abhorrent adjective in the description, and identified himself with every witness at the Inquest. He faintly moaned, "I am done for," as the victim, and he barbarously bellowed, "I'll serve you out," as the murderer. . . . He enjoyed himself thoroughly, and we all enjoyed ourselves, and were delightfully comfortable.

The scene is set approximately in the 1820s, and Dickens might have had Thurtell and Weare in mind as he wrote. But it is intended to be typical and could just as well have occurred forty years later, in any place where sensational newspapers were found.

Dickens assumes an affectionate though slightly patronizing stance toward the group at the Three Jolly Bargemen: It is in part the stance of Pip, the novel's narrator, who has long since moved into the larger world and seen worse horrors face-on. But Mr. Wopsle and his auditors are also the descendants of the credulous peasants with whom Gothic novelists routinely adorned their stories. Such ignoramuses were an ancient cliché, and fiction of all kinds hasn't yet tired of them: Anything strange, horrid or not, is supposed to enthrall bumpkins. The middle class fancies itself more sophisticated, yet at least in the mid-nineteenth century, even the upper reaches of the bourgeoisie were not immune to the appeal of true horror stories.

In his memoir *Father and Son* (1907), Edmund Gosse provides a vivid, largely affectionate account of growing up middle-class in the 1850s and 1860s. His father, Philip Henry Gosse (1810–1888), was an admired naturalist and the author of several popular books illustrated with his own delicate, precise watercolors. He was also, however, a leader of a religious sect called the Plymouth Brethren that believed in the literal truth of the Bible, especially the account of creation in Genesis. The clash between Philip Henry's staunch fundamentalism and his love of nature's variety led him to write

Omphalos (1858), in which he proved (to his own satisfaction if no one else's) that the earth had indeed been created in six days, but that God had equipped it with a fossil record that made it look millions of years old—in order, apparently, to test the faith of nineteenth-century scientists.

The ridicule that greeted *Omphalos* ruined Philip Henry's reputation and permanently embittered him. To some readers of *Father and Son*, he has seemed a madman who sabotaged his own career and subjected his only child to bizarre cruelties, all in the cause of an inflexible, untenable faith. Edmund's memoir chronicles his father's excesses without mercy, yet *Father and Son* is also free of rancor, and it includes several interludes of what can only be called middle-class domesticity. For instance, the two Gosses frequently engaged in "long cosy talks together over the fire":

Our favorite subject was murders. I wonder whether little boys of eight, soon to go upstairs alone at night, often discuss violent crime with a widower-papa? The practice, I cannot help thinking, is unusual; it was, however, consecutive with us. We tried other secular subjects, but we were sure to come round at last to "what do you suppose they really did with the body?"

Philip Henry told Edmund the famous story of Burke and Hare, the resurrection men, whose manufacture of fresh cadavers had come to light two decades before Edmund was born. Father and son chatted about the equally notorious case of Maria Manning, "who killed a gentleman on the stairs and buried him in quick-lime in the back-kitchen"; alongside her accomplice and husband, Frederick, she was hanged late in 1849, when Edmund was a few months old.

The Gosses mulled over current cases, too, as newspaper reports gradually unfolded them. Fifty years later, Edmund professed puzzlement about one, "the Carpet-bag Mystery," which he and Philip Henry "discussed evening after evening":

I have never come across a whisper of it since, and I suspect it of having been a hoax. As I recall the details, people in a boat, passing down the Thames, saw a carpet-bag hung high in air, on one of the projections of a pier of Waterloo Bridge. Being with difficulty dragged down—or perhaps up—this bag was found to be full of human remains, dreadful butcher's business of joints and fragments.

Details had grown blurry for the fifty-eight-year-old Gosse,

> but clear enough is the picture I hold of myself, in a high chair, on the
> lefthand side of the sitting-room fireplace, the leaping flames re-
> flected in the glass-case of tropical insects on the opposite wall, and
> my Father, leaning anxiously forward, with uplifted finger, emphasiz-
> ing to me the pros and cons of the horrible carpet-bag evidence.

The carpet-bag was no hoax: On October 9, 1857, a pair of Thames
boatmen spied one caught on an abutment of the Waterloo Bridge
and hauled it down. It contained, "in addition to a complete suit of
men's attire save for hat and shoes, twenty human pieces, which
upon being reorganized were found to constitute the whole body,
except for the head, of a dark-haired adult male." Neither victim nor
murderer was ever identified, and the head was never found.

GHETTOS OF FEELING

Given the reticence on such matters displayed by mid-Victorian
fiction and drama, it is rather surprising to find the period's true-
crime stories going in with such gusto for the clinical details of
mutilation and dismemberment. The twentieth-century stereotype
of Victorian home life makes no provision for family chats about
missing heads. Yet nineteenth-century journalism more than
matched its latter-day counterpart in reporting the minutiae of murder, and a fascination with them compromised neither respectability nor, as in Philip Henry Gosse's case, religious rectitude. Fifty
years after the fact, Edmund Gosse thought it odd that his straitlaced
father should have regaled an eight-year-old with speculations on
hacked-up bodies. But his memories of those distant evenings,
though vivid, had no terror in them; they were, he wrote with only
gentle irony, "cosy."

And Mr. Wopsle's listeners, including young Pip, are "delightfully
comfortable" while "abhorrent" adjectives flood them. Both
scenes—one recollected, the other fictional—are set by the fireside, ancient emblem of emotional as well as physical warmth, light
in the midst of darkness, safety from what may lurk in the cold
outdoors. It seems the archetypal place for telling tales of dread; far
from dissipating the coziness, they enhance it by contrast. Modern

legend supposes that our cave-dwelling ancestors gathered in just such a charmed circle to hear about lions, tigers, and bears. Down the ages, in the same sacred site, a thousand generations of youngsters shivered happily as their elders spun stories of ghoulies and ghosties. These, so the legend runs, are the timeless roots of scary fiction.

In fact, however, though the fireside may always have had this significance, and though scary stories may always have been told there, it became an emblem only in the nineteenth century, when its reality was rapidly fading. The Gothic novel had nothing to say about cozy firesides; nor did horrid melodrama, at least in its early years. But as both novels and plays grew increasingly domestic, as they more and more fervently asserted the primacy of home and family, the hearth became the mythical center of an eternal order that, according to the myth, had just recently come under assault. As rural populations drained into cities and the pressure of urban life rose, stretching and tearing traditional social bonds, fiction grew more and more sentimental about that lost little group before the fire.

It may be true that, at least in some minds, barrages of news about butchery at home inspired qualms about the survival of bourgeois civilization. But if that was their sole effect, only a perverse and widespread desire for qualms can explain the immense popularity of such news. Most likely, Dickens and Gosse came closer to the mark, with their evocations of comfort, even in Gosse's strained, unhappy household. By portraying outlandish acts in familiar settings—especially by declaring that their tales are factual—true-crime stories fortify rather than undermine the reader's unwarranted belief that no such nightmare can ever visit him. The sense of well-being induced by murder mysteries (a genre that sprang directly from nineteenth-century journalism) has often been traced to the same source.

Even in the 1860s, however, when English "sensational" fiction discovered the wealth of potential subjects that lay ready in the annals of domestic crime, novelists showed great restraint in their treatment of mayhem. Wilkie Collins's *The Woman in White* (1860), which is often called the first English sensation novel, owed its central plot device to an eighteenth-century French case that Collins had read about in Maurice Méjan's *Recueil des causes célèbres* (Collection of Famous Cases). Collins provided a villainous Italian nobleman, Count Fosco, who instead of gliding about, as Italians customarily did in horrid English novels, merely smiles a great deal and keeps white mice; Sydney Greenstreet played him in an annoyingly stately 1948 American film. But there is also a villainous English nobleman, Sir Percival Glyde, whose dark visage and slinking ways recall Montoni, Romaldi, and their Italian ilk. *The Woman in White* is bloodless, however: Its intrigue concerns property, not passion, and only one murder is committed in it, by a cabal of Italians.

Mary Elizabeth Braddon went a bit further in a journalistic direction with the second founding novel of English sensationalism, *Lady Audley's Secret* (1862). Here the villain is a woman, Lucy Audley, whose "liquid blue eyes," "rosy lips," and "profusion of fair ringlets" are made much of throughout. But this paragon of feminine delicacy is a bigamist who attempts to murder her inconvenient first husband by pushing him down a well. Later, she sets fire to an inn, aiming to kill only one occupant but ready to incinerate guests and staff alike. She fails on both counts, and the novel's bloodshed remains metaphoric, as in this misleadingly ominous description of Audley Court:

> A fierce and crimson sunset. The mullioned windows and the twinkling lattices are all ablaze with the red glory. . . . Even into those dim recesses of briar and brushwood, amidst which the old well is hidden, the crimson brightness penetrates in fitful flashes, till the dank weeds and the rusty iron wheel and broken woodwork seem as if they were flecked with blood.

The shock value of *Lady Audley's Secret* derives not from police-report horrors but from its subversion of a feminine stereotype. Braddon also intimates that a young woman can take energetic action on her own behalf—indeed, that she might be justified in doing so.

There were exceptions, of course: Dickens had dwelt on violent death in *Oliver Twist* (1838) and totally disintegrated a character in *Bleak House* (1853); in the late sixties he returned to Bill Sikes's bludgeoning of Nancy with a series of public readings that terrified audiences and probably hastened Dickens's early death in 1870. On the whole, however, even at its most sensational, the midcentury

English novel preserved the reticence of its Gothic forebears regarding bloodshed and decay as well as sex. They ordered these matters differently in France, where a proverbial freedom of sexual reference was matched by the apparent willingness of genteel readers to stomach descriptions of horror that their English counterparts would tolerate only from newspapers.

Sometimes, French novelists brought sex and rot together in a liaison unthinkable to the English. Near the end of Honoré de Balzac's *La Cousine Bette* (1846), for instance, Valérie Crevel succumbs to "a disease so horrible that a mere description of it is enough to make one shudder"; virtually overnight, she turns from a beautiful woman into a "rotting mass." As Dr. Bianchon reports,

> Her teeth and hair are falling, she looks like a leper and she even horrifies herself. Her hands are a dreadful sight, bloated and covered with greenish pustules; her nails are loose and become imbedded in the wounds she scratches. In short, pus is eating away at her extremities and slowly destroying them.

What's worse (and still more un-English), Valérie has been deliberately infected with this venereal disease by the Baron Montès de Montejanos, who possesses a cure unknown to European medicine. It is murder of a particularly loathsome kind.

No doubt recalling the death of Valérie, Emile Zola inflicted an extravagantly disgusting end on the prostitute heroine of *Nana* (1880):

> What lay on the pillow was a charnel-house, a heap of pus and blood, a shovelful of putrid flesh. The pustules had invaded the whole face, so that one pock touched the next. Withered and sunken, they had taken on the greyish colour of mud, and on that shapeless pulp, in which the features had ceased to be discernible, they already looked like mould from the grave.

This, the novel's penultimate paragraph, goes on for several more lines of relentless autopsy. It is Zola's ghastly revenge on the "Venus" he himself has created, and the glee with which he despoils his icon of female sexuality is, at least to a twentieth-century reader, far more horrifying than the symptoms of terminal smallpox. Zola's imagery, however, harks directly back to the Graveyard poets, and it makes a revealing error. No "charnel-house" displayed pus and blood; only dried-out, relatively sanitary bones went on show in such places. By 1880, no functioning charnels remained in Western Europe, though the name still carried a charge.

In the last third of the twentieth century, when horror films began to feature graphic images of mayhem and dissolution, they seemed to many observers a fresh sign of cultural degeneracy. It was not generally noticed that the less assaultive medium of print had been treating Western readers to a steady diet of similar horrors for a century and a half. Nineteenth-century French novelists felt justified in portraying the extremes of physical ruin for the same reason that sex was not beyond their range: The real world undeniably contained such things, and the whole real world was the province of fiction. English-speaking countries adopted that creed with great reluctance and fought about it chiefly in regard to sex. Not until the 1950s, when battles over sexual explicitness had been raging for decades, did portrayals of the body's mutilation rather than its proper functioning become controversial there. Even then, the contended field was a marginal one—comic books.

Anglo-American culture seems to be governed by the perverse belief that portrayals of the body's abuse or destruction are harmless, even fortifying, while those that show the body in pleasure act like poison. But from early in the nineteenth century onward, that culture regarded with increasing suspicion all representations— written, pictorial, or performed—that sought to elicit *any* visceral response from their audiences. In middle-class eyes, such gestures came to look crude, suited only to the coarse tastes of the lower classes or the unfledged sensibilities of children. At best, works that jerked tears or gasps were trivial, suitable perhaps for an idle moment's diversion but not to be taken in large doses—certainly not to be taken seriously. Within a century of Sterne's rhapsody on a caged starling, any such shameless burst of feeling had turned from a noble symptom into an embarrassment.

In the English novel, for instance, there is no doubt that considerable artistic progress occurred during the middle decades of the nineteenth century, between the start of Dickens's career in the late 1830s and the flowering of George Eliot's in the 1870s. But that progress entailed a shift from the wholesale stirring-up of emotion to the analytic contemplation of social arrangements and psychological states. The famous crowds that gathered at the New York docks in 1840 and 1841, keyed up into sentimental frenzy over Little Nell's fate in *The Old Curiosity Shop*, were not summoned by Dickens's darker, more satirical novels of the 1850s and 1860s. Till the end, however, he displayed something of a lowlife streak, particularly when it came to sympathetic tears—secretions that Eliot had no time for. Her interests were altogether higher, broader, more austere; her novels, especially *Middlemarch* (1872) and *Daniel Deronda* (1876), lent English fiction an intellectual clout it may have needed, but they also drove a thick wedge into the widening split between highbrow and lowbrow. Thanks to Eliot, Oscar Wilde was able to remark, in 1895, "One must have a heart of stone to read the death of Little Nell without laughing."

The quip was meant to shock, of course, but only because it stated, in plain if arch terms, what everyone of importance already took for granted. In the theater, where Wilde achieved his greatest success, the shift from sentiment to contemplation had come belatedly, though by 1895 it was virtually complete. Indeed, by the time of *The Importance of Being Earnest*, laughter was the only physical response that remained genteel—as it still is today. Weeping, shrieking, and hissing the villain had been relegated to provincial, low, or juvenile audiences, where they remained until movies made them respectable again. Anglo-American culture ghettoized strong emotion, driving it out to the margins of polite entertainment and segregating it in compartments with appropriate labels. Shivers at carnage belonged to journalism, tears of sympathy to ladies' magazine fiction, gasps of awe to boys' own stories, and none of these to gentility. Already by the end of the nineteenth century, a space had been cleared for horror movies, though decades would pass before it got filled.

In 1907, when Edmund Gosse looked back over fifty years to those cozy fireside chats, he expressed mild astonishment that their subject had been hacked-up bodies. Perhaps he felt some indignation that his fundamentalist father could talk happily about human flesh only when it had been butchered; more likely, though, Edmund was surprised to remember that a stiffly respectable man in 1857 waxed hot about such low-class matters. In 1907, Edmund had transcended all that, as the respectable culture he grew up to epitomize had also done. But when fear came home, it was not tamed. The Victorian age turned ruined castles into artifacts and missing heads into reassurances, yet it found a new, wilder horror: the mind.

VAULTS OF HEART AND BRAIN

Contrary to twentieth-century stereotype, the Victorian age was not the heyday of fictional fear. Compared to the late eighteenth and late twentieth centuries, the years between about 1840 and 1880 formed, in fact, a slack season in the history of scary entertainment. Real-life horror stories crowded Victorian newspapers, and some became the basis for plays, short stories, and novels; the supernatural, however, steadily lost its importance on the stage, and it rarely appeared at all in book-length fiction. Even the ghost story, at which the Victorians are supposed to have excelled, did not reach its peak until the last decades of the nineteenth century and the first of the twentieth. The mid-nineteenth century has put in much better service as the setting for later horror fictions than as a source in its own right. Indeed, it has become for the twentieth century what the Middle Ages were for Horace Walpole: a distant yet nearby, alien yet creepily familiar past, studded with crumbling gingerbread mansions instead of Gothic castles.

What we chiefly owe to the Victorians is our inherited system of ranking all fictions, as well as sorting them by type—a system that did not deal kindly with fear. Except for the ghost story, the Victorians downgraded frightening entertainments, attaching to them the air of lowness and juvenility they still bear today. In this, of course, they only completed a process that began when scary fiction did: Eighteenth-century horrid novels had been addressed mainly to immature readers like Catherine Morland, and some had been written by them; the specters and demons of early-nineteenth-century melodrama had been devised to thrill riffraff. Perhaps there is something essentially vulgar or childish about scary fiction; that, at least, has been Western culture's verdict on it. In her own day, Ann Radcliffe, the fountainhead, won praise from high and low alike, but the entire nineteenth century failed to produce a single first-rate novelist who specialized in chills; the best the twentieth century can do in that line is Stephen King. History has also relegated Radcliffe's imitators— along with the entirety of horrid melodrama—to oblivion.

The ingrained conservatism of scary entertainment, its characteristic habit of telling the same old story, using devices that were hackneyed two hundred years ago, no doubt owes something to its confinement to a cultural ghetto. In that sealed-off place, news of artistic progress comes slowly, if at all. Few innovations by the twentieth-century literary avant-garde, for instance, have had any significant impact on the narrative methods of today's horror writers. The relative isolation of frightening entertainment has, conversely, made it a fertile reservoir for mainstream and even elite art, which loves to borrow its stock techniques, adapting them to higher or at least different purposes. On rare occasions, a mainstream entertainer has seemed to cross over entirely into a lower realm, as Alfred Hitchcock did with *Psycho* in 1960. In that famous case, shock was doubled and redoubled. Not only did Hitchcock apply his extraordinary skill to tricks that would have been humdrum in clumsier hands; he also scared his first audiences half out of their wits simply because *he* was doing it.

In the nineteenth century, the boundary between elite and popular culture was still forming, and it wavered. "Popular" culture, indeed, had not yet been clearly defined as such, nor had it been parceled out into the categories we recognize today. Affective entertainment—which aims to stir your feelings and can be labeled according to the feeling it goes after—gradually slid down the scale of respectability, until it hit rock bottom in the popular ghetto. On the way, however, it was not immune to changes that beset high art. Domestication was one; another, which went in tandem, was a growing tendency to psychologize human action, to interpret what people do as a symptom of what they think, and to conceive of thinking as an obscure process that consciousness hardly knows and that action only cryptically signifies. At the very end of the century, Freud began to construct a universal theory on this basis; the result would set the course of late-twentieth-century art, criticism, and schlock—perhaps the last elite system to exert such an across-the-board effect. Freud often declared that artists had seen the truth before him. He might have added that schlock peddlers saw it, too.

In the eighteenth-century horrid novel and the melodramas that grew from it, only villains exhibit a psychology in anything like the post-Freudian sense. Like the castles they inhabit, villainous minds are dark, intricate, and easy to get lost in; they are also restless, perturbed by contrary impulses that do not torment heroes and heroines. Yet the most complex of Gothic villains, Schedoni in Ann Radcliffe's *The Italian*, can submit his mind to thorough inventory:

> He considered the character of his own mind with astonishment, for circumstances had drawn forth traits, of which, till now, he had no suspicion. He knew not by what doctrine to explain the inconsistencies, the contradictions, he experienced, and, perhaps, it was not one of the least that in these moments of direful and conflicting passions, his reason could still look down upon their operations, and lead him to a cool, though brief examination of his own nature.

Even then, Radcliffe adds, Schedoni fails to see that pride remains "the master-spring of his mind"—just as it had been for Milton's Satan, whose mental processes Schedoni's quite deliberately resemble.

Gothic villains may be self-blind, but their minds are all of a piece. No part leads a separate, hidden life, as the fiendish dark sides of innumerable post-Freudian psychopaths do. To a twentieth-century reader this openness looks shallow, and it quite literally is: Horrid novelists did not imagine that even the most intricate mind possessed depths in which nameless forces lurked. On the early-nineteenth-century stage, where villains obligingly informed the audience of their nefarious schemes, villainous shallowness became almost ludicrous—though, of course, stage villains were no more superficial than were the good guys they menaced. In horrid novels and plays alike, when the past rose up to thwart present evil, it came in the objective, external form of ghosts, demons, and long-incarcerated earls. These were not the repressed memories that haunt latter-day wrongdoers; supernatural or human, they could be seen and touched.

It's fashionable to read these old scenarios allegorically, to interpret the vengeful ghost, for instance, as a stand-in for the villain's guilty conscience. Such readings are plausible because on this point, traditional wisdom conveniently agrees with twentieth-century views. As the playbill for *The Gamblers* proclaimed, "Murder, though it have no tongue, will speak with most miraculous organ." The source is *Hamlet*, though the quotation might easily refer to the return of the repressed. This way of reading early horrid fictions obscures the slow migration of evil, lasting most of the nineteenth century, from external to internal, vengeful ghost to avenging conscience. As horror left the Apennines and settled next door, forsaking the mind of a bandit chief for that of someone you might pass on the street, it also dove down into dark regions that anybody might harbor, because nothing showed above.

The change is detectable in all grades of art, highest to lowest. High art made everything psychological; just after the turn of the twentieth century, Henry James would demonstrate that a rowboat trip and a rubber of bridge could furnish occasions for thrilling mental dramas. Lower forms proceeded more cautiously, and frightening fictions never wholly gave up the ancient idea that the scariest things are those that jump at us from outside. But the domestication of fright led inevitably to its psychologizing: If, as newspapers said, people like you and me were committing inconceivable crimes, the difference between us must lie in the criminals' warped psyches. Very likely, the criminals were—*mad!*

From the early nineteenth century onward, madness gradually grew into scary entertainment's most serviceable convention. The wildest contrivances of plot can be explained away on the grounds that the contriver was mad and therefore paid no attention to common sense or probability. Early horrid fictions rarely used that expedient: For them, simply being Italian or Spanish was enough to explain any amount of odd behavior, especially if one was also a cleric. Even the ancestor of all twentieth-century mad scientists, Victor Frankenstein, is far from mad; nothing, for that matter, is wrong with the Monster's powers of reason. The erroneous implanting of a criminal's brain was an innovation of the 1931 film; both Victor's and the Monster's original problems had been matters of philosophy, not pathology.

In the same year as Mary Shelley's *Frankenstein*, "S. N. E." of Warwick caught a glimpse of the future in *The Murdered Maid.* Though the villain, Thornville, carries on in the ubiquitous Romaldi manner—"Which way shall I fly, where hide myself? . . . Ha! what voice was that? Hark!"—his end breaks the mold. Acquitted of Marie Ashville's murder, he is bragging to some bystanders about his legal immunity when, without warning, a "Chorus of Spirits" arises and presents an elaborate vision, with songs, of the dead Marie:

Ha! what form is that which rises from the tomb!—a murdered, mangled corse!—Stiff from the icy hand of rapine, come, whip me ye demons that surround my heart!—rack me,—use me as you please,—thus—thus I join you! *Draws a concealed Pistol, and shoots himself,—he drops without uttering a word,—all start up in horror.*

This curious hodgepodge combines the appeal of real-life bloodshed, the old thrill of castle specters, a wish-fulfilling dash of divine retribution (the real Thornville, Abraham Thornton, emigrated to America), and a surprising psychological touch. Though the audience sees the vision in all its blue-fiery ghastliness, Thornville's companions feel no horror until the shot rings out. Guilt, not God, has wrought revenge.

Shakespeare, of course, portrays something similar in Act III of *Macbeth*, when Banquo's ghost sits in Macbeth's place and only Macbeth can see him. It took more than two hundred years, however, for this device to become fit for recycling; it would take decades to catch on as a theatrical cliché. By 1852, *The Corsican Brothers*, one of the last successful ghostly melodramas and perhaps the most durable, had polished highly the technique of staging old-style horrors while justifying them as mental phenomena. The play's theatrical gimmick is that Acts I and II occur simultaneously, on Corsica and in Paris. The psychological gimmick is that the brothers, Fabien and Louis, are identical twins: When one dies, the other will know instantly. At the end of Act I, Fabien, on Corsica, sees Louis's rising ghost, thanks to the Corsican trap; he then has a vision of him lying dead, near Paris, killed in a duel. Act II reveals what really happened, ending with the same tableau as Act I, this time real rather than imagined. In Act III, Fabien avenges Louis's murder, and the ghost rises again, bidding farewell as Louis ascends into heaven.

The Corsican Brothers achieves a near-perfect compromise between the blatant supernaturalism of *The Castle Spectre*, more than fifty years earlier, and the thoroughgoing psychologism of Ibsen, almost thirty years later. Louis's ghost is undeniably real—and his rise won such plaudits that stages all over Europe were gutted and rebuilt to accommodate it—but he is also the spawn of Fabien's mind. The apparition doesn't get explained away in the Radcliffean style, but its objective existence isn't granted either. The play opts instead for a third possibility, a new one: The ghost is real and yet not real, there because Lucien sees it, nowhere unless he does. The remarkable endurance of *The Corsican Brothers* is due, along with extremely clever plotting, to its reliance on the twilight zone where reality and fantasy blur into one. Theatergoers of 1852 responded with a shock of recognition; nearly a century and a half later, we recognize it with a nod, as if we'd always known it.

By 1871, only the lowest playhouses were still staging actual specters, and only the lowest novels centered on deeds rather than thoughts. One of the biggest English and American theatrical hits of that year was Leopold Lewis's *The Bells*, adapted from *Le Juif polonais* (The Polish Jew) by Emile Erckmann and Alexandre Chatrian. The play became a war-horse, and a meal ticket, for Henry Irving, who went on performing the lead, the repentant villain Mathias, until just before his death in 1905. The play remained popular well into the twentieth century; it was filmed at least half a dozen times, most notably in a 1926 American version with Lionel Barrymore as Mathias and Boris Karloff as the Mesmerist. Though *The Bells* faded from the theatrical and cinematic repertoire after the 1930s, its main gimmick, like that of *The Corsican Brothers*, has been honored by countless recyclings.

Mathias is a wealthy innkeeper and burgomaster of an Alsatian town. In Act I, his daughter, Annette, is about to marry the dashing though impecunious Christian; Mathias prides himself on the hefty dowry he intends to bestow on this pure love match. In fact, however, he can afford such largess because, fifteen years earlier, he murdered and robbed an itinerant Polish Jew. At the end of the act, the past returns, though at first Mathias doesn't see but only hears it:

> What is this jangling in my ears? What is tonight? Ah, it is the very night—the very hour! [*Clock strikes ten.*] I feel a darkness coming over me. [*Stage darkens.*] . . . Shall I call for help? No, no, Mathias. Have courage! The Jew is dead!

Behind him, "*the back of the scene rises and sinks,*" revealing a ghastly pantomime:

> the JEW *is discovered seated in sledge . . . the horse carrying Bells;*
> *the* JEW's *face is turned away; the snow is falling fast; the scene is*

seen through a gauze; lime light . . . vision of a MAN *dressed in a brown blouse and hood over his head, carrying an axe, stands in an attitude of following the sledge; when the picture is fully disclosed the Bells cease.*

Reassured by the silence, Mathias rises and turns, only to confront the truth of his past:

[*He*] *starts violently upon seeing the vision before him; at the same time the* JEW *in the sledge suddenly turns his face, which is ashy pale, and fixes his eyes sternly upon him;* MATHIAS *utters a prolonged cry of terror, and falls senseless. Hurried music.*

The bells torment him throughout Act II, and by the start of Act III, they have completely unhinged him. As the sounds of Annette's wedding feast are heard offstage, Mathias fantasizes a trial scene, complete with judges, clerks, and a "PUBLIC" in Alsatian costumes; there is also a Mesmerist, who hypnotizes Mathias and leads him to perform his old crime publicly:

The Bells! The Bells! He comes! [*He bends down in a watching attitude, and remains still—a pause—in a low voice.*] You will be rich—you will be rich—you will be rich! [*The noise of the Bells increase (sic)—the* CROWD *express alarm simultaneously—all at once* MATHIAS *springs forward, and with a species of savage roar, strikes a terrible blow with his right hand.*] Ah! ah! I have you now, Jew! [*He strikes again—the* CROWD *simultaneously express horror.*]

At the end, the wedding guests break into Mathias's room to find him dressed in his bloodstained brown clothes; the bells are heard for the last time, and he expires.

The Bells must have made an irresistible showcase for Irving—as it would for any actor who does not overrate restraint—but it can have made sense to its first audiences only because they knew how to distinguish between real and imagined events, even when both were performed with the same degree of stage realism. The pantomime that closes Act I signals its fantastic nature with gauze and limelight, but almost the whole of Act III is played realistically; only the sound of offstage revelry reminds the audience that the trial is taking place entirely in Mathias's guilt-tortured mind. Scores of films, from *The Cabinet of Dr. Caligari* (1919) to *The Shining* (1980) and beyond, would play tricks with the convention that hallucination and fact can be represented in exactly the same way.

The technique was new to the stage in 1871; it had partial precursors in fiction, like Poe's narratives by madmen, but as recently as 1852, *The Corsican Brothers* had still represented the psychic world in ghostly, external terms. *The Bells* presupposes that complex, thickly peopled dramas can be enacted wholly inside the mind, and that an ordinary audience will interpret them not as ghosts but as symptoms. The play employs stage machinery that dates back to *The Castle Spectre*, and its musical tactics are not much different from those of *A Tale of Mystery*. But Mathias is no moustache-twirling Romaldi or Woodville. He is a generous, loving man who got away with a heinous crime, a commonplace fellow (not unlike the husbands and fathers in newspaper crime reports) who once axed a man to death and threw his hacked corpse into a lime kiln. Mathias is not a subtle psychological portrait, but on the face of him he unnervingly resembles the commonplace man next door.

By the last quarter of the nineteenth century, the unseen horrors of the ordinary mind had permanently joined the repertory of scary entertainment. They never wholly supplanted the old troupe of ghosts, demons, depraved noblemen, and scheming clerics; their commonplace habitats would prove quite compatible with the old backdrops of crumbling castles and crypts, and their predilection for dismemberment merely lent immediacy to the Graveyard poets' clutching skeletons. In an 1880 letter to his German translator, Henrik Ibsen made a typical and quite modern-sounding declaration:

> Everything that I have written has the closest possible connection with what I have lived through, even if it has not been my own personal experience; in every new poem or play I have aimed at my own spiritual emancipation—for a man shares the responsibility and the guilt of the society to which he belongs.

He went on, however, to add a quatrain that translated these sentiments into the terms of old-fashioned horrors:

To *live* is to battle with trolls
In vaults of heart and brain;
To *write*—that is to pass
Judgment on one's self.

The *Ghosts* that Ibsen would summon in his 1881 play clanked no
rusty chains, but they were specters even so.

At bottom, there is little difference between the realistic, psychological tactics of many latter-day scary entertainments and the far-
fetched fantasies that chilled Regency damsels like Catherine
Morland. All rely upon an uneasy awareness of the body's penchant
for turning inexplicably, in an instant, from a familiar human form
into something uncannily other. The body may disintegrate, spilling
garish blood and intricate guts; it may simply die and rot, in which
case the transformation comes more slowly but with even greater
horror because it is inevitable; or the mind that strangely inhabits
the body may come to frightening independent life, strewing death
around it. From sensational crime reports to melodramas to tales of
ghosts and madness, scary fictions draw repeatedly, unceasingly,
on that bottomless reservoir of fear.

I don't mean, however, to write off everything that raises a chill as
merely the reflex of a single social neurosis. The variety of scary
fictions is far more interesting than whatever common roots they
possess; the roots may, indeed, lie so deep that unearthing them
reveals little about any growth they sprout. Frightening fiction can
perhaps be accounted for as a symptom of Western culture's recoil
from the facts of mortality. But that doesn't explain why for more
than two hundred years, millions of people have reveled in fictional
things that would dismay or sicken them if they were real. In 1918,
Virginia Woolf summed up several generations of commentators
when she marveled at "the strange human craving for the pleasure of
feeling afraid." Later observers agree: How strange (and yet how
human) it is that fear can be pleasant! What a delightful mystery!

The solution lies on the surface—not in the details or intentions
of scary entertainments but in the social context where such things
enjoy their only real existence. Unlike high, serious art, which one
savors alone even in the midst of a crowd, scary fiction works when
it is shared. This was obviously true for horrid melodramas, but it
also applied to printed horrors when they were read aloud to a circle

of eager listeners or debated by a father and son before the flickering fire. Such communal shuddering faded from mainstream Western culture in the late nineteenth and early twentieth centuries, as the arts and even journalism slipped into polite silence. But it powerfully revived with the arrival of film, where it still flourishes, as anyone knows who has joined the raucous, extremely impolite audience of a contemporary horror film.

Sharing the fear softens it, turning it into comfort. The mechanism is ancient, perhaps, but it remained disorganized and unselfconscious until the nineteenth century, when the newborn entertainment industry recognized the commercial possibilities of artificial fear and set about exploiting them. The most artful contrivers of scary entertainment implanted in their fictions a hint that the convivial ring around the fire did not cancel death's dominion. But those entertainers were either artists, launched on quests after truth that happened to traverse fear's domain, or else they merely played with their audience's expectations, sowing seeds of unease because they knew how comforting shared fear was expected to be. That cat-and-mouse game became standard practice after the first quarter of the twentieth century, especially because large profits came in when Dracula, Frankenstein, Jason, or Freddy refused to die.

On the whole, scary entertainments endured a fallow season in the mid-nineteenth century. In one form, however, fear grew stronger. There alone it not only enjoyed wide popularity but even, sometimes, got elevated to the rank of high art. As novels and plays passed it by, fear flourished in the short story, a nineteenth-century invention that customarily appeared in another new product, the magazine. Spawned just as the horrid novel was fading, the horrid short story proved to be the ideal home for effects that longer fictions could not or would not sustain. Until the arrival of horror films in the 1930s, horror stories dominated the field; indeed, it was short fiction that first defined horror as a genre, the way we know it today.

The vampire Millarca attacks an innocent young victim. (ILLUSTRATION BY
D. H. FRISTON, FROM *The Dark Blue,* 1871–1872.)

6

Genceficɑtion

SMALL CHANGES

In life, fear obeys no deadline, but in fiction its term is brief. Even today's specialized horror novels and films seldom attempt to sustain fearful emotions longer than a few pages or minutes at a stretch. In the late eighteenth and early nineteenth centuries, fear took its place as one among the many strong feelings aimed at by horrid novels and melodramas. Its favorite companions in those old works were patronizing chuckles at the antics of servants and peasants, along with sighs of sad or joyous care for beleaguered young lovers. Such types became standard in all melodramas, horrid or not, and they remain with us. The shocking novelty of late-twentieth-century horrors like *Night of the Living Dead* (1968) and *The Texas Chainsaw Massacre* (1974) derived in part from those films' deliberate omission of these expected, soothing fellow travelers with fear.

At its topmost pitch, of course, fear cannot last long, in reality or fiction. At some point, if the source will not relent, the frightened one passes out. The heroines of Gothic novels do so frequently—though their readers were probably not expected to follow suit—and it became a prime selling point of scary shows, from Dickens's readings in the late 1860s through the Grand Guignol Theater at the turn of the twentieth century, that they had driven spectators, especially women, to faint away. Similar claims were made for Lon Chaney's unmasking scene in *The Phantom of the Opera* (1925), and as late as 1959, tombstone-shaped lobby cards assured prospective viewers of *The House on Haunted Hill* that somebody had died from the film's impact. In recent years, this ploy has been neglected, probably because today's horror-movie audiences arrive so well armed against scare tactics that nothing can faze them.

They have had, of course, plenty of warning. Today's horrid entertainments come with labels: Horror-movie trailers, posters, and ads declare exactly what the effect is intended to be; books do the same by means of cover art, their authors' patented names, or the section of the bookstore—usually HORROR—where they wait for buyers. It's easy to forget that marketing by genre is a recent development. A century ago, when a reader bought or borrowed *Dracula*, she found herself in Catherine Morland's position, trusting the testimony of better-versed friends. She might have read reviews or leafed through a few pages in a bookstore, where *Dracula* lay among NOVELS, if it was classified at all. Not until the 1930s were horror movies put in a category; before then, even F. W. Murnau's *Nosferatu: Eine Symphonie des Grauens* (Nosferatu: A Symphony of Horror, 1922) had been simply a film that frightened—not a member of a preordained class or species.

In one form of entertainment, however, the desire to frighten declared itself much earlier as an identifying mark and a marketing tool—short stories. From the early nineteenth century well into the twentieth, short stories furnished the primary vehicle for scary fictional effects; they slipped into second place when horror movies took the lead, but even in our postliterate age they enjoy great popularity. Short stories were also the first form to develop— and sustain—a subcategory that promised gooseflesh before all else. Spawned just as the horrid novel was fading, in the second and third decades of the nineteenth century, the horrid story went through ups and downs, but it never slipped into oblivion. Horrid stories also developed a self-conscious tradition that paralleled the mainstream of fiction and occasionally barged in on it.

On several counts, short fiction very early proved the appropriate form for artificial fear. The nature of the emotion, with its limited lifespan, suited itself well to stories that could be read in one sitting. Most early- and mid-nineteenth-century horrid stories seem diffuse to a latter-day reader, but by the turn of the twentieth century, when the short story had won the status of an art form, some writers lent it remarkable concision and concentration. W. W. Jacobs's deathless "The Monkey's Paw" (1902), for instance, gets its creepy business done in three thousand words; in his chilling "August Heat" (1910), W. F. Harvey hits what is probably rock bottom, around two thousand.

Traditionally, tales of ghosts and marvels had been brief, often appearing as episodes or digressions in longer works. Classical literature held scores of examples, including Book 11 of *The Odyssey*, in which Odysseus visits Hades and offers lamb's blood to "the blurred and breathless dead." Ovid's *Metamorphoses* contained several hair-raising anecdotes, and goosefleshy interludes could be found in the works of Petronius, Apuleius, and many other Roman writers. *The Arabian Nights Entertainments*, first translated into French and English in the early eighteenth century, provided a gold mine of exotic horrors, all told briefly. And the nationalist antiquarianism of the late eighteenth and early nineteenth centuries, especially in Germany and England, the fad that Chatterton and Macpherson sought to batten on, unearthed plenty of ghastly tales and ballads, ready for exploitation.

This last source was particularly valuable to commercial purveyors of horrid fiction, who gave an air of authenticity to their stories by claiming to have drawn them from some local, usually oral tradition. In English, Sir Walter Scott was the first to make extensive use of the device; it soon became standard. Early in his literary career, Scott published *Minstrelsy of the Scottish Border* (1802–1803), a three-volume compilation of ballads. Though heavily edited and polished up by Scott and his associates, many of the tales had been obtained from interviews with illiterate, talkative country folk. After 1805, Scott turned his attention to fiction, but most of his poems and novels remained grounded in Scottish history or legend. Often, their genuineness was asserted by a figure like Jedediah Cleishbotham, supposed parish clerk of Gandercleugh, who introduces six of Scott's novels, including two of his most famous, *The Heart of Midlothian* (1818) and *The Bride of Lammermoor* (1819).

Scott is often credited with having invented the English ghost story, if not the very genre of the short story in the modern sense. The "earliest masterpiece" of a ghostly kind, as two recent anthologists call it, is his "Wandering Willie's Tale," which first appeared, as such tales had done for centuries before it, as an interpolation in a full-length work, *Redgauntlet* (1824). This epistolary novel (an old-fashioned form by then) is set in the late 1740s or 1750s. Willie Steenson, a blind fiddler, tells Darsie Latimer in elaborate detail how wicked Sir Robert Redgauntlet made good his pledge from beyond the grave. Latimer reports the tale verbatim to his friend Alan Fairford—an unlikely feat, since it goes on for some seventy-five hundred words. Besides, most of it is told in an approximation of broad Scots: "But they werena weel out of the room, when Sir Robert gied a yelloch that garr'd the Castle rock!" Genteel nineteenth-century English readers had a high tolerance for transcribed dialect, though they prided themselves on speaking the queen's version. They took rural language as genteel writers like Scott and George Eliot meant it, as a sign of rude truth. "Wandering Willie's Tale" is further vouched for by Willie's testimony that the events happened to his grandfather and father, not far from where Latimer hears the tale.

In *Redgauntlet*, it serves mostly as a big splash of the quaint local color for which Scott was famous. The story could easily be detached from the novel, and Scott—the most enterprising of early-nineteenth-century writers—quickly did so, revising it slightly for inclusion in a collection of supernatural tales called *Legends of Terror* (1826). For over a century, "Wandering Willie's Tale" held its own; as late as 1931, introducing *The Supernatural Omnibus*, Montague Summers excused its absence on the grounds that it was "too easily accessible to be given here." By then, Scott's fiction had fallen into general neglect, surviving mainly as adventure stories for rather patient boys; it lost even that low status not long thereafter, and today hardly anybody reads Scott. To its first readers, "Wandering Willie" offered the safe pleasure of a peasant's tale: It was authentic because a rustic told it and dismissible for the same reason. The homogenized twentieth century has little feeling for those charms and little patience with the likes of Wandering Willie.

Another of Scott's short stories has fared better; indeed, it stands as the archetype of a still-flourishing tradition of ghostly fiction. "The Tapestried Chamber" was first published in *Blackwood's Edinburgh Magazine* in 1818; ten years later, substantially revised, it appeared in *The Keepsake*, a posh Christmas annual. With typical thrift, Scott saw it through the press a third time, adding it to the first series of *Chronicles of the Canongate* when that volume joined his collected works in 1831. In 1986, Michael Cox and R. A. Gilbert placed "The Tapestried Chamber" at the head of *The Oxford Book of English Ghost Stories*; during the intervening century and a half, the tale had never lost its popularity.

Reading "The Tapestried Chamber" in the late twentieth century is an uncanny experience. Everything looks familiar: the ancient, partly ruined castle, the unexpected overnight guest, the horrid midnight visitant, the truth next morning. Yet one can hardly say how one first learned this simple story—except that experience didn't teach it. There have been so many fictional versions, and so many variations, that the plot seems ageless, like an inheritance through the blood rather than the media. Stories, however, are not inherited, though the desire for them may be. The dateless legends of all nations offer anecdotes about haunted rooms, buildings, and objects, but "The Tapestried Chamber" is a commercial product with no other link to the deeper past than Scott's finely tuned awareness that such stuff sold well.

The story is brief, around five thousand words, and simple. Sometime in the mid-1780s, General Richard Browne, home from the American war, has embarked on a tour of western England. Near a charming little town, he spots a picturesque castle of fifteenth-century vintage, which he decides to investigate. Local inquiry reveals that the place belongs to Lord Woodville—a delightful coincidence, since Frank Woodville was Browne's fag at Eton and his friend at Oxford. Warmly welcomed, the general is lodged in a "comfortable, but old-fashioned" room with seventeenth-century furniture including "tapestry hangings" that "gently undulated as the autumnal breeze found its way through the ancient lattice-window." As he prepares for "a luxurious night's rest," the narrator interrupts: "Here, contrary to the custom of this species of tale, we leave the general in possession of his apartment until the next morning."

"This species of tale" is, of course, the horrid novel, in which tapestried chambers routinely thwart the repose of frightened but stalwart heroines. In *Northanger Abbey*, Henry Tilney's jocular list of the horrors awaiting Catherine Morland includes a "gloomy chamber . . . hung with tapestry exhibiting figures as large as life" and concealing a secret door. But at Northanger Abbey, Catherine finds nothing more ominous than modern window curtains that "seemed in motion" only during a violent storm. Scott highly admired Austen (*Northanger Abbey* was published the year before "The Tapestried Chamber"), but he didn't need her prompting to make the sly joke of sending a battle-weary soldier to bed in a species of room that fiction had reserved for defenseless maidens.

Next morning, General Browne shows up late for breakfast, looking "haggard and ghastly in a peculiar degree." He has also suddenly remembered "indispensable business" that compels an immediate departure, despite his promise to stay at the castle a week or more. When Woodville interrogates him, the true story comes out. The night before, as he was dozing off, he saw, between his bed and the fireplace, a woman wearing "an old-fashioned gown." At first, he thought she must be an oddly dressed servant, but then she turned:

> gracious heaven! my lord, what a countenance did she display to me! There was no longer any question what she was, or any thought of her being a living being. Upon a face which wore the fixed features of a corpse, were imprinted the traces of the vilest and most hideous passions which had animated her while she lived.

Rudely, the hag darted toward the bed and squatted on it, "advancing her countenance within half a yard of mine." The general's response was classic—a bit maidenly, too: "all firmness forsook me, all manhood melted from me like wax in the furnace, and I felt my hair individually bristle. The current of my life-blood ceased to flow, and I sank back in a swoon."

Rather rudely in his own right, Woodville informs his guest that these midnight terrors were the result of "an experiment." The Tapestried Chamber, rumored to be haunted, had been closed for two generations. On Woodville's recent succession to the estate, he had reopened it, and the unexpected arrival of an old friend had provided an opportunity to dispel the rumors by stationing a stalwart soldier there. Browne takes no permanent offense—though he refuses to prolong his stay—and later, in the portrait gallery, he identifies a painting of "the accursed hag who visited me last night!" Which brings a tantalizing explanation from Woodville:

That is the picture of a wretched ancestress of mine, of whose crimes a black and fearful catalogue is recorded in a family history in my charter-chest. The recital of them would be too horrible; it is enough to say, that in yon fatal apartment incest and unnatural murder were committed. I will restore it to the solitude to which the better judgement of those who preceded me had consigned it . . .

The twentieth-century reader would like to hear more about "incest and unnatural murder," but simply mentioning such crimes was sufficient for Scott's purpose and his audience's sensibilities. On that unsatisfying note, "The Tapestried Chamber" comes to its neat end.

"The Tapestried Chamber" amounted to a brief diversion for the tireless Scott, and it makes only the mildest demands on its readers' intellect or emotions. For those well versed in Gothic horrors, however, it plays clever little jokes. Not only does Scott postpone narrating the ghost's visit (a conventional horrid writer would have told the general's adventures straight through), he also reverses conventional sex roles by making the swooner a man, the evil visitor a woman. This may not be much to hang a tale on, but it served for *Blackwood's* and *The Keepsake*, which had no desire to overtax their readers. And it is typical of the genre to which "The Tapestried Chamber" contributed its first throwaway masterpiece.

For two centuries, horrid short stories have been one-note compositions, reducible to a gimmick apiece. Their length, of course, compels simplification, along with a narrow focus of emotional appeal. But the most durable horrid stories also tend to employ a specialized kind of strategy. They seldom try anything radically new; instead, they ring small changes on tricks their readers have already mastered. Just as "The Tapestried Chamber" presupposes familiarity with Gothic conventions, so later horrid stories depend on prior acquaintance with the haunted-chamber gimmick, the ancient-crimes gimmick, and the most popular gimmick of all, the sturdy fellow who denies the existence of ghosts until one leaps up and grins in his face. This blockhead—of whom "The Tapestried Chamber" offers two rudimentary examples—flourished in science-fiction films of the 1950s, when he denied existence not to ghosts but to block-long grasshoppers.

All generic fictions develop through the accumulation of small changes that are both new and old—new enough to avoid mere repetition, yet close enough to the old pattern that they remain familiar. Similar strategies operate in the modern genres of mysteries, romances, and spy thrillers, as well as in TV sitcoms and of course horror movies. In a sense, these fictions do not develop at all; they fill in territory left unexploited by the past. After a while, they may peter out, as the genteel detective novel did in the 1950s and the television Western in the 1970s. They never die; isolated revivals remain possible long after a genre's vitality has faded, and spoofs and parodies may extend its life yet further. Or the conventions of one genre may be taken over by another, stripping them of their generic associations. A process of this kind seems to be under way at the end of the twentieth century, as graphic bloodshed— once the identifying mark of self-proclaimed horror films— becomes commonplace in everything (so far) except comedies.

The first modern genre to run out of steam was the horrid novel, which was already moribund by 1820. But many of its techniques survived decades longer in melodrama, which bequeathed them to film. And the horrid story can be regarded as simply a pared-down, streamlined version of the bulky genre from whose ruins it rose. Mrs. Radcliffe's distinctive blend of exotic scenery, sublime decay, sham supernaturalism, and quivering sensibility was known in its heyday chiefly for one of the many emotions it sought to inspire—terror. Increasingly, writers of horrid stories focused on that emotion to the exclusion of all others. By the end of the nineteenth century, they had come close to perfecting the only genre of entertainment that gets its name not from its setting or subject but from the feeling it creates. "I felt my hair individually bristle," says Scott's General Browne, speaking for the ideal reader of horrid short fiction.

POE'S JOKES

By the 1830s, especially in Britain, short stories of all kinds had become standard magazine fare. The pace was set by *Blackwood's*, founded in 1817, which appealed to a broad range of middle-class tastes with a monthly smorgasbord of reviews, topical articles, and fiction. This successful formula was widely imitated on both sides of the Atlantic. In England, the *London Magazine* (1819–1829), *Fraser's Magazine* (1830–1882), and *Bentley's Miscellany* (1837–1869), among many others, offered similar menus; in the United States, such monthlies as *Godey's Lady's Book* (1830–1898), the *Southern Literary Messenger* (1834–1864), and *Graham's Magazine* (1839–1858) followed the pattern, often supplementing it with fashion plates intended to attract female subscribers.

Established writers frequently contributed to these journals, but in Britain they did so casually, following Scott's example. Until the last quarter of the nineteenth century, the British regarded short fiction as at best a sideline or a laboratory where ideas for novels might be tested; the short story did not yet rank as an art form, and no significant reputation could be grounded solely on it. In the United States, short fiction paid just as poorly and won as little respect; nevertheless, it attracted two of the nation's finest writers, Nathaniel Hawthorne (1804–1864) and Edgar Allan Poe (1809–1849). In his own time, Hawthorne was best known for his five novels, but Poe wrote only one, *The Narrative of Arthur Gordon Pym* (1838), a failure. Poe enjoyed some repute as a perceptive if cantankerous critic, and "The Raven" (1845) at once became the schoolroom nemesis it remains. But his two collections of stories, *Tales of the Grotesque and Arabesque* (1840) and *Tales* (1845), fell flat.

In part, they failed because their contents bore too plainly the marks of magazine fiction, throwaway writing. Hawthorne also had trouble marketing his collections; his stories, however, employed their lurid materials in the interest of moral allegory. They were therefore palatable to an audience of serious middle-class readers. Poe's stories, by contrast, often seemed to revel in the horrid for its own sake, to offer no redemption of visceral force by spiritual teaching. To make matters worse, rumor had it that Poe was a drunkard, an opium addict, a connoisseur of dissipation. Twentieth-century scholarship has shown that, in fact, his life was "one of the dullest any figure of literary importance has lived in the past two hundred years," but to an age that read all fiction as emanations from its authors' souls, Poe's fondness for obsessed, deranged, drug-induced states of mind automatically suggested that he knew them from personal experience. Poe did little to discredit the connection.

For decades after his death, Poe and his stories retained, in American eyes at least, a curious aura of mingled triviality and unwholesomeness. This attitude was well summed up by Henry James in an 1876 essay on Charles Baudelaire, who had translated Poe into French and admired him extravagantly:

> With all due respect to the very original genius of the author of the "Tales of Mystery" [Poe never published any such title], it seems to us that to take him with more than a certain degree of seriousness is to lack seriousness one's self. An enthusiasm for Poe is the mark of a decidedly primitive stage of reflection.

This assessment is hard to argue with, though a late-twentieth-century reader is likely to find it considerably less damning than James's contemporaries did. Thanks to such opinions, however, Poe's influence on Anglo-American fiction took a long detour through France, coming home only at the end of the nineteenth century.

James was right to deny Poe the merits of reflection. Poe's stories do not reflect on the minds and situations they portray; they simply portray them, without apology, sometimes nearly without context. They don't encourage reflection in the reader either. After finishing a Poe story, the reader may mull it over or not, as she pleases; while it is being read, all the story demands is surrender to the given mood or scene. Poe is the most purely affective, least analytic of writers, and to take him seriously may be, as James said, a symptom of primitive intellectual development. Poe's ongoing popularity among high-school students and college freshmen supports that view. Yet Poe himself was always serious, even when he wrote semiparodies like "Metzengerstein" or perpetrated hoaxes like "The Facts in the Case of M. Valdemar." He had serious designs on his readers' individual hairs, intending to make them bristle.

In many ways, Poe resembled the melodramatists of his time and later, who also aimed at the audience's gut, not its intellect. Like them, he wrote hastily and often carelessly. But it's as if he had been assigned just the scary bits of a play that, complete, would add episodes of lovemaking and low comedy. There is no lovemaking in Poe; he is comic only in retrospect. His stories purvey a single emotion, usually fear, loathing, or sheer horror, that starts out at a high pitch, rises to the utmost, and stops. In the magazines where they first appeared, his stories came sandwiched between sentimental sonnets and fashion plates; taken together, the ensemble made a banquet not much different from an evening at the contemporary theater. Read singly, Poe's stories can be powerful; read in sequence, they rapidly become ridiculous.

Poe is also, before Stephen King, the most derivative of horrid writers; his work draws far more from other writing than from anyone's real or possible experience. King relies on a gagging excess of verbiage, Poe on a premodern minimum, but both implicitly trust their readers' familiarity with the conventions of the genre in which the two writers place themselves. King's reservoir of ideas is the ghost or horror story as twentieth-century anthologies have defined it; Poe's was much smaller—the horrid novel, melodrama, and the casual fiction of Scott, Dickens, and the anonymous hacks who wrote for *Blackwood's* and other English magazines. And though Poe is always serious, unlike the literal-minded King he uses his borrowed ideas to make jokes. Many of his stories are pure tissues of clichés, but (in the manner of "The Tapestried Chamber") they are clichés with a twist.

Poe's first published story, "Metzengerstein," which appeared in the *Philadelphia Saturday Courier* in January 1832, seems to have been intended as a parody of the threadbare fad for blood and thunder with vaguely East European settings. Yet nothing in the tale itself—except perhaps its extravagance—betrays parodic intent. Taken seriously, "Metzengerstein" is a thorough, if somewhat frantic, recycling of *The Castle of Otranto*, including rival families, an ancient curse that no one understands, a dissipated baron, and a picture (in this case a tapestry) that comes to life. At the end, like Otranto, the Palace Metzengerstein is destroyed, but instead of an enormously dilated Alfonso, "a cloud of smoke settled heavily over the battlements in the distinct colossal figure of—*a horse.*" "Metzengerstein" is most notable, however, for what it omits: There are no family history, next to no intrigue, and no love. Indeed, the story altogether lacks female characters; the sole passion on display is Baron Frederick's for the ghastly animal that finally undoes him.

"Metzengerstein" is a joke because, like "The Tapestried Chamber," it plays with familiar conventions—copying some, bending others, highhandedly ignoring the rest. Many of Poe's later, better-known stories turn similar tricks, though with greater subtlety and sophistication. "The Fall of the House of Usher" (1839), for instance, recycles *Otranto*'s doomed family and castle in what can only be called an original way, by merging them. The House itself is a standard Gothic structure, marked by "excessive antiquity" and "extensive decay"; it comes complete with a "valet, of stealthy step," "many dark and intricate passages," and "numerous vaults" inside its walls. Like Radcliffean castles, the House is also far too large for its current residents, who number only two, Roderick and Madeline Usher, besides that stealthy valet.

But instead of reproaching them with its grandeur, the House has, in some "shadowy" manner, become enmeshed in their souls. As the nameless narrator paraphrases Roderick, there is

an influence which some peculiarities in the mere form and substance of his family mansion had, by dint of long sufferance, he said, obtained over his spirit—an effect which the *physique* of the gray wall and turrets, and of the dim tarn into which they all looked down, had, at length, brought about upon the *morale* of his existence.

What this means is far from clear, even to the narrator, but the outcome is plain: As the House goes, so go the Ushers, and terminal decay has ruined them all. "The Fall of the House of Usher" is garrulous by Poe's standards, running close to eight thousand words and providing an unusual amount of background information. But at bottom it is another joke, perhaps merely an extended pun on two senses of the word "house." Again there is no plot to speak of, and the place of the conventional lovers has been taken this time not by a man and his horse but by a brother and sister, both dying.

Some of Poe's tales offer so little ordinary storytelling that the reader must supply nearly everything. "The Tell-Tale Heart" (1843) seems to begin in mid-conversation: "True!—nervous—very, very dreadfully nervous I had been and am; but why *will* you say that I am mad?" It goes on to describe, with no scene setting whatever, how a young man first loved, then hated an old one (neither has a name), and how he plotted to kill him, then did it, solely on account of the old man's "vulture eye." Most of this very short story is devoted to a twist on the stock horrid-novel situation of the heroine threatened in her bedroom by a lustful lord or a gliding monk; Mrs. Radcliffe contributed the model in *The Italian*. Here, however, innocent Ellena has become a vulture-eyed old man, and the murder actually occurs (horrid heroines always escape).

"The Pit and the Pendulum" (1843) also begins abruptly: "I was sick—sick unto death with that long agony." The reader only gradually learns that he is on familiar horrid territory—a dungeon of the Spanish Inquisition. "Ligeia" (1838) carries lack of specification to a nearly self-defeating extreme. The unnamed narrator starts by confessing that he cannot remember when, where, or how he met Ligeia; he never even knew her family name, though he married her. This may be a joke on the obsession of all English fiction, horrid or not, with genealogies. But the narrator's memory is so impaired that it ought to disqualify him from narrating: "I cannot, for my soul, remember . . . my memory is feeble . . . I cannot *now* bring these points to mind . . . I have *never known* . . . I but indistinctly recall . . . I have utterly forgotten," he says, all in the first paragraph. He remembers none of the things that conventional horrid fiction would provide in surplus. He does recall that Ligeia died, he married again, and his first wife's spirit possessed his second wife's corpse; perhaps, though, he's only mixing up the two women. "Ligeia" is the closest Poe came to a love story.

Poe's joking does not make him funny; only his style does that. Neither amused his American contemporaries, most of whom regarded him as the hack he plausibly resembled. And if Baudelaire saw any jokes in Poe, he did not mention them. Baudelaire saw himself in Poe:

> There is in man, he [Poe] says, a mysterious force which modern philosophy does not wish to take into consideration; nevertheless, without this nameless force, without this primordial bent, a host of human actions will remain unexplained, inexplicable. These actions are attractive only *because* they are bad, dangerous; they possess the fascination of the abyss. This primitive, irresistible force is natural Perversity, which makes man constantly and simultaneously a murderer and a suicide, an assassin and a hangman . . .

Baudelaire was not Poe's first French translator (loose, anonymous renderings of "The Murders in the Rue Morgue" had appeared as early as 1846), but he was certainly his fondest acolyte. Between 1856 and 1863, he translated five volumes of Poe, mostly prose but including the inevitable "Raven." He attached wildly laudatory prefaces to each volume, chatted Poe up among his literary friends, and launched a craze that hasn't fizzled yet, to the perennial puzzlement of American observers.

Baudelaire loved Poe because he saw in his incompleteness, his omission of "a reasonably sufficient motive" for the deeds he portrayed, some "remarkably satanic subtlety" that made him profound. The subtlety was an illusion, generated partly by wish fulfillment and partly by ignorance of the Anglo-American hack tradition in which Poe's stories belong and to which they make playful reference. But there was another quality in Poe, one he actually possessed, that fascinated Baudelaire, Guy de Maupassant, Stéphane Mallarmé, and his other French admirers; it also rescued him for twentieth-century English and American readers. Poe often confined his stories to the testimony of a single participant, whose frantic prose casts automatic doubt on his sanity. The narrators of "The Tell-Tale Heart" and "Ligeia," for example, must be either deranged or drugged; those of "The Black Cat" (1843) and "The Cask of Amontillado" (1846) are certainly suspect. They seem to call into question the very nature of reality, or at least of human knowledge, a trick that twentieth-century culture hasn't yet grown weary of.

In fact, they do no such thing; Poe's trust in the sufficiency of reason was quite conventionally strong, as he proved in his tales featuring M. Dupin, the ratiocinative sleuth. But for the artistic avant-garde of the late nineteenth century, Poe's unreliable narrators made a refreshing change from the omniscient voices that ruled mainstream Victorian and Edwardian fiction. Poe seemed ahead of his time in his apparent exploration of the mind's scary twilight zones, an area that the rest of Western culture began to find thrilling only a generation after him. In retrospect, Poe the hack looked like Poe the harbinger; his short, sad life became, as Baudelaire said, a "grievous tragedy." And Poe's stories served to transport the clichés of early-nineteenth-century magazine fiction directly into the horrid-entertainment industry of the twentieth.

THE HORRORS OF CHRISTMAS

Magazine clichés, however, also had their own career, which followed the same general course as those of horrid melodrama, down from the Apennines into the home and the normal heart. As magazines multiplied during the latter half of the nineteenth century, short fiction boomed; especially in England, scary stories constituted a distinct and reliably popular subspecies. Frederick Marryat's "The White Wolf of the Hartz Mountains" (first published in the *New Monthly Magazine* in 1837, as an episode in his serialized novel *The Phantom Ship*) is typical of the old-style horrid story, with its romantic Continental locale of which "many strange tales are told." Such stories continued to be published, but the field belonged more and more, as it did on the contemporary stage, to hauntings and horrors in nearby places, among people with easily pronounceable names.

The new style was represented by Richard Barham's *Ingoldsby Legends*, which began publication in 1837 in *Bentley's Miscellany* (which was then edited by the twenty-four-year-old Charles

Dickens). These loosely linked stories and poems—all connected with the mythical estate of Ingoldsby, in Kent—proved immensely popular in both Britain and the United States; in book form, three series were published between 1840 and 1847 and frequently reprinted throughout the nineteenth century. Then they fell into obscurity and out of print. Summers's *Supernatural Omnibus* (1931) was the last twentieth-century horrid anthology to include any Ingoldsby stories, and even the obdurate antiquarian Summers wrote defensively about Barham as the sole property of "Ingoldsby enthusiasts"; today we would call him a cult figure, and he faded fast.

Barham's tales are well written—even his poems can still be read with mild pleasure—but the quality that endeared him to nineteenth-century readers turned nauseating later: jocularity. He initiated a strain of English fiction that borrows horrid techniques in order to make them cute; the tradition survives, debased but not degraded, in *Count Chocula* and *Frankenberry* cereals. It was widely practiced throughout the nineteenth century by such hacks as the stunningly prolific Sabine Baring-Gould (1834–1924), who in addition to nearly one hundred novels, travelogues, and inspirational books cranked out stories with ghostly themes, which he collected in *A Book of Ghosts* (1904). These workmanlike productions include "Jean Bouchon," about a deceased French waiter who comes back to snitch tips, and "A Professional Secret," about a novelist haunted by his characters, a surprising anticipation of Luigi Pirandello's *Six Characters in Search of an Author* (1921).

A Book of Ghosts typifies the largely forgotten Victorian subgenre of the heartwarming horrid story, which reached its British peak in Margaret Oliphant's "The Open Door" (1881) and Oscar Wilde's "The Canterville Ghost" (1891). The American Mary E. Wilkins Freeman excelled at this difficult fusion of fear and pathos, particularly in "The Lost Ghost" (1903), with its "pretty harmless little sort of ghost" that can nevertheless chill the blood. These and a few other such stories have survived in reprints, but latter-day anthologists have tended to pass them over in favor of sterner stuff, perhaps feeling that horror is compromised when it is paired with tender sentiments. Nineteenth-century readers saw no incongruity there, any more than they did at the theater when ghastly specters shared the bill with pairs of sappy young lovers. The horrid short story, however, had a particular affinity for the holiday that epitomized Victorian domesticity at its smuggest, Christmas. By the end of the century, in heaps of Christmas supplements and annuals, the season had become a fictional saturnalia for ghosts, in what Summers nostalgically called the "good spooky yarn of the real old Christmassy kind."

Late-century writers and readers took for granted that, as Henry James wrote in "The Turn of the Screw" (1898), a tale told "on Christmas Eve in an old house" should be both "strange" and "gruesome." M. R. James, whose strange, gruesome stories count among the best of the early twentieth century, used to read them aloud to circles of friends every Christmas Eve. Both Jameses and their readers seem to have assumed that the custom was ancient and quintessentially English—assumptions that have annoyed later scholars because they rest on no historical evidence. In her 1977 study of "The Rise and Fall of the English Ghost Story," Julia Briggs tussles for a while with the mysterious link between Christmas and the telling of ghost stories; she can find, however, no proof that there was any before the famous Dingley Dell episode in Dickens's *Pickwick Papers* (first published, a bit belatedly, in January 1837). "Certainly," Briggs concludes with a shrug, "the tradition was re-established" under Dickens's influence.

He certainly worked hard to cultivate it. His own five Christmas books—which began with *A Christmas Carol* in 1843—powerfully reinforced this new tradition, and in the Christmas issues of the weekly journals he edited, *Household Words* (1850–1859) and *All the Year Round* (1859–1870), he regularly published ghostly tales by Wilkie Collins, Amelia B. Edwards, and other middlebrow writers. Dickens deserves credit for virtually inventing the cozy, round-the-fire Christmas that is still called "Dickensian"; there's no reason to suppose he didn't invent the Christmas ghost story, too. Whenever he referred to it, of course, he endowed it with the utmost antiquity: In *Pickwick Papers*, for instance, the custom is said to have been observed by the Wardle family "from time immemorial." Horrid fiction is adept at fabricating a venerable past for itself, but Dickens also had personal motives.

In the first Christmas issue of *Household Words* (1850), he published an odd little item, "A Christmas Tree," that helps to clarify them. The essay purports to be the meditations of a middle-aged man—Dickens was thirty-eight at the time—who has been watching children play "round that pretty German toy, a Christmas tree." The twentieth-century reader may stumble over the phrase "German toy," but the custom of hauling evergreens into the house was fairly new to England in 1850: It had been popularized by the highly Germanic Prince Albert, starting in 1840. This, however, does not prevent Dickens's narrator from inviting his readers to join him in summoning up what "we all remember best upon the branches of the Christmas Tree of our own young Christmas days"—a tall order for any contemporary reader more than ten years old.

First, he remembers toys, most of which seem to have scared him silly. There was the Tumbler doll, with his "lobster eyes"; there were the "demoniacal" Jack-in-the-box, the "horrible" jumping frog, and the "ghastly" cardboard man. By far the worst was "that dreadful Mask," which he found "hideous," "intolerable," "insupportable," because when anyone put it on, he glimpsed "the universal change that is to come on every face, and make it still." The narrator's memories soon turn cozier, but the first impression he conveys is that his childhood Christmases were relentless rounds of horror. The horrid mood returns in the last third of the essay, when (transformed now into "a middle-aged nobleman") he provides a catalogue of "Winter Stories—Ghost Stories, or more shame for us—round the Christmas fire." All the clichés are here, as fresh in 1850 as they are today: the "old houses, with resounding galleries, and dismal state-bedchambers, and haunted wings shut up for many years," un-washable bloodstains, doors that will not close, legends of murder and unslaked revenge. The essay ends with a brief paean to "the branches of the Christmas Tree, which cast no gloomy shadow!" Yet fully half of "A Christmas Tree" is devoted to gloom, fear, and reminders of death.

It has often been suggested that Dickens's own unhappy childhood—in which toys were few and Christmas trees nonexistent—fueled his adult fantasies of snug hearthside do-mesticity. But his major fiction offers very few portraits of intact, secure families; domestic happiness is usually a distant goal, not a fact of life, and it can be achieved only after terrible struggle. The importation of ghosts and graveyards into Christmas no doubt served the same purpose as the reading of horrible murder reports by the fire, fortifying the illusion of safety by toying with its opposite. The true Dickensian Christmas, though, was a peculiarly ambivalent feast, with rather too many death's-heads at the table. "The Story of the Goblins Who Stole a Sexton," for example, which enlivens Christmas Eve at Dingley Dell, takes place mostly in (and under) a graveyard. It also features a little poem that Monk Lewis might have relished:

> Brave lodgings for one, brave lodgings for one,
> A few feet of cold earth, when life is done;
> A stone at the head, a stone at the feet,
> A rich, juicy meal for the worms to eat . . .

It takes all Dickens's skill (and strong wishing on the reader's part) to blot out *that* in the hearth's ruddy glow.

It isn't surprising that Dickens felt a graveyard chill at Christmas. His personal Ghost of Christmas Past had small warmth to remind him of, and his Christmas Present was a willed illusion; for him as for Ebenezer Scrooge (as for us, every one), some future Christmas promised the inevitable earth. The curious thing is that Dickens's huge middle-class public embraced the package with gusto and kept the season horrid for well over half a century. Annuals like *The Keepsake* had been publishing end-of-the-year ghost stories long before *Pickwick Papers*, but it was Dickens who, through editorship as well as his own stories, forged a tradition and made it seem timeless. After the turn of the twentieth century, it dwindled; by 1931, it had become matter for Summers's artificial nostalgia. But it isn't wholly dead: American television digs it up each year, with obligatory reruns of the various *Christmas Carol* films.

BACK TO THE GRAVEYARD

Dickens's readers may have welcomed his Christmas horrors because they shared his unease with the domestic myth he both loved and hated. Perhaps scaring each other on Christmas Eve was a harmless outlet for aggressions that otherwise would have led to reports in the *Illustrated Police News*. Whatever the reason, Christmas annuals and special magazine issues formed the chief English forum for horrid short fiction until late in the nineteenth century. Short stories remained a sideline for most English and American writers. Even when, like Henry James, they turned out scores of them, they saved their finest efforts for novels, where the largest public (and payment) lay. Toward the end of the century, partly thanks to French influence, short fiction rose in artistic repute; still, however, very few English writers specialized in it, let alone its horrid subspecies.

On the whole, English horrid stories also preserved the gentility of their Gothic forebears. Though the Radcliffean habit of explaining away the supernatural fell into disfavor, the ghosts who glided through late-Victorian galleries seldom had dire designs on the living. Many simply wished to make known an ancient wrong and get it righted; that done, they slept as the dead should. Domesticity prevailed in most of these stories, as it did in the novels and plays of the period. Oddly, however, the psychologizing trend that triumphed in the novel and transformed even melodrama, that Poe had adapted to short fiction in the 1840s, made hardly a dent in the English horrid story until after the turn of the twentieth century. By then, too, the walking dead were bringing back more than information.

Among the steadiest practitioners in the domestic style was Mrs. J. H. Riddell (1832–1906), the author of some forty realistic novels, all now forgotten. Her horrid fiction—four short novels and more than a dozen stories—fared poorly at the hands of twentieth-century anthologists; it would be forgotten, too, except for the efforts of E. F. Bleiler, who edited most of it for paperback reprints in the 1970s. Riddell belonged to the populous tribe of Victorian women who scribbled ceaselessly to support their ailing or incompetent menfolk. Like Margaret Oliphant and Mary Elizabeth Braddon, she wrote rapidly and, often, to formula; like their work, hers is much better than, given such conditions, it has any right to be. Riddell made a minor specialty of Christmas horrors: her ghostly novellas filled four issues of *Routledge's Christmas Annual* between 1873 and 1878. The first, *Fairy Water* (reprinted as *The Haunted House at Latchford*), may be her best; it also offers an abundant stock of clichés that later generations know well, even if they've never heard of Mrs. J. H. Riddell.

There are two houses in the story, from which it got its two titles. Fairy Water is a charming place, haunted only by Captain Trevor's will, which forbids his young widow, Mary, to marry again. Crow Hall near Latchford, however, presents a very different picture. The owner, Valentine Waldrum (who falls in love with Mary), can hardly bear to talk about the house. Years before, his father was walking in the garden when "he suddenly stopped, and declared he saw a woman looking out of the window of a room where no living woman was." A "mania" set in; the elder Waldrum "began to 'see things' and to talk strangely." Swift decline followed, and he died apparently mad. No one inhabits Crow Hall now but an old caretaker, who "has the reputation of being a witch."

The narrator, Hercules Stafford Trevor, barrister, resolves to do his unhappy young friend a good deed. An effete but lineal descendant of Scott's General Browne, Trevor buys Crow Hall and moves in, determined to make the land pay and to dispel the house's evil aura. From the first, ominous signs appear—"*I never awoke that night, or any other night I spent in the house, with a feeling of being alone*"—but Trevor persists. The caretaker, Mrs. Paul, turns out to be a talky rustic in the Radcliffe mold; she tells him a rambling story covering two centuries of Waldrum family history. The upshot is that Valentine's great-grandmother, along with her legendary jewelry, disappeared from Crow Hall one night many years ago, and since then "nothing has prospered with the family." The house is also said to contain secret passages, built to hide Catholics and later used for smuggling.

After numerous involvements that seem designed to pad *The Haunted House* out to its forty thousand words, a hidden staircase is uncovered in the room where the ghostly woman walks. It leads to a "subterraneous passage," in which Trevor and the workmen make a gruesome discovery:

> "Show a light here, Bill."
> Without troubling Bill, Mr. Tuft skipped across the floor, and threw a glance across the entrance of the subterranean passage.

"It's bones, ain't it?" asked the discoverer, looking up in Mr. Tuft's face, "and bits of glass."

This is shorthand, because the reader has already been treated to a full version in Trevor's nightmare of following the long-dead Mrs. Philip Waldrum through the wall and down the stairs:

> at last we found ourselves in a square room that smelt like a charnel-house, and was close and suffocating as the grave. In a passage leading out of it something lay in a heap. She pointed to it; and, looking more closely, I saw these were bones on which jewels sparkled as on the hands and neck of my companion. As I stood, the face of Philip's wife changed—her cheeks dropped in, her eyes grew lustreless, her mouth fell, the skin tightened over her forehead. While I looked her countenance altered to that of a grinning death's-head; then the whole body collapsed, and I was alone with a heap of bones.

In the end, the salvaged jewels solve Valentine's financial problems, a new will found at Fairy Water lets Mary and Valentine wed, and the Haunted House at Latchford is razed.

Almost all of Riddell's horrid tales, long or short, take the same pattern. In *The Uninhabited House* (*Routledge's Christmas Annual* for 1875), the haunted building is modern, and the man who made Mr. Elmsdale a ghost still lives; "Nut Bush Farm," which Riddell included in her *Weird Stories* (1882), offers a ghost who prefers the outdoors, near the thicket where his unburied skeleton lies. Riddell's living characters, even the hardiest, automatically feel a chill when revenants arrive; usually it runs down or up their spines, and sometimes it haunts them ever after. From the twentieth-century reader's point of view, this is an overreaction, because the story has made clear in advance that the ghosts intend no harm. Riddell, however, means to have it both ways, to scare and soothe in equal measure, without letting one emotion cancel the other. Magazine readers of the 1870s and 1880s evidently saw nothing objectionable in the arrangement.

Riddell's well-intentioned ghosts may owe something to the contemporary fad for summoning the dear departed into drawing rooms and cajoling them to rap tables. From the 1850s onward, spiritualism enjoyed a tremendous middle-class vogue in both England and the United States, where it had originated. It came in several forms, from table rapping to Ouija boards to formal séances and the photographing of materialized spirits; it attracted many ardent advocates—including Elizabeth Barrett Browning and, late in his life, Arthur Conan Doyle—along with even more numerous debunkers. Marriage to Elizabeth, for instance, did not prevent Robert Browning from composing the most vitriolic of antispiritualist satires, "Mr. Sludge, 'The Medium,' " though he published it only in 1864, three years after her death.

The literature of spiritualism is enormous; it branches out into theosophy, various brands of occultism, and the study of psychic phenomena like long-distance card reading and the bending of spoons. On the whole, however, spiritualism in all its forms has had remarkably little influence on the tradition of scary entertainment. Spiritualists seldom appear in frightening fiction, and when they do they are ridiculous. The treatment is epitomized by Shirley Jackson's planchette-wielding Mrs. Montague in *The Haunting of Hill House* (1959). "I deplore fear in these matters," she tells her husband.

> You know perfectly well . . . that those who have passed beyond *expect* to see us happy and smiling; they *want* to know that we are thinking of them lovingly. The spirits dwelling in this house may be actually *suffering* because they are aware that you are afraid of them.

Exactly wrong, of course, about whatever dwells in Hill House—though the fatheaded Mrs. Montague never finds that out.

Spiritualism sprouted from the urge toward domestic coziness that permeated mid-nineteenth-century culture. The urge could be easily subverted in some areas—gory newspaper reports, for instance, or ghastly tales on Christmas Eve—but when it lurched beyond the grave, it threatened to abolish scary entertainment altogether by making death cozy, too. Mrs. Riddell must have known about séances and such (the Society for Psychical Research was founded in 1882, the year of her *Weird Stories*), but she kept them out of her fiction. And though her ghosts hurt no one, they are terrifying simply because they are ghosts. Intentions don't matter; as brave young Patterson says in *The Uninhabited House*, any ghost is "that which no man can behold unappalled."

The appalling thing, however, is not so much the apparition as the decayed human flesh from which it emanates and to which it points. When Riddell wanted to make her readers' hair stand on end, she wrote passages like Trevor's nightmare in *The Haunted House at Latchford*; she simply repeated devices that the Graveyard poets had already been recycling nearly a century and a half before. The secret staircase, subterraneous passage, and charnel-house atmosphere had been staples of horrid novels around the turn of the nineteenth century. The body that suddenly rots away was invoked by both Young and Hervey in the 1740s; Monk Lewis trotted it out (also in a dream narrative) for *The Castle Spectre* (1797); Poe did an especially gruesome version in "The Case of M. Valdemar" (1845). If Riddell knew about these precedents, she did not let on. Like the innumerable later stories and films that have portrayed exactly the same scene—like *Raiders of the Lost Ark* (1981), with its melting Nazis—*The Haunted House at Latchford* treats this tableau as if it were brand new. For many of the story's first readers, it probably was.

Riddell only occasionally indulges in charnel-house horrors, but when she does, she anticipates a trend in horrid short fiction that began at the end of the nineteenth century and continues. Generalizations are risky in such a crowded field, but after 1900 there developed a drive toward ever more explicit evocations of both bloodshed and rot, especially rot. Many factors contributed to this trend: the decline, on all fronts, of genteel reticence; the rejection of what had come to seem Victorian hypocrisy; the need to spark novelty in a genre where too much had already been done. In that genre, French influence brought not only a reassessment of Poe but also the example of writers like Maupassant and Villiers de l'Isle-Adam, many of whose tales are unabashedly gruesome even when they do not involve the supernatural. The dismissal of spiritualism had a special side effect. Spiritualists summoned up entities who were either wholly immaterial or composed of floaty white stuff like gauze (often, it really was gauze).

Drawing-room ghosts were clean, odorless, and well behaved, presentable in polite company. Increasingly, English and American fictional ghosts played dirty.

F. Marion Crawford's anthology war-horse "The Upper Berth" (1886) offers an early instance. At bottom, the story is yet another recycling—nautical this time—of "The Tapestried Chamber." But Crawford's persistent drowned man not only knocks people down; he also neglects personal hygiene. As the narrator, Brisbane, reports his first contact with the berth's occupant:

> I remember that the sensation as I put my hands forward was as though I were plunging them into the air of a damp cellar, and from behind the curtains came a gust of wind that smelled horribly of stagnant sea-water. I laid hold of something that had the shape of a man's arm, but was smooth, and wet, and icy cold. But suddenly, as I pulled, the creature sprang violently forward against me, a clammy, oozy mass, as it seemed to me, heavy and wet, yet endowed with a sort of supernatural strength.

This creature has no information to impart, no designs either benevolent or wicked on the living. And he makes a terrible mess in the stateroom.

Crawford's nasty revenant had numerous progeny in the works of Montague Rhodes James (1862–1936), who, more powerfully than any other single writer, set the course of Anglo-American horrors for the twentieth century. James brought to the horrid short story an element of physical loathing (and occasional ghastly violence) that had been rare since Monk Lewis and was uncommon even in Poe. He revived the charnel-house chill of the mid-eighteenth century, certified it with antiquarian learning, and packaged it in understated, irreproachable prose. Not since the Gothic novelists had anyone conveyed so plainly the scary strangeness of the past, simply because it *was* past. Not since the Graveyard poets had death been portrayed as such a lively state. For a century, in English at least, the horrors of death had undergone a steady course of mollification, splitting, and dispersal; in James's stories, they pulled themselves together again.

By profession a medievalist and bibliographer, James found the spare time to write four slim volumes of horrid tales: *Ghost Stories of an Antiquary* (1904), *More Ghost Stories of an Antiquary* (1911), *A Thin Ghost and Others* (1919), and *A Warning to the Curious* (1925). James's horrors come in many forms, but most are physically loathsome, even when they are half-seen or dimly heard. In "The Ash-Tree" (1904), for instance, something visits Sir Richard Fell during the night:

> There is very little light about the bedstead, but there is a strange movement there; it seems as if Sir Richard were moving his head rapidly to and fro with only the slightest possible sound. And now you would guess, so deceptive is the half-darkness, that he had several heads, round and brownish, which move back and forward, even as low as his chest. It is a horrible illusion. Is it nothing more? There! something drops off the bed with a soft plump, like a kitten, and is out of the window in a flash; another—four—and after that there is quiet again.

The kittens turn out to be monstrous spiders, spawned from the rotted corpse of a witch hidden in the hollow ash tree.

In "The Treasure of Abbot Thomas" (1904), no such mayhem is done, and the horrid creature can hardly be described. It feels like leather to the touch, "dampish" and heavy, and it has arms; it may or may not have a face, but it certainly stinks. As Mr. Somerton, whom it grabs, explains: "I was conscious of a most horrible smell of mould, and of a cold kind of face pressed against my own, and moving slowly over it, and of several—I don't know how many—legs or arms or tentacles or something clinging to my body." Since the sixteenth century, this creature has been waiting for someone to violate the abbot's treasure. Once loose, it seems to desire only to stand guard by the violator's door, infecting the air with "the hideous smell of mould." It promises no violence; its horror is purely that of a dead thing that can move and cling.

James did not singlehandedly engineer the trend toward physical disgust that characterizes English horrid fiction around the turn of the twentieth century. Less-known writers went the same way—like Perceval Landon, whose "Thurnley Abbey" (1908) recycles "The Tapestried Chamber" yet again, with the memorable twist of a skeleton nun who gets nearly pulverized, only to reassemble herself bone by fractured bone. Similar gruesomeness marks H. G. Wells's "The Cone" (1897), Arthur Conan Doyle's "The Leather Funnel" (1900), Bram Stoker's "The Squaw" (1914), and many other stories of the period. But the trend might not have become definitive if James hadn't patented its perfect—and perfectly inoffensive—formula. In his manicured hands, head-sized venomous spiders gained admission into polite society, because, though the spiders grossly misbehaved, James himself was never vulgar. Not all his followers would imitate him in that.

James's individual volumes sold well, and his *Collected Ghost Stories* has not gone out of print since it was published, in 1931. He owed even more of his influence, however, to a new vehicle that came into being after the First World War: the horrid anthology. From the first, James's stories found an automatic place in such collections, a place they retain today. Horrid anthologies, along with the scholarly studies of supernatural and Gothic fiction that started appearing at about the same time, have defined the genre for three generations of Anglo-American readers and writers. In films, they virtually created it, for the entire world. At the end of the twentieth century, we know how to spot a horror movie, TV show, or novel mainly because, eighty-odd years ago, horror stood up and announced itself. That it took so long is curious enough; the surprising thing is that editors and scholars made it happen.

CANONIZATION

Anthologies of poetry had been in existence since the Classical era, but they took their modern form late in the eighteenth century, about the time of the Gothic fad. Modern anthologies, like Oliver Goldsmith's *The Beauties of English Poesy* (1767), were aimed at the same audience that lapped up Mrs. Radcliffe's phony lore: the rising middle class, for which history was a novelty and literature an acquisition, not an inheritance. Anthologies offered quick and easy access to a long, not always enthralling tradition; true to their name (from the Greek for "a gathering of flowers"), they contained only the finest blossoms, plucked by editors who presumably possessed the erudition and taste their readers lacked. The popularity of such shortcuts grew steadily during the nineteenth century and peaked, in English, with Francis Palgrave's *The Golden Treasury* (1861) and the first *Oxford Book of English Verse* (1900), edited by Arthur Quiller-Couch. In the twentieth century, especially for poetry, anthologies have determined what most moderately educated readers know about the literary past.

Anthologies interact in complicated ways with the bodies of work they survey. Editors and readers must share the belief that there is a tradition already in place before selection begins; the tradition must also be either so large or so scattered (perhaps both) that only a specialist can command it. But anthologies shape the tradition while seeming only to skim it. The tradition changes in retrospect, thanks to changing patterns of inclusion and exclusion. Anthologies also respond to contemporary fashions, and later anthologies bounce off earlier ones, tracing a tradition of their own. John Donne, for instance, did not appear in Palgrave's 1861 *Treasury*; Donne became standard only after 1921, when Herbert J. C. Grierson revived him in *Metaphysical Lyrics and Poems of the Seventeenth Century*. Yet today's college students, finding page after page of Donne in their compulsory textbooks, may well assume that he influenced the development of English poetry far more significantly than he did.

Canon formation—the process by which posterity sifts the past, enshrining some inheritances and consigning others to the vault—is a vexed topic at the end of the twentieth century, especially on American college campuses. The site is appropriate, because since World War I, in the United States at least, college professors have been almost exclusively entrusted with the task of defining and conveying the literary tradition. Until lately, this caste was happy to keep on repeating a fable about how white men (the fablers were white men) had written this, then that, engendering history. In the last twenty years, the composition of the caste has changed, and so has the fable. It has lately been learned that women were writing alongside canonical history, and that men and women whose skin was not white did some writing, too. The result has been a wholesale invasion of the vault and, for the comprehensive literary anthology, a crisis. Since its first edition in 1962, the *Norton Anthology of English Literature*, standard in many American colleges, has ballooned; it was bulky at birth, but the fifth edition, published in 1986, threatens to burst its bindings at fifty-two hundred pages in two volumes. If it gets any fatter, it will die.

The vicissitudes of the literary canon have had small impact on horrid short fiction. That kind of writing gets excluded from even the most catholic literary anthologies, except for the inescapable Poe and politically provocative stories like Charlotte Perkins Gilman's "The Yellow Wallpaper" (1892). Nevertheless, literary scholarship has powerfully influenced the nature of twentieth-century horror, perhaps even determined it. Until academics discovered that there had been a tradition of horrid fiction, writers who wished to raise gooseflesh were compelled to rely on their personal encounters with earlier efforts in that line. Because such work usually appeared in ephemeral formats like magazines, the knowledge of would-be horrid writers had to be spotty, confined largely to recent examples. It makes sense to suppose, for instance, that "The Treasure of Abbot Thomas" might have drawn on F. Marion Crawford's "The Upper Berth," because M. R. James loved to rummage through old magazines, where he might have found Crawford's story.

But only amnesia or plagiarism can account for the resemblance of Bram Stoker's "The Judge's House" (1914) to Joseph Sheridan Le Fanu's "An Account of Some Disturbances in Aungier Street." Le Fanu's story first came out in the *Dublin University Magazine* in 1853; *In a Glass Darkly* republished it in 1872. Stoker must have read it somewhere; two stories that center on a hanging judge reincarnated as a giant rat in a spooky old house can hardly have arisen from separate bursts of genius. Yet unlike Poe, Stoker presumes no prior knowledge on the reader's part. Like Mrs. Riddell, Stoker started at ground zero—as he no doubt felt entitled to do, since precious few of his readers, if any, could have been aware of Le Fanu's precedent.

Le Fanu (1814–1873) was only moderately prolific by mid-Victorian standards, grinding out seventeen books in twenty-five years. He was unusual, though, because he concentrated on tales of suspense and terror, often invoking the supernatural. Popular in his own day as a contributor to magazines, he fared less well with his novels, of which only *Uncle Silas* (1864) saw frequent reprinting. The rest became collector's items, and rare ones at that, while his stories went the common way of ephemeral work, into oblivion. Even Le Fanu's most fervent late-twentieth-century admirers can't disguise their embarrassment that this supposed forerunner of the modern horrid tale seems to have been practically unknown for two generations after his death. Jack Sullivan, for instance, calls Le Fanu's influence "appropriately ghostly and indistinct"—a clever way of saying that he had none.

M. R. James knew of Le Fanu, however, and he plainly shows that knowledge in his own work. In 1923, James edited *Madam Crowl's Ghost and Other Tales of Mystery*, which introduced the long-dead master's short fiction to a larger audience than it had had for fifty years. Anthologists soon followed. Vere H. Collins's *Ghosts and Marvels* (1924), the first major English collection of "uncanny tales," included Le Fanu's "Schalken the Painter" (1839), along with an appreciative introduction by James. Dorothy L. Sayers's popular *Omnibus of Crime* (1929) served "Green Tea," which Sullivan, writing half a century later, would call not only Le Fanu's best story but also "an ideal introduction" to "the entire ghostly school that he spawned." To judge from late-twentieth-century horrid anthologies—none of which is complete without Le Fanu—it does look as if he spawned a school. But the spawning must have been glacially slow.

Scholarship made Le Fanu a founder of the modern horrid story, and anthologists have kept him available. These two influences did not begin their work, however, until late in the genre's ramshackle, amnesia-prone history. The first academic study of the subject, Dorothy Scarborough's *The Supernatural in Modern English Fiction*, did not appear until 1917; the byways of the Gothic novel were first explored at length by Edith Birkhead's *The Tale of Terror* (1921). Before these books and the chronological anthologies that soon joined them, horrid stories formed no real tradition. Later practitioners could gain, at best, fragmentary access to the fiction that had preceded them; except for classics like Scott, Dickens, and to some degree Poe, horrid stories languished in libraries' dustiest corners, where commercial writers were unlikely to seek them out. Scholars, however, haunted such places. When they dug up the "tale of terror," they rewarded it with a pedigree.

Scarborough's pioneering effort aims at comprehensiveness, and posterity has not always agreed with her judgments. She spends what seems an inordinate number of words on John Kendrick Bangs, for instance, and she never mentions Le Fanu. But in general her horrid canon has remained intact: the Gothic novel first; Poe, Hawthorne, and Dickens toward the middle of the nineteenth century; Algernon Blackwood, Rudyard Kipling, H. G. Wells, Crawford, and W. W. Jacobs in more recent years. Collins's *Ghosts and Marvels* helped to canonize Jacobs's "The Monkey's Paw," which it put in company with stories by Scott, Marryat, Robert Louis Stevenson, and M. R. James. Sayers reprinted the story, as did Phyllis Fraser and Herbert Wise in the long-lived Modern Library volume *Great Tales of Terror and the Supernatural* (1944). It remains an inevitable classic, though it is also probably the only story by W. W. Jacobs that most readers have ever heard of.

Not all later anthologies offer the same contents, of course; each new one has to be at least slightly different, if only to excuse the existence of yet another horrid anthology. Some are idiosyncratic—like Dashiell Hammett's peculiar *Creeps by Night* (1931)—while all get erratic as their surveys approach the date of their own publication. But certain writers have become de rigueur, even when they are known for only a single story, like Jacobs, or at best half a dozen, like F. Marion Crawford. Crawford (1854–1909) published more than forty books in his busy hack's career, most of them romances with exotic settings. All were in print when his lone volume of supernatural tales, *Wandering Ghosts*, appeared posthumously in 1911; all rest in the back stacks today. *Wandering Ghosts* itself has never been reprinted, but at least three of its seven stories—"The Screaming Skull," "For the Blood Is the Life," and the ubiquitous "Upper Berth"—have enjoyed such an active anthology life that Crawford's name survives as that of a horrid writer, an immortality he would very likely not have welcomed.

By the mid-1930s, frightening fiction had become solidly established as a genre with a venerable past that writers and readers could explore without braving the back stacks. The tradition was principally composed of short stories, with a few novels thrown in, like *Otranto* and *Udolpho* from the eighteenth century and *Frankenstein* and *Dracula* from the nineteenth. Plays never made it into the horrid canon at all. Their texts were hard to find and made dull reading without blue fire to illuminate them; most horrid plays also contained too much love and comedy for the increasingly narrow tastes of anthologists. Scholars of the Gothic brought Continental works into their surveys, but for the ordinary reader of English the tradition was (and remains) overwhelmingly Anglo-American.

The specter of respectability lurked in these developments. Though the stories on which anthologists foraged were quite genteel, most had been of minor importance for both their writers and their first readers. When anthologists began to call them "great" and to crown "classics" in the genre, a chill came into the air. The genteel tradition continued, especially in England, and it lives. But in the United States, the period of horrid canonization also saw the building of a new—and very old—forum for goose-flesh. Like parodic shadows of high-toned anthologies, cheap magazines sprang up; their garish covers and crude illustrations promised horror in hot, rude doses. They also promised to vanish quickly, because there was nothing great or classic about them. Probably without knowing it, pulp magazines—named for their coarse, short-lived paper—harked back to the Gothic chapbooks of the early nineteenth century, the penny dreadfuls of a few decades later, and the boys' adventure magazines of decades later still. Their immediate source, however, was the same self-conscious turn that spun off polite anthologies and scholarly studies: the new awareness that there was a special kind of fiction devoted to raising hairs, that it had a large, open reservoir of techniques at its disposal, that its effects could be sharpened and deepened to the point of public outrage.

Among the earliest horrid pulps was *Weird Tales*, which began as a monthly in March 1923 and went on, with frequent lapses, till 1954. In recent years, the magazine has gone the apparently inevitable late-twentieth-century route and been canonized itself, at least by cultists, because it published early stories by H. P. Lovecraft, Robert Bloch, Richard Matheson, and many other favorites. *Weird Tales*, however, helped to create the notion of an entertainment cult by publishing stories that only a few readers would like, hoping they would like them fiercely. There was nothing new about cultism, but it came fresh to horror: Now initiates learned to adore a sensation, not a person or a creed, and the ephemeral embarked on its strange journey from worthlessness to great price.

The cultural roots of a twentieth-century horror story may be so ramified and tangled that the labor required to comb them out exceeds anything *Hamlet* demands. Worse, the labor promises no enlightenment beyond proof that the story caught whatever wind was blowing out of the lengthening past. Worst of all, when the story aimed to die after a month or two, as those in *Weird Tales* did, it comes to a belated reader so armored in its moment that the sharpest analytic tool glances off. The oddest feature of the early *Weird Tales* is the flowery extravagance of their language; it is characteristic of the work of Lovecraft and his imitators, though it was widespread in the magazine as a whole, particularly during its first decade. When dire and ghastly things came into view, adjectival hell broke loose.

Poe provided the chief precedent, but the quirk also reflects a deep linguistic conservatism. Respectable fiction, even of the horrid kind, had undergone a steady loosening of syntax from the mid-nineteenth century onward. Sentences and paragraphs grew shorter; the meandering rhythms of Radcliffean prose gave way to a more staccato, declarative style. And the piling on of urgent adjectives came to seem shrill and rude. These developments, however, occurred much more slowly in the cheaper grades of fiction, which held on stubbornly to eighteenth-century modes. The antiquated style of many *Weird Tales* suggests that, for pulp, the whole nineteenth century might as well not have happened.

A famous example is C. M. Eddy's "The Loved Dead" (1924), which was revised by Lovecraft and possibly imbued with his personal brand of verbal hysteria. But it is not untypical of the norm. Obviously imitating Poe, the story presents a monologue by a nameless necrophile and mass murderer hiding in a graveyard:

Around me on every side, sepulchral sentinels guarding unkempt graves, the tilting, decrepit headstones lie half-hidden in masses of nauseous, rotting vegetation. Above the rest, silhouetted against the living sky, an august monument lifts its austere, tapering spire like

the sepulchral chieftain of a lemurian horde. The air is heavy with
the noxious odors of fungi and the scent of damp, moldy earth, but
to me it is the aroma of Elysium.

And so on.

He proceeds to recite his autobiography, from a "wan, pallid,
undersized" childhood, through the discovery of his love for death
and interrupted employment as an undertaker's assistant ("One
morning Mr. Gresham came . . . to find me stretched out upon a
cold slab deep in ghoulish slumber, my arms wrapped about the
stark, naked body of a fetid corpse!"), to his career as a corpse
manufacturer, the latest atrocity, and the pursuit that has driven
him to this hiding place. At the end, cornered, he pulls out a
bloodstained razor and slashes his wrist: "Warm, fresh blood
spatters grotesque patterns on dingy, decrepit slabs . . . phantasmal hordes swarm over the rotting graves . . . scorched tongues of
invisible flame sear the brand of hell upon my sickened soul . . . I
can—write—no—more."

"The Loved Dead" is highly modern, even modernist, in its
desire to slap the reader's bourgeois face. It is more explicit in its
physical horrors than a polite tale of 1924 would have been,
especially with its heavy aura of perverted sexuality. Eddy may
have owed a debt to Richard von Krafft-Ebing's *Psychopathia
Sexualis* (1886), which contains case histories of a similar cast.
But practically every other aspect of the story, like Eddy's style, is
antique. Poe provides the crazed narrator and overheated tone.
The messy, moldy graveyard has more in common with a Graveyard poem than with any twentieth-century cemetery. There are no
ghosts, but in good old melodramatic fashion, "phantasmal
hordes" engulf the villain at the end; they drag him down to the
same hell that swallowed Lewis's Ambrosio more than a century
before. And, in a way that hadn't changed in 150 years, "The
Loved Dead" depends for its horror on the uncanny frightfulness
of death.

By about 1930, scary entertainment had amassed its full inventory of effects. It had recognized its history, begun to establish a
canon, and even started rebelling against the stultification canons
bring. Horrid short stories would continue to flourish; they would
spawn a score of subtypes, including science-fiction and fantasy

tales; adaptations would proliferate on radio and later on television. But the primary vehicle of late-twentieth-century fright—
film—got off to a surprisingly slow start. Before 1930, horrid
movies hardly claimed a shelf in the genre's warehouse; by 1940,
they owned the place.

Lon Chaney's Man in the Beaver Hat pays a house call. (STILL FROM *London After Midnight*, © 1927 TURNER ENTERTAINMENT CO. ALL RIGHTS RESERVED.)

7

Scream and Scream Again

DEAD END

On the evening of April 13, 1897, a theater with an agenda opened in the rue Chaptal, Paris. Its impresario, Oscar Méténier, drew on several sources, chiefly Emile Zola's Naturalism and the recently defunct Théâtre Libre (Free Theater) of André Antoine. For nearly twenty years, Zola had been urging French playwrights to drop moldy conventions like pleasing the public. As he wrote in 1880, playwrights ought to imitate Naturalist novelists, who said to their readers: "That is reality: shudder or laugh at it, draw from it some lesson or other if you will; the sole task of the author has been to put true documents before your eyes." At the Théâtre Libre, Antoine attempted to practice Zola's precepts, often portraying—as his master's novels did—the depths of urban squalor. He also championed the foreign avant-garde: August Strindberg's *Miss Julie* had its French premiere at Antoine's theater in 1893. That same year, the Théâtre Libre went bankrupt.

Méténier would make no such mistake. His theater wouldn't educate its patrons; it would merely kick their hearts up and down the rue Chaptal. Above all, he intended to shock; he used even architecture for the purpose. The theater's eighteenth-century house had been built as a convent and still sported angels on the ceiling and "pseudo-gothic designs cut into the thick oak doors." In such venerable, pious surroundings, the offensiveness of depravity and violence on stage would be multiplied. But Méténier went further. He named his new theater after a puppet show, tacking on *"big"* or *"great"*: Grand Guignol.

Méténier's formula slated as many as eight short plays in an evening, drastically shifting gears from comedy to horror to realistic drama and back again. In 1898, the Grand Guignol was taken over by Max Maurey, who cut the number of plays down to four or five and put the emphasis on horror. According to Mel Gordon, Maurey intended to make the Grand Guignol "a place where every social taboo of good taste was cracked and shattered":

> This formula would attract the French public that slaked its blood lust and fascination with the morbid by devouring pulp novels and unlikely tabloid exposés. This clientele, in other times, flocked to country freak shows and wax museums that featured chambers of horror and sensational crime. Now, watching live realistic and gory enactments of mutilation, rape, torture, and murder, each spectator could play out his fantasies of victimization and retribution.

Maurey did not dispense with comedies and farces, but under his management (1898–1915) and that of his successor, Camille Choisy (1915–1928), the phrase "grand guignol" became synonymous with the most grotesque extremes of bloody horror. It retains that meaning today, even for those who have never heard of the Grand Guignol Theater.

The name may have traveled well, but the style didn't. In its earlier years, the French company toured widely, visiting Rome and London (briefly) in 1908, London again in 1913, and Montreal and New York in 1923, with small success. Attempts were made to set up native Grands Guignols in both Britain and the United States; the most successful, Sybil Thorndike's London experiment, lasted only three years, 1920–1923. Several short French films of

Grand Guignol plays appeared before the First World War, and some British versions in the 1920s. In that medium, too, however, the special aura of the little theater in the rue Chaptal proved either inimitable or repellent. Gordon makes a valiant effort to establish the Grand Guignol's "major impact" on European and American films through at least 1935. But the qualities he cites— "unexpected brutalities," "gratuitous violence," "unhealthy atmosphere"—were hardly trademarks. Horrid short fiction had developed them independently, and horrid films probably did the same.

When the Théâtre du Grand Guignol finally shut down, in November 1962, it had been for at least three decades little more than a sideshow. Perhaps, despite the stern aims of its first managers, that's all it had ever been. Ironically, however, the whimpering end of the Grand Guignol coincided with the advent of grand guignol in popular film. Gordon would like us to believe that such horror-movie landmarks as Alfred Hitchcock's *Psycho* (1960) and Herschell Gordon Lewis's *Blood Feast* (1963) owe something to Méténier, Maurey, and company. In fact, the Grand Guignol's case resembles those of Poe, Le Fanu, and other belatedly unearthed forebears in the amnesiac history of modern fright. Like the early-twentieth-century writers who seemed to imitate Le Fanu without having read him, horrid filmmakers from the 1960s onward produced "grand guignol" with only the vaguest notion, if any, what that phrase originally meant. The potential for gross physical horror had been implicit in the genre since Walpole, whether or not anyone exploited it. Those few who did, like Lewis, Maturin, and Poe, remained isolated figures, exercising no necessary influence on writers who trod that ground after them. The same is true of the Grand Guignol: It got there first, perhaps, but it staked no claim.

In fact, the Grand Guignol looks more like the end of a tradition than the source of one. Its crowded, varied programs duplicated the smorgasbord of theater evenings in the 1820s and 1830s, though in concentrated form. Its blatant acting style was also a throwback, running distinctly (and consciously) counter to the naturalism that prevailed in mainstream theaters. It was the death rattle of horrid melodrama. Yet it did look forward, if by accident, to effects that theater would seldom seek again and that movies would discover only sixty years later. The Grand Guignol's first managers may have wished to shake up their audiences à la Zola, by rubbing their noses in squalor and degradation. Instead, they forged a style of extremely realistic mayhem that was nevertheless archly artificial. To attend the Grand Guignol meant to steel one's stomach against the skills of actors and stage technicians; they, in turn, aware of that strategy, redoubled their efforts; spectators parried the thrust, and so on. The outcome was a cat-and-mouse game that exactly anticipated the sparring between makers and viewers of late-twentieth-century horror movies. And in both cases, instead of sober reflection, high hilarity reigns.

On the whole, however, the Grand Guignol was an antique practically at its inception. Many of its playlets came from old or at least familiar sources—like Poe, a favorite. The most famous Grand Guignol horror play, for example, André de Lorde's *Le Système du Dr. Goudron et du Prof. Plume*, first performed in 1903 and filmed in 1912, derived its plot (and its title) from Poe's facetious 1845 story "The System of Dr. Tarr and Professor Fether." In both Poe and Lorde, outsiders visit a private lunatic asylum operated under a revolutionary new "system." Poe employs his customary nameless narrator; Lorde splits him into two buffoonish reporters, Jean and Henri, on the trail of scoops for the *Journal de Paris*. In both story and play, the visitors meet several odd personages, all of whom heap praise on what Poe's asylum director calls the "soothing system."

Inmates here are kept under minimal restraint; instead of straitjackets and cold showers, they get indulgence. The result has been a recovery rate far higher than any conventional institution can claim. Everything the director says sounds reasonable, yet everything is slightly askew; the truth, of course, is that the inmates have taken over the asylum. The so-called director is mad, as are his "very good friends and assistants." This fact slowly dawns on Poe's narrator (any half-awake reader spots it pages ahead of him) at a banquet where the dishes are as crazy as the guests. Poe's tone is jocular—offensively so to a late-twentieth-century reader, since he handles madness very much in the manner of 1845, as an amusing spectacle. At the end, when pandemonium has exploded in the banqueting hall, the windows are suddenly broken in by "a perfect army of what I took to be Chimpanzees, Ourang-Outangs, or big black baboons of the Cape of Good Hope." These are the asylum's guards, whose simian looks come from their having been tarred and feathered. The sham director, M. Maillard, used really to hold that office; two or three years ago, however, he went mad and joined the inmates. Then he led their rebellion.

Lorde's play preserves Poe's structure of suspicion and discovery, but he dramatizes it and makes it characteristically Grand Guignol. Poe sprawls across time and space; Lorde confines himself to a single room, Dr. Goudron's study. He borrows Poe's character names and a few lines of dialogue, but there is no humor, and a heavy air of foreboding overhangs the whole. Terrifying screams are heard from outside; groans sound from the adjoining room, where Goudron has just been engaged in some secret business. As the lunkheaded reporters gradually tumble to the madness of the Doctor's "highly valued collaborators," a thunderstorm rises, making the lunatics crazier and the tension tighter. Finally, in a burst of violence without precedent in Poe, the inmates go wild, Goudron attempts to gouge out Henri's eye—"The blood is flowing. Ha, ha!" he cries—and when the guards rush in, the secret in the next room is revealed:

> At this moment, the third guard drags out the director's body, a horrible corpse, mutilated, gory, the face completely slashed by a razor. Everyone shrinks back from this horrifying sight and turns his head as the corpse is dragged across the stage. And we hear in the background the shrill screams of the lunatics who begin to laugh and sing again. The curtain falls slowly.

After this, the Grand Guignol's audience was no doubt glad for a bit of comic relief.

Those who bemoan the graphic bloodletting of late-century horror films, who see it as a symptom of terminal degeneracy in Western culture, should take a lesson from the Grand Guignol Theater, where equal horrors went on display ninety years ago. Today's films may give ghastlier close-ups, but no film can match the gruesome impact of real people getting stabbed and slashed just a few feet from the audience, gushing stage blood by the potful. As for redeeming social value (famously missing from latter-day gore films), the Grand Guignol pioneered there, too. In its horror plays, the only aim was to make the spectators sick; their basest prejudices, especially fear of mental illness, served the purpose best and were lavishly drawn upon. Nothing in the annals of horror films can beat the Grand Guignol for lack of conscience.

What's remarkable is that, with few exceptions, films were so slow to exploit Grand Guignol techniques. The very notion of a horror film developed late, lagging several years behind that of horror fiction. And even when, by the mid-1930s, horror films had emerged as a distinct genre, they generally exhibited a reticence in regard to bloodshed that makes them look squeamish by comparison with stories published in the same period. In part, this delicacy was due to the squeamishness of the whole film medium, which clung to genteel standards long after written fiction had jettisoned them. But film's conservatism had a special effect on the cultivation of gooseflesh. Instead of forging on into uncharted realms of horror, film persistently harked back to a tradition far older than itself, recycling it in quantities that put the horrid novel to shame.

FUN IN THE OLD DARK HOUSE

Late-century horror aficionados turn testy when they consider how tardily filmmakers—Americans in particular—got around to exploiting the shock potential of their medium. In *The Encyclopedia of Horror Movies* (1986), for example, editor Phil Hardy sniffs at "the vogue for haunted-house spoofs which more or less smothered any real flowering of horror movies during the silent cinema's years of maturity in America." Ramming the point home, the *Encyclopedia* dismisses the "standard haunted-house routine" that mars *The Phantom of the Opera* and slaps playwright Crane Wilbur, "whose tiresome spoof horrors dogged the last years of the silent movie in America." The attitude is typical. In retrospect it does seem perverse that American films—which would dominate the horror field in the thirties and set the tone for the international vogue from the fifties onward—frittered away their energies on bastard blends of chills and laughter.

Most of these movies look silly today: Their repertoire of scary effects is extremely narrow, hardly varying from film to film, and their comedy has lost whatever tickle it once had. Compared to German products like *The Cabinet of Dr. Caligari* (1919) and *Nosferatu* (1921), they look lily-livered as well, skittish about the consequences of dispensing with the bug-eyed servants or bumbling cops who inevitably take the edge off fear. From that viewpoint, it's reprehensible that *Caligari*'s central story about a weird somnambulist and his sinister keeper comes framed as a madman's fantasy. And though European filmmakers could spin out purer horrors than their American counterparts, they rarely did so. Often enough, they too threw in a dash of low comedy, as in the 1922 Swedish epic *Häxan* (*Witchcraft through the Ages*), which summons up a scary Satan only to have him pull crude pranks. Even most Europeans failed to recognize what seems obvious now: that the resources of film far exceed those of print or live performance for the raising of individual hairs.

The belated recognition of film's horrid power occurred on a large scale first in the United States, and it came as a by-product of the very works that latter-day mavens disdain, spooky-house comedies. Frequently based on stage plays, they made a direct link between nineteenth-century melodrama and twentieth-century film, the clearest case of continuity in the lurching history of scary entertainment. Although today they look like hybrids, jumbling slapstick, detective stories, and ghostliness, in fact they are the original stock from which those specialized types were later bred pure. And the old spooky-house genre has had a much longer life than its detractors would like to admit.

Allardyce Nicoll traces the whole "popular school" of " 'crook,' 'crime,' 'detective,' 'mystery,' and 'thriller' " plays back to a single source: William Gillette and Arthur Conan Doyle's *Sherlock Holmes*, which premiered on Broadway in November of 1899 and moved to London two years later. It became a steady vehicle for Gillette in the lead role, and it was revived in London and New York as recently as 1974. The dramatic thriller may have copied the figure of the master criminal from Doyle's Professor Moriarty, but its other personnel had an older pedigree. The standard young lovers, beset by difficulties, came from nineteenth-century melodrama, which had inherited them from the horrid novel; the standard comical servants arrived by the same route. The supernatural effects that inevitably turned out to be natural harked straight back to Mrs. Radcliffe, forgetting the century of horrid fiction that had intervened. Above all, however, the spooky house where most such plays were set defined the genre and furnished its derisory name. And that was a Gothic prop, passed down from *The Castle of Otranto* in a state of eerily perfect preservation.

If anything holds the scary tradition together, it is the spooky house, which has stood fast for 250 years while the world around it has gone through unimaginable changes. Already in Walpole's *Otranto*, the spooky house was uselessly huge, confusingly intricate, and full of secrets. In Radcliffe and her imitators, it came into the flower of its rottenness, a vast decaying body that was history's reproach to the shrunken later generation lost among its galleries. Scott, Dickens, Le Fanu, Riddell, Stoker, and most other nineteenth-century fear mongers haunted the same scene, and sensational journalists strove to evoke it whenever a corpse had been found under floorboards or pavement. Early-twentieth-century plays and films bought the setting wholesale. The only difference was that, instead of castles, they tended to stage their horrors in places "furnished after the substantial custom of forty years ago."

That phrase comes from the stage directions for Ralph Spence's play *The Gorilla*, which enjoyed great success on Broadway in 1925 and was adapted to film in 1927, 1930, and 1939, the last version starring the Ritz Brothers. It was perhaps the zaniest of the spooky-house comedies, equipped with every generic cliché: superstitious servant, stupid cops, wisecracking reporter, master criminal ("the Gorilla"), sliding panels, clutching hands—the works. Spence also threw in a real gorilla, named Poe, tapping into another, inexplicably popular source of comic fear. The device worked poorly onstage, but from the 1920s through the early 1950s, a remarkable number of funny-scary films featured gorillas on the loose, sometimes in the jungle but often in substantial old houses. Often, too, as in *The Ape Man* (1943), the beast was a transformed human being.

Murderous gorillas had been popular in nineteenth-century horrid journalism as well, but they hit their apotheosis in *King Kong* (1933), which ought to have killed the fad but didn't. Finally, like many such devices, it petered out in silliness; the nadir—though not the end—came in 1952, with *Bela Lugosi Meets a Brooklyn Gorilla*, whose title testifies to both stars' degradation. Distasteful as the fashion now appears, during its heyday "the ape" (a catch-all name that covered any simian bigger than Cheetah) made the ideal vehicle for horrors that were harmless after all. Poe's "Murders in the Rue Morgue," which every American adolescent knew, may have spurred it, but Poe's orangutan is really a murderer, as most cinematic apes were not. Evolutionary theory—common Western knowledge by then—may have lent creepiness to the resemblance between apes and human beings. Robert Louis Stevenson's *Strange Case of Dr. Jekyll and Mr. Hyde* (1886) is thick with Darwinesque shadows, and in the 1931 film version Fredric March's Hyde looks distinctly apelike, especially around the mouth.

On the whole, however, stage and film apes were figures of fun, all the more so because they were obviously costumed people. The real terror in such plays and movies came from human sources: sometimes a criminal mastermind seeking treasure concealed in the spooky house, sometimes a homicidal maniac escaped from the asylum nearby, often a deranged or merely fiendish relative determined to inherit the estate or cover up an old crime. In most cases, as in Radcliffean novels, the scariness of the building itself is pure decor; only hysterical spinsters and servants (in American examples, usually black) waste any time on ghosts. Real danger comes from outside, often wearing a familiar face when the lights are on and, in the dark, a black hooded cloak. This outfit serves to hide the villain's features until the denouement; it also gives him a curious resemblance to the Schedonis and Ambrosios who glided through the horrid novels of 120 years before.

Spooky-house comedies reached their peak in the middle and late 1920s; by 1925, their conventions were already so familiar to theatergoers that Spence could spoof them in *The Gorilla*. One of the earliest and best was *The Bat* (1920), by Mary Roberts Rinehart and Avery Hopwood, derived from Rinehart's 1908 novel *The Circular Staircase*. It was filmed in 1926, supplied with sound as

The Bat Whispers in 1930, and sprung upon the public again in 1959, with a screenplay by the durable Crane Wilbur. But *The Bat*'s greatest success occurred on the stage, where its virtually nonstop round of thunderclaps, surprise entrances, and plot reversals lent it an appeal that transcended the genre it helped to found.

Like *The Gorilla* (which blatantly imitates it), *The Bat* pays less attention to inspiring fear than to showing off its own clever construction. Both plays are so tautly suited to the resources and restrictions of live theater that they go slack on film. John Willard's *The Cat and the Canary* (1922) is far simpler and slower-paced; it was a stage success, too, though it owes its fame and influence to the 1927 silent film, directed by Paul Leni. There were recyclings, of course—a sound remake (*The Cat Creeps*) in 1930, a vehicle for Bob Hope and Paulette Goddard in 1939, a bungled update in 1978—but Leni's version became the archetype of the spooky-house film, and later entries in the genre harked back to it as if precursors and rivals hadn't existed. The major reason for their preference is that Leni's *Cat* tries as hard as it can to be a movie, not just the filming of something that belongs on a stage.

Leni had worked with Max Reinhardt in Berlin theater and had directed the much-esteemed *Das Wachsfigurenkabinett* (Waxworks, 1924) starring Werner Krauss, who had acted Dr. Caligari in an earlier *Cabinet*. When Leni emigrated to Hollywood in 1926, he brought with him a notion of scary entertainment that diverged sharply from the Anglo-American brand. Bred on Poe in his Baudelairean guise, and on his French and German imitators, Leni had learned to see fear as a symptom of the beholder's eye, free from the Radcliffean tease about whether the ghosts are real or not. And he knew how to guide a camera to reinforce feelings instead of merely catching them; despite the example of D. W. Griffith, few American film directors could manage that feat in 1927. "Drawing on his expressionist resources," says Phil Hardy, Leni struggled to defeat the tackiness of Willard's vulgar play. In fact, the avant-garde spurt called Expressionism made its slight mark on history mainly because Leni and a few others dragged it westward and forcibly mated it with trash like *The Cat and the Canary*.

Leni's film is a crossbreed and shows it. The screenplay, by

Robert F. Hill and Alfred A. Cohn, sticks close to Willard's original, a compact little tale about a midnight will-reading, a supposed escaped lunatic, and a plot to drive the heiress insane so the next in line can inherit. Willard's black servant, Mammy Pleasant, keeps her name and pointless venomous glances, but she is played by a white actress, to distinctly odd effect. The hero, Paul Jones, has been given a somewhat stiffer backbone, and spinsterish Aunt Susan—quite unsympathetic in the play—becomes a slapstick old maid who runs off in hysterics crying "GHOSTS!" Otherwise, Willard's machinery of sliding panels, clutching clawed hands, and a clock that strikes after twenty years of silence remains largely intact.

On stage, the effect must have been the thoroughly familiar one of a few small jolts muffled up in laughter. The film's sets and camera work, however, insistently suggest that something less soothing is really going on, just out of sight. The spooky house, for instance, which is shot in silhouette at the start and periodically throughout, cannot be a real house, certainly not one on the Hudson River, as it is said to be. It is, more likely, a psychological structure reflecting the reputed madness of its builder and urging madness on those who visit there. The house has at least eight witch-hatted towers, madly jumbled together; it's also thick with cobwebs both inside and out. The rooms, several of which are shown, as well as a long windowed gallery and a monumental staircase, are suitably neo-Gothic and huge. Yet they bear no clear spatial relation to one another and none whatever to the house's exterior.

The camera takes advantage of these oddities, panning across them and into dark corners with a portentous gravity that the film's plot does little to justify. In fact, the decor of Leni's *Cat* is far scarier than the hijinks that occur within it; the house has emotive strength of its own, independent of—often at odds with—the story for which it seems to provide merely a setting. Leni drew on his Expressionist experience for some aspects of the film; he even made an in-joke by having the "doctor," who arrives late and leaves quickly, made up to look like Krauss's Caligari. But the spookiness of *The Cat and the Canary* derives from an older source. It was among the first films of its ilk to let the house play a major role, to go back to Walpole, Radcliffe, and Poe for an atmosphere of "intricate desolation" that in nearly two centuries had lost none of its power to chill.

Many American films of the late 1920s and the 1930s—especially those, like Leni's, produced at Universal—show the influence of Expressionism in their deployment of impossible architecture, warning shadows, and oblique camera angles. But the spooky-house inheritance was not the property of a single school, nor was it strictly European. Americans, of course, faced the difficulty that their relatively young country had only ersatz castles. To compensate, however, Americans enjoyed a telescoped sense of time that could see antiquity in anything after fifty years or even five. When Poe and Hawthorne wished to conjure up an abysmal, threatening past, they usually set their stories in Europe, which to American eyes looked so old that it repelled and allured in equal measure. In *The Scarlet Letter* (1850) and *The House of the Seven Gables* (1851), Hawthorne wrung plausible Radcliffean chills from New England's colonial days, barely two centuries gone when he wrote. H. P. Lovecraft—Hawthorne's and Poe's truest twentieth-century follower—squandered steaming heaps of adverbs trying to make Providence, Rhode Island, and the mythical towns of Arkham and Dunwich, Massachusetts, look older than the hills they sat on. He needn't have bothered.

Instead, he could have followed the example of Tod Browning (1880–1962), whose lack of concern for history and geography enabled him to forge a kind of spooky setting that was timeless, placeless, and yet distinctively American. Best known today as the director of *Dracula* (1931), Browning had worked as an acrobat and clown before becoming an assistant to D. W. Griffith about 1915. Circuses and carnivals appeared in many of the films he directed, including *Freaks* (1932), *The Unholy Three* (1925, sound version 1930), and *The Unknown* (1927). Circus experience must also have honed Browning's sense of how to entertain an audience that demanded thrills pure, simple, and strong. And it made him the ideal director for Lon Chaney, who was a special sort of clown in his own right.

Browning did not direct Chaney's two most famous performances, *The Hunchback of Notre Dame* (1923) and *The Phantom of the Opera*; big-budget projects like those went to safer directors. But the ten films they made together between 1919 and 1930, several based on Browning's own stories, established the actor as the Man of a Thousand Faces and the director as a trademark name for offbeat, rather unwholesome excitement. Near the end of the silent era, in 1927, they ventured for the first time into the territory of the spooky house. The result was *London after Midnight*, which went a step beyond even *The Cat and the Canary* in exploiting the terror of decor for its own sake. No prints of *London after Midnight* are known to survive, but a good sense of the film can be put together from Browning's sound remake, *Mark of the Vampire* (1935), and Philip J. Riley's book-length reconstruction.

Again the story is Browning's, originally called "The Hypnotist." Chaney plays two roles: Inspector Burke of Scotland Yard (pompous and bespectacled) and "the Man in the Beaver Hat," a fearsome creation with bulging, black-rimmed eyes, two full rows of sharp, canine teeth displayed in a perpetual grin, a bat-winged black cloak, and that silly hat, which makes him even scarier. Even in stills, sixty years later, the effect is strong; it must have been all the more so on moviegoers prepared for Chaney's tricks but unused to this kind of ghastliness. He is a vampire, the first in American film—at least he's supposed to be one.

He has just moved into the Balfour House, where Roger Balfour was murdered five years ago, a crime Inspector Burke failed to solve. In that short time, the Balfour House has fallen into a remarkable degree of disrepair: It is shrouded in cobwebs, set about with broken urns, and given over to bats and other creatures of the night. It is also a remarkable house to find in a London suburb. Unlike Leni's mansion on the Hudson, the Balfour House has no fantastic towers or secret passages; there is nothing psychological about it. The place looks more like a ruined castle than a suburban mansion—especially the long, broad staircase down which the vampire and his pallid female companion make their first entrance. Neither modern nor plausibly ancient, the Balfour House invokes straight decay and rot, with a family of walking corpses in its midst.

True to the spooky-house fashion, *London after Midnight* provides comical, credulous servants and a not-half-bad mystery satisfactorily solved; true to Mrs. Radcliffe, the vampires are actors employed to frighten a confession out of the murderer. But even more powerfully than Leni's grotesque mansion, the Balfour

214 THE THRILL OF FEAR

House seems to stand apart from the shenanigans staged in and around it. To judge from the available evidence, Browning's direction of *London after Midnight* was seldom inventive; as he evidently did in *Dracula* and *Mark of the Vampire* (which follows much of *London* scene by scene), he must have told the camera crew just to point at the set and shoot. Yet at times in all three films, cinematic clunkiness wields a power that sophistication could not achieve. When Browning trained his cameras not on hysterical chambermaids or pontificating inspectors but on cobwebs, he pressed a button that made him and his culture jump.

Browning "*loved* cobwebs," art director A. Arnold Gillespie recalled decades later. "We had designed and built a special hand-held cobweb machine for Tod." Cobwebs, indeed, come close to stealing the show in Browning's three spooky-house films, abetted by the desolate chambers they festoon and the vermin that creep among them. *Dracula* comes alive only toward the beginning and at the very end, when Castle Dracula and Carfax Abbey give Karl Freund's camera the chance to glide through scenes of grand decay, up and down vast stone staircases. It hardly matters that, besides rats and spiders, Castle Dracula houses armadillos. Their presence is absurd, but they scuttle across the cobwebby floor, and anything that does that suffices. Empty of history, logic, and sometimes sense, Browning's spooky scenes offered American audiences a frisson not very different from what Walpole's guests had felt at Strawberry Hill nearly two centuries before.

THE GREAT RECYCLING MACHINE

Spooky-house comedies flourished throughout the 1930s. Sound remakes gave them a boost early in the decade, and one of the best such films, *Topper Returns* (1940), came at the very end. In addition to Roland Young, Billie Burke, and Eddie "Rochester" Anderson (on loan from the Jack Benny radio show), it provides an unlikely anticipation of *Psycho* by murdering Joan Blondell half an hour into the action; she comes back, however, as a ghostly sleuth. Most later entries emphasized laughter rather than chills. The 1939 *Cat and the Canary*, for instance, cast Bob Hope in the reluctant hero's role; having, as he says, acted in melodrama, he wisecracks about coming plot twists and grins when they arrive on schedule. By 1939, audiences could be expected to know spooky-house conventions well enough to get—if not to laugh at—Hope's lame jokes.

Staples of the horrid warehouse, spooky-house comedies never went wholly out of stock. But they sank in popularity and prestige as the devices that once raised gooseflesh turned funny in their own right. Films of that kind descended to the level of B pictures, low-budget companions to better-financed, usually better features. They joined the march of series with comic stars: The East Side Kids made three—*The Ghost Creeps* (1940), *Spooks Run Wild* (1941), and *Ghosts on the Loose* (1943)—the latter two featuring a declining Bela Lugosi. Dean Martin and Jerry Lewis perpetrated *Scared Stiff* in 1952, and a sort of nadir came four years later with *Francis in the Haunted House*, which sent the talking mule clopping down cobwebby corridors alongside hapless Mickey Rooney.

The next decade brought further debasement with the TV series "The Addams Family" and "The Munsters" (both 1964–1966). The spooky house itself still retains its power, but after the 1930s the traditional alternation of shrieks and laughter became unstable, then untenable. The stage abandoned it, except for tongue-in-cheek revivals of *The Bat*; movies sorted themselves out into genres of horror and comedy. Later haunted-house films like *The Haunting* (1963) and *The Legend of Hell House* (1973), both based on novels, have no time for laughs; spoofs like *Saturday the 14th* (1981) and *Bloodbath at the House of Death* (1983) have time for little else. And though it contains no spooky houses, the bravest recent attempt to reunite the old emotional partners, *An American Werewolf in London* (1981), seems to have bewildered more moviegoers than it pleased.

In part, this trend was due to the genrefication of horrid fiction that solidified during the 1920s and invaded movies a few years later, extending and confirming the century-old horrid ghetto. But it also happened by accident. In 1923, Hamilton Deane secured the dramatic rights to *Dracula* from Stoker's touchy widow; on

Valentine's Day 1927, his play *Dracula* premiered in London, where it ran nearly a year, starring Raymond Huntley as the vampire. For the American version, Deane joined John L. Balderston to concoct *Dracula: The Vampire Play*, which opened at New York's Fulton Theatre on October 5. The star was Bela Lugosi, whose Hungarian birth put him pretty close (geographically if not linguistically) to the Count's Transylvania. On both sides of the Atlantic, *Dracula* scored a great success. A film was therefore inevitable.

Tod Browning had been interested in Stoker's novel for some time, intending to cast Lon Chaney in the lead. Chaney's sham vampire in *London after Midnight* suggests how different the history of horror movies would have been if the great actor hadn't died in 1930, before a *Dracula* film could be made. Chaney's Man in the Beaver Hat is horrific in every detail but especially in those of his face, with its mouthful of sharp teeth and round, staring eyes. He is purely a creature of darkness, at home among cobwebs and nowhere else. Lugosi's Count, by contrast, glides across drawing rooms and crypts with equal aplomb; no charnel-house air clings to him. His face is rather handsome, in a vaguely decadent, lounge-lizard style, and he never shows a fang. Lugosi attempted to evoke ideas of aristocratic corruption rather than the literal rot of the grave. He created a long-lived type—in which he found himself hopelessly cast—but he also neglected the deepest source of the vampire's power to chill.

In retrospect, *Dracula* looks like a transitional film, stuck between spooky-house comedies and the more singleminded cinematic horrors that would soon follow. The "play script" (credited to Garrett Fort but also worked on by several others) goes back to Stoker for the scenes in Transylvania and for Dracula's voyage to England but otherwise leans heavily on Deane and Balderston's stage version. The result is a peculiar hybrid of a movie, an atmospheric first half grafted onto a talky, static second, with a brief resurgence of atmosphere at the end. It discards Deane and Balderston's worst sillinesses: they bring Dracula to England via a "three-engined German plane" and give Harker, on arriving in Carfax Abbey, the supremely foolish line, "The place smells horribly of bats." But the film retains the comical servants, who seem out of place in the midst of what should be genuinely dire doings.

That, perhaps, is *Dracula*'s chief failing, both on stage and in the Browning film. It strives to break out of the spooky-house district, in which the ghosts are all figments, into a realm where, as Dr. Van Helsing says at the end of the play (cut from the film), *"there are such things."* But it gets, at best, only halfway out. The film's commercial success, however (especially opportune in the hard-pressed spring of 1931), led Universal Pictures to hunt around for a follow-up. They found one in *Frankenstein*, directed by James Whale and starring Boris Karloff as the Monster, which went quickly into production and premiered in New York on December 4. Again, accident helped determine horror-film history: Fresh from *Dracula*, Lugosi seemed a prime choice to play the Monster, and he might have ended up doing so if he hadn't been such a recalcitrant actor. He insisted on designing his own makeup, which Edward Van Sloan recalled years later as "more like something out of *Babes in Toyland*!"

Within months, and at the behest of a single Hollywood studio, moviegoers had been introduced to four icons of twentieth-century horror: two books and two men. None was quite new to films, of course. *Dracula* had inspired *Nosferatu* and strongly influenced *London after Midnight*; *Frankenstein* had been filmed under that title in 1910 and adapted as *Life without Soul* in 1916. Lugosi had been making movies since 1923 in the United States; William Henry Pratt became Boris Karloff about 1910 and had his first film role in 1919. Actors had been wedded to roles many times before, but never in theatrical history had the marriage proven so definitive or durable. Lugosi died in 1956, Karloff in 1969, yet even today their faces and voices are recognizable to American children who haven't a clue where Europe is.

Karloff's career fared better than Lugosi's, perhaps because his *Frankenstein* makeup buried his face and his voice was confined to grunts and roars. Audiences knew only his name, which became vaguely associated with horror but did not pin him down to any one spot on that broad field. Karloff played the Monster twice more, in *Bride of Frankenstein* (1935) and *Son of Frankenstein* (1939); he also, however, appeared as the drunken, lascivious butler in *The Old Dark House*, the desiccated Egyptian in *The Mummy*, Sax Rohmer's Oriental mastermind in *The Mask of Fu Manchu* (all three in 1932), and in scores of other roles that had little in common but the design of raising gooseflesh. By 1941, his name and face had become such trademarks that he could appear as a Boris Karloff lookalike in Joseph Kesselring's play *Arsenic and Old Lace* and win applause for the resemblance.

At first, Lugosi did nearly as well, escaping from Dracula to star as Murder Legendre in *White Zombie* and Dr. Mirakle, the killer ape's master, in *Murders in the Rue Morgue* (both 1932). But his Hungarian accent, his supposedly mesmerizing eyes, and especially the black cloak he swirled so well combined to hem him in; they were too specific, too closely identified with a single character, to allow him Karloff's relative freedom. Though Lugosi played many other roles throughout the thirties and forties—including the Monster in *Frankenstein Meets the Wolf Man* (1943)—Dracula haunted him, and he fell back repeatedly on the image that first made him famous.

He spoofed it twice with the East Side Kids and reprised it for *Return of the Vampire* (1944), *Abbott and Costello Meet Frankenstein* (1948), and *Old Mother Riley Meets the Vampire* (1952); he also appeared as Dracula in revivals of the play, at Las Vegas casinos, and on TV variety shows. Dracula even dogged him after death. When Lugosi died, he had filmed only a few scenes of what would become Edward D. Wood's ineffable *Plan 9 from Outer Space*; it is said that the director's wife's chiropractor did the rest. Those who attended the film on its release, in 1959, saw a stalking figure that bore no resemblance to Lugosi except for the black cloak. Sadly, however, the cloak sufficed.

The careers of Karloff and Lugosi illustrate a general trait of moviemaking that has been particularly strong in horror films: the tendency to recycle everything, people as well as ideas, until it turns tedious or ridiculous. Karloff escaped the worst, which Lugosi succumbed to; both, however, became identified with a kind of response they might make fun of but could not shake off. Other actors suffered typecasting as villains or heroes, swashbucklers or bumblers; constrictive though these types were, they permitted considerable range within their limits and could fairly easily be transgressed. Horror films, however, have spawned a tribe of actors, mostly men, to whom horror clings no matter what they try their hands at. In varying degrees, Lionel Atwill, Dwight Frye, George Zucco, Lon Chaney, Jr., Peter Lorre, Gale

Sondergaard, Vincent Price, Christopher Lee, and Barbara Steele, among many others, have felt the grip of horror's typecasting.

The same tendency marks horror films themselves, which drain dry every character, theme, or gimmick that yields the slightest popular—that is, financial—success. In recent years, the recycling of horror has gone to the extreme of eight *Friday the 13ths* between 1980 and 1989. By 1991, the *Nightmare on Elm Street* series, launched in 1985, had reached its sixth installment; there had been three sequels, at least in title, to the popular and effective *Halloween* (1978); and Leatherface, the busy butcher of *The Texas Chainsaw Massacre*, had spun off into two star vehicles of his own. Following suit, the whole American film industry now seems bent on tacking a *II* to anything that made money last year. But from the moment *Dracula* and *Frankenstein* established the genre "horror movie," recycling was its hallmark. *Dracula* bred *Dracula's Daughter* (1936); *Frankenstein* met its *Bride*; *White Zombie* spawned *Revolt of the Zombies* (1936); the list could go on for pages. Even the originals, of course, had been recycled from earlier plays, novels, or films, and that kind of plundering reached a frantic pitch after *Dracula* and *Frankenstein* proved that "horror" made money.

Between 1931 and 1935, in addition to the vampire and the man-made monster (and the spooky-house comedy, which was still going strong), Hollywood refashioned just about every other available horrid cliché and did its best to beat them all to death. *Dr. X* (1932) furnished the mad scientist, a *Frankenstein* variant that would have a long life of its own. *Dr. Jekyll and Mr. Hyde* had been filmed under that name twice before, but it came back again in the horror stampede of 1932, winning an Academy Award for Fredric March. Poe contributed *Murders in the Rue Morgue* and *The Black Cat* (1934)—at least their titles—while H. G. Wells's *The Island of Dr. Moreau* (1896) became *Island of Lost Souls* (1933). This list, too, could be extended a long way.

The phenomenon is remarkable, and several explanations have been offered for it. Mired in the Great Depression, audiences may have sought escape into fantasy—though their attraction to fantasies that stood their hairs on end remains hard to account for (perhaps it was homeopathic medicine). The advent of talkies may have helped horror, since howling wolves and creaking doors could now be portrayed, not merely suggested. The demarcation of "horror stories" may have allowed movies to batten on that, as they did on everything else. No doubt all these factors contributed to the explosion of horror films in the early 1930s, but probably the main cause was simple novelty. Though far from new in inspiration, these films launched an assault on their audiences' nerves that indeed *was* new; they thrilled in double measure for that reason. And not since the horrid melodramas of the early nineteenth century had large and diverse audiences gathered to scare themselves in perfect safety.

WINDING DOWN

The "horror films" of the thirties and forties have little in common beyond an evident intention to scare, usually signaled by their titles and especially their advertising. Some early entries staged elaborate promotions, like the uniformed nurses hired to sit in theater lobbies for both *Dracula* and *Frankenstein*, or the dead-looking actors who paraded in front of New York's Rivoli Theater, where *White Zombie* premiered. The primary vehicles, however, were newspaper ads and posters, which promised far heavier shocks than any fiction could deliver. Though the films of the period did not get noticeably more violent or gruesome with time, ad writers found themselves locked into one-upmanship, with eventually ludicrous results. In 1931, *Dracula* billed itself tamely as "The story of the strangest Passion the world has ever known!" and *Frankenstein* was just "THE MAN WHO MADE A MONSTER." By 1934, *The Black Cat* was ungrammatically trumpeting "THINGS YOU NEVER SAW BEFORE OR EVER DREAMED OF!" And by 1940, *Chamber of Horrors* shrieked about "A beautiful girl, helpless victim of a madman, who uses torture to get her secret!" In Britain, where it was made, *Chamber of Horrors* came forth as *The Door with Seven Locks*, a more accurate label for this rather sedate adaptation of an Edgar Wallace novel.

The trend was far from monolithic, of course, and if you were cloistered enough to take posters at their word, you probably never went to movies anyway. But it was chiefly by these means that horror films defined themselves and located their audiences. Whether or not a film delivered what its ads promised, promises sold tickets. By steadily raising the would-be stakes, advertising helped to narrow the appeal of such films, especially the low-budget, starless ones. Advertising thereby contributed to the strangulation of horror that was setting in already by 1935 and had virtually wiped it off the screen a decade later.

Horror also strangled itself, in typical Hollywood fashion, by riding a few once-successful types into the ground, exhausting their novelty and coaxing sighs instead of screams. Reviewers reflected growing disaffection and impatience. In 1932, for example, the *New York Daily News* called *Murders in the Rue Morgue* a "horror film" as if that were something new and effective on anyone who saw it. In 1941, the trade journal *Film Daily* advised that only theaters whose audiences "go for this type of film" should book *The Black Cat*, a spooky-house item that owed nothing to Poe and little to the 1934 film beyond Lugosi and its title. Mrs. Radcliffe's imitators had run the same course, battering the horrid novel from a genteel shock to a low-grade bore in about twenty-five years; movies covered the same ground in ten at most. By 1820, the horrid novel was dead, its remains dispersed into melodrama, pantomime, and even serious fiction. By 1940, the horror film had died, too, though its posthumous progeny would take two decades to sprout.

World War II may have had some impact, but the most likely culprit is boredom, born of repetition and reticence. Having found that vampires, zombies, mummies, werewolves, mad scientists, and cobwebby vaults made money, moviemakers ground them out in quantity. Somewhere along the dwindling line, moviemakers may have recognized that all these icons of horror embodied the invasion of life by death, that fear of death was their sole source of power, that the source was therefore bottomless. If so, they kept the knowledge to themselves. Instead of plunging deeper into the source, they swaddled their horror figures in thickening layers of insulation against fear, until they all became laughable, then tedious.

With very few exceptions, Hollywood's first wave of horror films maintained a degree of reticence that makes Victorian horrid

fiction look rowdy; they seem positively namby-pamby compared
to the disgustingness of the pulp fiction of their own time. Occasionally, a film like the 1932 *Dr. Jekyll* exhibited some slight
frankness about sex. Rarely, as in *Island of Lost Souls* and *The
Black Cat* (1934), something akin to genuine "grand guignol" was
evoked. Overly shocking scenes were cut from *Frankenstein* and
King Kong before their general release, then restored half a century later, and *Freaks* was shelved entirely for more than two
decades. On the whole, however, self-censorship guaranteed that
in their very conception films would dull the horrors of violence
and rot. Like horrid novels before them, horror films of the thirties and forties constantly intimated that dismemberment, bloodshed, and decay were to be found nearby in time or space, though
the camera almost never caught them.

The baroquely prudish Production Code of 1930—in full opera-
tion by 1934—partly dictated Hollywood's squeamishness across
the board. Its rules met no serious challenge until 1953, when
Otto Preminger refused to delete incendiary words like "virgin"
from *The Moon Is Blue*, and United Artists backed him. The Code,
however, focused on sex, a marginal concern for most horror
films. Their reticence sprang from the same belief that, for all its
hypocrisy, the Code also honored: Movies were universal entertainment, truest to themselves when they delighted young and
old, sophisticates and hicks. Explicit sex might offend many people and corrupt some others; explicit horror would repel practically everyone, including those who enjoyed horror when it was
intimated rather than shown. Foreign films left their tiny audiences mourning mankind's lot or puzzling over ironies, but Hollywood meant to please in the directest terms. Scenes like Dr.
Pretorius dining among cadavers in *Bride of Frankenstein* got by
only when they outwitted their overseers.

The belief was grounded in greed, but it nevertheless produced
an astonishing number of films that give pleasure fifty years later
and are likely to go on doing so. Time has gilded *The Wizard of
Oz* and *Gone with the Wind*; it has ossified *Son of Frankenstein*,
though all three films were released in the same year, 1939.
Ironically, the blunting of horror for the sake of universal appeal
led to the opposite outcome. Horror movies degenerated into feed
for stunted appetites; viewers had to be crippled in some way if

they could be satisfied by the dreck they were being served. Late-century horror mavens venerate the seven films produced by Val Lewton at RKO between 1942 and 1946, the leanest years of Hollywood horror. In retrospect, certainly, they are striking films, but they're also decadent. They could be made only when the wellspring—this one about ten years old and wholly derivative—had dried up.

Lewton's films wear garish titles like *Cat People* (1942) and *The Curse of the Cat People* (1944), but the films themselves make few bids, cheap or otherwise, for strong responses. Instead, they are slow-moving and decorous, emphasizing eerie atmosphere rather than shocks. The most luridly named example, *I Walked with a Zombie* (1943)—"FORBIDDEN VOODOO SECRETS SENSATIONALLY REVEALED!" gasped the poster—is perhaps the politest of them. Eschewing the charnel-house gruesomeness that had blotched earlier entries in the zombie line, director Jacques Tourneur provides distant drums, ominous innuendo, and a good deal of trekking through the cane fields by moonlight. The title turns out to be accurate, but it seems highly unlikely that the spunky heroine, who goes on that dire stroll several times, would ever make such a rude announcement. Besides, the zombie in question poses no threat to anyone but herself; she got into her walking-dead state through an act of misguided compassion she hardly merited. In the end, she is released into real death, and just deserts are distributed all around.

I don't mean to denigrate either *I Walked with a Zombie* or Lewton's other productions. Despite their evident low budgets, they are coherently made, and they sometimes achieve mild chills that can still be appreciated today. They also lack the low comedy endemic in other would-be horror films of the period. Their very tastefulness was a novelty, perhaps the only kind available after a decade of unimaginative stereotyping. Yet they claim membership in a worn-out genre, only to disdain and rise above it; in a sense, they are parodies. Forty years later, horror aficionados would praise Lewton's films as being ahead of their time, bemoaning their lack of contemporary influence. They are certainly untypical of the 1940s in skill and unity of tone, but they reflect exhaustion far more plainly than even *The Ape Man*, released in the same year as *I Walked*. In that wretched film, Lugosi glues on a wig and a beard that make him look rather like an unkempt Disraeli, in order to storm about a basement laboratory and break a few vials. *The Ape Man* is stupid; at least, however, it trots out the ape and the mad scientist as if they still had some life in them.

Typical of what happened to American movie horror in the 1940s is a film that's usually regarded as an endpoint, though for its stars it made a new beginning. *Abbott and Costello Meet Frankenstein* premiered in New York on July 28, 1948, the eighth and final appearance by the Monster in a feature from Universal (now Universal-International). After the fourth, *The Ghost of Frankenstein*, in 1942, the studio had taken to sending out the Monster with monstrous attendants, as if he were too feeble to leave home alone. He had met the Wolf Man in 1943, teamed up with the Wolf Man and Dracula in *The House of Frankenstein* (1944), and joined the same crew again in *House of Dracula* (1945). This time, he couldn't complain of loneliness; in addition to Bud Abbott and Lou Costello, Glenn Strange's Monster enjoyed the company of the Wolf Man (Lon Chaney, Jr.), Dracula (Lugosi), and, briefly, the Invisible Man.

It was certainly the end of the line for the charnel-house creation who had required nurses in the lobby seventeen years earlier; it also marked a low point for his once-fearsome companions. But *Abbott and Costello Meet Frankenstein* pumped fresh blood into the career of its two comic stars. They had made a run-of-the-mill spooky-house comedy, *Hold That Ghost*, in 1941; the new film's commercial success launched them on an orgy of monster meeting, as if their producers were determined to trash every scary figure Universal had popularized in the thirties. *Abbott and Costello Meet the Killer, Boris Karloff* (1948), *Abbott and Costello Meet the Invisible Man* (1951), *Abbott and Costello Meet Dr. Jekyll and Mr. Hyde* (1953), *Abbott and Costello Meet the Mummy* (1955): The list is as repetitive and depressing as the films. They even *Go to Mars* in 1953, evidently intending to catch the newborn craze for outer-space thrills and smother it in its cradle.

Curiously, their rendezvous with Frankenstein can still be watched with more than antiquarian pleasure, provided the viewer has a tolerance for sardonic Bud and pudgy, whiny Lou. According to Gregory William Mank, in his definitive history of Universal's Monster series, the film allowed its tired old bugaboos "to make a gracefully comic exit as the more contemporary horrors of the atomic age made their entrance." To some degree, this is true, though in film, those new horrors were seldom as contemporary as they looked, and often they weren't horrors at all. Abbott and Costello's *Frankenstein* does not ridicule its passé monsters; it lets them run through their trademark shticks (Dracula rising from his coffin, the Wolf Man's face painfully changing) without mockery. Costello's bug eyes cast no shame on a long roster of scared servants; his fright seems as genuine as it could be, under the circumstances. And some of the settings, especially Dracula's swamp-encircled castle, might have gratified Mrs. Radcliffe.

After *Abbott and Costello Meet Frankenstein*, however, there was nowhere for the tradition to go. Other nations, notably Britain, produced a number of films that can be classified as "horror," but the United States patented the "horror film," grinding it out in quantity and exporting it with great profit. Imaginative poverty, opportunism, and fake gentility conspired to use up American resources in record time. More than a century earlier, the horrid novel had similarly died from imitativeness and boredom. But that short tradition fired the odd, premature genius of Monk Lewis, who shocked polite Western culture by filling in Mrs. Radcliffe's gaps before she had left off leaving them. Amid the horde of American horror films made between 1931 and 1948, only a few took timid forays in Lewis's direction. The industrial climate of Hollywood was hostile to any brand of oddness, as the famous case of Orson Welles illustrates. To judge from his performances as *The Shadow* on radio (1937–1938) and from the quirky Gothicism of *Citizen Kane* (1941) and *The Magnificent Ambersons* (1942), Welles might have become the Monk Lewis of American horror. But the odd genius that did so, though it was already ripe, would wait twenty years more to annex horror's territory.

FRESH BLOOD

Nothing dies in the realm of fear; even the ravages of Abbott and Costello could not kill the American horror film. It merely slept for a while, awaiting resurrection. Starting in 1950 with *Rocketship XM*, Hollywood's thrill mongers turned their attention toward the

perils of technology, in a decade-long barrage of what are collec-
tively known as science-fiction films. "Science fiction" is a looser
label than "horror," comprising outer-space adventures, invasions
from outer space, atomic energy gone berserk, and various breeds
of deranged men with PhDs. Though these films attempted to urge
gasps from their audiences, very few went for the charnel-house
chill that characterizes the horrid tradition. Instead, they unleashed overgrown ants (*Them!*, 1954), spiders (*Tarantula*, 1955),
birds (*The Giant Claw*, 1957), people (*The Amazing Colossal
Man*, 1957; *The Attack of the Fifty-Foot Woman*, 1958), and lumps
(*The Blob*, 1958). In the lucrative market for simulations of large-
scale wreckage, Hollywood faced early competition from Japa-
nese filmmakers, who exported their *Gojira* (*Godzilla*) in 1955
and brought the huge lizard back for several sequels.

Some science-fiction films took a craftier, and cheaper, approach. They featured ordinary-looking people who either were
Martians in disguise or had been possessed by malevolent extraterrestrial powers. Such films as *Invaders from Mars* (1953), *Invasion of the Body Snatchers* (1956), *It Conquered the World* (1956),
and *I Married a Monster from Outer Space* (1958) have been
analyzed as allegories of anti-Communist hysteria—plausibly
enough, since neither adherence to an ideology nor possession
by Martians requires special makeup. Whatever their allegorical
design, these films, too, rarely drew on the resources of the scary
tradition. When they did, science-fiction films copied the old
techniques. The giant ants in *Them!*, for instance, keep out of
sight for the first several minutes; they are known only by their
fondness for sugar, the eerie buzzing sound they make, and a
traumatized little girl's shriek, "Them!" Even after the ants have
been shown, their size remains less unnerving than their home
life, which goes on in dark, intricate underground nests. At the
end, they must be hunted among the drainage tunnels under Los
Angeles—new versions of the queasily visceral subterraneous
passages that the Gothic novelists loved to deploy.

Science-fiction films have their own long history, entwined with
that of the horrid tradition but gradually growing apart from it; by
the 1950s, the genres were distinct enough that one could seem to
supersede the other in wresting screams from American moviegoers. By then, however, the moviegoing public itself had splin-

tered. The old ideal of a universal audience, which had done its part to doom American horror films in the 1940s, now belonged to television; the old bane of timidity went with it and still hamstrings television four decades later. After the 1948 Supreme Court decision breaking up Paramount's vertical monopoly on production and distribution, Hollywood itself was no longer monolithic. Independent producers multiplied through the fifties; there was also a rising flood of foreign films, both the "art-house" kind and flashier items like *Godzillas* from Japan and *Herculeses* from Italy.

Belatedly, Hollywood producers recognized that films could turn profits without appealing equally to grandmothers and babies. The big money now filled the pockets of teenagers, who went to the movies more often than their elders and who presumably had different tastes. Thomas Doherty, who has tracked these trends in detail, calls them "juvenilization": "Since the 1950s, moviemakers have been forced to narrow their focus and attract the one group with the requisite income, leisure, and garrulousness to support a theatrical business." "Teenpics" boomed from the mid-fifties onward, branching into subspecies from dramas like *Rebel without a Cause* (1955) to the mildly erotic idiocy of Annette Funicello and Frankie Avalon in the sixties. Teenagers' money still rules: "Without the support of the teenage audience," says Doherty, "few theatrical movies break even, fewer still become hits, and none become blockbusters."

Television joined in burying old Hollywood, but it had the opposite effect on the dormant horror film. From the start an avid recycler of movies, television acquired in 1957 a package of "52 of Universal's greatest spine-tingling films," including that studio's first *Dracula* and *Frankenstein*. Many stations set up local, late-evening "Shock Theatres," usually hosted by a comical ghoul like New York's Zacherly, who wisecracked during the frequent commercial breaks. (That gimmick, too, had an afterlife: It was revived for cable television in the late 1980s by "Commander USA's Groovy Movies" on the USA network and in 1990 by "Mystery Science Theater 3000" on the Comedy Channel.) Aimed chiefly at teenagers, such series offered them a first look at horrors that, not yet thirty years old, were already being called "classic." Television may have shrunk the American attention span down to an eye's blink, but it did for horror films what anthologies had done for horrid short fiction in the 1920s. Television gave horror films a history and a museum for displaying it; in the 1980s, videocassettes would complete the transformation of film into a medium just as archival as the printed word.

The TV recycling of "classic" horror movies in the late 1950s coincided with a resurgence of film horror on several new fronts, including Mexico. In 1930, Mexican moviegoers had been treated to a Spanish-language *Cat and the Canary* called *La Voluntad del Muerto*; it was reputedly superior to the sound remake in English, *The Cat Creeps*. The next year, they saw a Spanish *Dracula*, filmed at night on the same sets the English-speaking cast was using during the day. According to David J. Skal, director George Melford handled cobwebs better than Tod Browning did, and he also retired the armadillos. For twenty-five years thereafter, Mexican horror consisted mainly of dubbed American exports. But in 1957, Fernando Mendez directed two films, *El Vampiro* (The Vampire) and *El Ataud del Vampiro* (The Vampire's Coffin), that signaled the birth of an international horror-movie industry.

These rather somber black-and-white films are set ostensibly in Mexico, though their trappings belong to Old Europe as Americans had imagined it in the 1930s. With *La Momia Azteca* (The Aztec Mummy, 1957), Rafael Portillo began a shoestring series of more adventurous movies that made a slight attempt to blend Hollywood clichés and local traditions. The Aztec Mummy, however, soon went the way of Godzilla; it is remembered today mainly for its last appearance, *Las Luchadoras contra la Momia* (The Wrestling Women vs. the Aztec Mummy, 1964), which has often been subjected to ridicule on American TV shows of the Shock Theatre ilk. The Mexican horror industry faded in the sixties under an avalanche of films from Italy and Spain. Most of them, in turn, imitated the first significant outpouring of horror from Britain. Not since Universal in the thirties had a studio devised a style so distinctive it wore the studio's name: Hammer.

The Hammer horror film made its debut in 1957 with *The Curse of Frankenstein*. The following year brought a sequel, *The Revenge of Frankenstein*, along with *Dracula* (released in the United States as *Horror of Dracula*) and *The Hound of the Baskervilles*. In 1959, the studio put its mark on *The Mummy*, and so on through the sixties and into the seventies, until it, too, wore out. These five films shared the same director (Terence Fisher) and cinematographer (Jack Asher). All five starred Peter Cushing and Christopher Lee, who bid fair to succeed Lugosi and Karloff as real-life icons of horror. Hammer's films made few innovations in the stories they told; by then, *Dracula* and *Frankenstein* had been put through so many twists and permutations that little remained to ring changes on. But Hammer lent the genre a visual style that made its films look new. Photographed in color—a rarity in horror movies before then—they went in for opulence on a grand, if actually inexpensive scale. The settings were vaguely nineteenth century and resembled the Technicolor Victorianism that Hollywood had dreamt up in the previous decade for would-be serious films like *A Song to Remember* (1944), with Cornel Wilde as Frédéric Chopin.

Rich purples, blues, and reds predominate. Bosomy young women display a great deal of rosy skin above their low-cut velvet gowns; spacious interiors glow with candlelight on glass and polished wood; night is very, very blue. Even alleyways drip atmosphere. The decor has little resemblance to the actual look of Victorian England, a much dimmer, grimier place. But for a generation that knew such scenes only from movies—the first generation, indeed, that had probably never met a Victorian—false accuracy passed for the real thing. The films therefore possessed what had been lacking from most American horror films for two decades: seriousness. Except for an occasional credulous peasant, Hammer's films also dispense with comic relief, the traditional counterpoise to dread. They are glamorously grim from first to last.

Hammer's most important innovation, however, is that when ghastliness occurs the camera doesn't shy away or fade to black: It zooms in. Lee's Dracula—a far more feral creature than Lugosi's—has fangs, bares them in a snarl, and seems to sink them into flesh, drawing blood that smears his mouth. In the 1958 *Dracula*, the extermination of a female vampire is shown complete: The stake drives in, blood gushes, the vampire howls and withers. The scene is almost as gruesome as Lucy's impaling in Stoker's novel. The Monster in *Curse of Frankenstein* (Lee again) shambles about, sloppily stitched and wrapped in stained bandages; except for defective speech, he is very much the charnel-house escapee of Mary Shelley's imagination. Compared to the carnage that would arrive in the next two decades, the gore in Hammer's first horror films looks decorous; often, it seems to be part of the scenery, a splash of red to round off the composition. But Technicolor blood did for the horror film what *The Monk* had failed to do for the horrid novel: It refreshed the whole genre.

Back in the U.S.A., a drift toward more explicit bloodshed was already underway and might eventually have transformed the field even without Hammer's imports. American ingenuity, however, flourished best on the promotional side. *Macabre* (1958) inaugurated producer-director William Castle's brief campaign to top the gimmick mongers of the past. It came furnished with nurses and hearses at some premieres, but the film's most adaptable trick was an insurance policy from Lloyd's of London, paying one thousand dollars to the beneficiary of any viewer who died of fright. In *The House on Haunted Hill* and *The Tingler* (both 1959), the gimmicks moved from the lobby into the movie. At the end of *Haunted Hill*, while Vincent Price turned complicated-looking reels on screen, a skeleton was supposed to slide on wires across the theater ceiling. This was billed as "Emergo." Near the end of the more inventive *Tingler*, the screen went black, and Price's voice mellifluously warned that the lobsterish Tingler (visceral essence of fear) had escaped into the theater. The only repellent was screaming, which Price urged. Some seats had been wired to generate low-voltage shocks, as if the Tingler were underfoot. This was "Percepto."

The House on Haunted Hill and *The Tingler* were unsuited to drive-in theaters, the chief teenage moviegoing haunt of the time. They also defied revival, even at indoor theaters, because their novelty was lost without the original, cumbersome gimmicks. But *The Tingler* looked beyond gimmicks in one sequence. A deaf-and-dumb woman (who cannot scream and kill the beast within her) awakes to a parade of clichés: a self-closing window, a knife-wielding corpse, a furry hand holding a cleaver. She flees into the bathroom, where all the faucets are running, though she can't hear them. Now, this black-and-white film is red and white. Viscous red flows into the sink; the medicine-chest door swings out, displaying her death certificate. She turns slowly toward the bathtub. It is three-quarters filled with foaming red, out of which, to her strangling horror, a slick, red hand and arm rise, clutching. She faints, dies, and eventually yields up the Tingler to Price's scalpel.

Hammer and Castle might have spawned a cinematic bloodbath on their own; *The Tingler*, after all, portrays a literal one. But the commercial success of these and similar films—along with that of the 1955 French import *Les Diaboliques*, called *Diabolique* in the United States, apparently the premiere of the ghastly bathroom— was being watched by a third party, whose unexpected intervention would decisively shove horror movies in the direction of gore. Alfred Hitchcock had begun asking everyone around him "how profitable they thought a first-class, low-budget shocker by a major director might be." The answers were probably equivocal; the outcome, however, was *Psycho*, based on Robert Bloch's 1959 potboiler and released to American theaters in the summer of 1960. More has been written about Hitchcock than any other film direc- tor, and more about *Psycho* than any of his fifty other films. It is perhaps his greatest work and undoubtedly a landmark in the history of movies. In the history of scary entertainment, it is an extreme rarity: a single entry that summed up nearly everything that had been done in the genre before, recast it, and sent it spinning into the future.

Psycho draws indirectly on the century-old tradition of horrid newspaper reporting: Bloch's novel had been inspired by the 1957 case of Ed Gein, a Wisconsin rustic who committed at least two murders, robbed graves, and inhabited a "house of horror" (as reporters called it) littered with skulls, tanned human skin, and other ghoulish playthings. Bloch buried his novel's link to the Gein case, and the film restored none of it. But the film's drably contem- porary black-and-white look—along with the announcement (pointless in the event) that it begins on Friday, December 11, at precisely 2:43 P.M.—gives it the you-are-there quality that sensa- tional journalism aims at. Into such a newsreelish world the Bateses' spooky house fits with remarkable smoothness. Gaunt and Victorian, it glowers down from a hill in the best Udolpho manner. The camera goes inside with ominous caution, exploring more deeply on each visit: first to the downstairs hall and a distant glimpse of the kitchen, then up the stairs (and down again), then into the bedrooms, finally to the cellar, where the worst horror waits.

Old and new coalesce everywhere in *Psycho*. The central gimmick, Norman Bates's identity with his mother, comes from Bloch,
who took it from *Dr. Jekyll and Mr. Hyde* and its many recyclings; it
hadn't been quite fresh when Stevenson used it in 1886. Bloch
gussied up the device with an overlay of street-corner Freudianism;
the film debunks Freud by squeezing him into the prosings of a
smug, callous psychiatrist who comes on near the end to dispel
shadows. Then the film undercuts him and Freud with shots of
Norman's staring, skull-like face and of a murder victim's car
(hacked, rotting corpse no doubt inside) being dredged from the
swamp where Norman tried to hide it forever. This, the film's final
scene, also completes a series of images—a flushing toilet, bloody
water swirling into a drain—that suggest fetid abysses everywhere,
drawing us irresistibly down.

It would be delightful to report that movies recycled Hitchcock's
genius. That, however, was inimitable. Instead, *Psycho*'s commercial success triggered a temporary boom in cinematic psychopaths
and a longer-lasting fashion for dwelling on the details of bloody
murder. There are only two murders in *Psycho*, and both are artfully
set up. But the artistry serves the single purpose of shocking and
disorienting the viewer, forcing him to watch what earlier films left
implied. The first and more famous murder, Janet Leigh's knifing in
a motel-room shower, shows the blade entering flesh in only one
split-second shot out of many. There is also implausibly little
blood, given the large-scale carnage apparently taking place. Blood
and the slashing blade are the scene's stars, however, ably abetted
by a madly jumping camera and Bernard Herrmann's piercing
music. Unlike the mild films to which decades of reviewers had
been applying the label "grand guignol," *Psycho* deserved it.

Hitchcock supervised the film's promotion masterfully, demon-
strating that he could beat Americans at their native game. During
shooting, he milked considerable publicity from a policy that for-
bade visitors on the set; in theaters, no one was supposed to be
admitted after the film had begun. And in the ads it was "Alfred
Hitchcock's *Psycho*," capitalizing on a name far more familiar to
Americans than that of any actor in it. *Psycho* was not a teenpic;
though shot on a low budget, it had what passed in Hollywood for
class. Because Hitchcock was a first-rate director, he seemed to
give permission for lesser lights to indulge in unlimited blood. The

film's popularity seemed to prove that the world's movie audiences lusted for just that. During the next two decades, moralists and would-be censors grew steadily more alarmed over the tidal wave of gore that *Psycho* unleashed. But that, too, like everything else in scary fiction's history, had happened before.

Fear is the same. (STILL FROM *The Evil Dead,* © 1983 NEW LINE CINEMA CORP. ALL RIGHTS RESERVED.)

8

Splat!

2000 MANIACS

After *Psycho*, bloody cinematic hell broke loose all over the world. Predictably, the least inventive entrants in the new horror sweepstakes came from established American studios, which sought to batten on Hitchcock's success with a horde of rip-offs. The most blatant was *Homicidal* (1961), produced and directed by William Castle. The gimmick this time was the "fright break," a one-minute pause before the supposedly unbearable climax, when patrons could get their money back if they had the good sense to flee. In 1962, *What Ever Happened to Baby Jane?* continued the lunatic fad and spun off a new one for the dubious spectacle of aging female stars in grotesque roles; the same producers also turned out *Hush . . . Hush, Sweet Charlotte* (1964) and *What Ever Happened to Aunt Alice?* (1969). Within seven years, Bette Davis, Joan Crawford, Olivia de Havilland, Mary Astor, Geraldine Page, Ruth Gordon, and Mildred Dunnock had all done goosefleshy stints. Davis and Crawford stuck with the genre for years thereafter; it became, indeed, the final phase of Crawford's long career. She went on to appear in *Strait-Jacket* (1963) and *I Saw What You*

Did (1965), both directed by Castle, as well as *Berserk!* (1967), in which, as a circus ringmistress, she showed off her improbably shapely legs.

Though they were certainly tacky enough, these films solicited mainstream patronage and remained inexplicit about the gore they relentlessly implied. In Britain, Hammer showed less restraint. That studio became the most assiduous recycler of *Psycho*, grinding out *Taste of Fear* (1961, released in the United States as *Scream of Fear*), *Maniac* (1963), *Paranoiac* (1963), *Nightmare* (1964), and *Hysteria* (1964). In 1965, Hammer joined the over-the-hill-star game by casting Bette Davis in *The Nanny* and Tallulah Bankhead in *Fanatic*; American moviegoers saw the latter as *Die! Die! My Darling*. Except for *Fanatic*, Hammer's *Psycho* copies were filmed in black and white, like the original. During the same years, the studio went on manufacturing and exporting—much to the benefit of the British film industry—its trademark blend of colorful decor and decorous bloodshed. *Dracula, Prince of Darkness* (1965), *Dracula Has Risen from the Grave* (1968), *Taste the Blood of Dracula* (1969), and *The Scars of Dracula* (1970), all starring Christopher Lee, brought the Count back again and again; *The Evil of Frankenstein* (1964), *Frankenstein Created Woman* (1966), and *Frankenstein Must Be Destroyed* (1969), all with Peter Cushing, kept on remaking the Monster.

There would be more of both and other horrors besides, including a trilogy of films vaguely based on Le Fanu's "Carmilla" that brought bare-breasted women into the formula, along with lesbian overtones. In 1973, Hammer dropped out of the horror industry, partly on account of Terence Fisher's death and Lee's refusal to don a cape again after *The Satanic Rites of Dracula*. But many of Hammer's later films show signs of the imaginative exhaustion that seems eventually to grip all contestants on the horror field. This time around, weariness took less than a decade to come on. In the 1958 *Dracula*, for instance, Lee had been scary because of his blood-smeared mouth and brutal stride, which made Lugosi look dainty. Ten years later, in *Dracula Has Risen*, these features possessed no novelty, and Anthony Hinds's screenplay further denatured Lee's Count by making him spend most of the film vainly attempting to get back into his own castle. In a worn-out hunt for newness, Dracula had been deprived of his Gothic arches, a fatal mistake.

By 1973, Hammer horror was a familiar style; the development hamstrung Hammer but had already spurred on imitators. Between 1960 and 1964, Roger Corman directed what he would later call his "Poe cycle," eight films very loosely based on Poe's inescapable tales. Corman, the perpetrator of *It Conquered the World*, had been cranking out amazingly inexpensive drive-in fare since his producer's debut with *The Monster from the Ocean Floor* in 1954. His Poe films were cheap, too, though they looked expensive; most of them owed little to their reputed source beyond a title and the germ of an idea. Corman turned Poe's stories back into the run-of-the-mill pulp they sprang from, filling in backgrounds and explaining motivation in wholly conventional ways. *House of Usher* (1960), for example, transformed Poe's nameless narrator into a handsome love interest for Madeline; it also offered a laborious explanation of how a centuries-old mansion had ended up in Massachusetts (shipped there from England, stone by stone). As in Hammer's films, however, what mattered in Corman's Poe was the look, not the logic.

Despite *Psycho*'s precedent, the splintered movie audience continued to break up into smaller and smaller segments. For more than a decade, the principal audience for "horror films," in the United States and Western Europe, remained adolescent; in the United States, the main showplace was drive-in theaters, where films vied for attention with popcorn ads and backseat fumbling. Horror movies that aimed at this market and its international counterparts could be made cheaply by independent producers; they required no big-name stars or famous directors, and they could be dubbed into any number of languages for worldwide distribution. Since nobody cared about the films' integrity, they could also be shortened or lengthened to suit the tastes of particular audiences. And their titles could be changed at will, not only from language to language but also from release to release. Some version of a single film might end up being shown under as many as a dozen different names.

A typical case is a pair of Italian-American horrors shown at American drive-ins during the summer of 1966 (twenty years later, they were packaged together, complete with refreshment plugs, for video mavens). *Il Boia Scarlatto* had played in Britain as *The Crimson Executioner*, a fairly close translation. Italian audiences, however, might also have seen it as *Il Castello di Artena* (The Castle of Artena); English aliases included *The Red Hangman*, *The Scarlet Hangman*, and the drive-in title, *Bloody Pit of Horror*. Its companion began as *Cinque Tombes per un Medium* and arrived in dubbed English, literally, as *Five Graves for a Medium*. But it was also called *Coffin of Terror*, *The Tombs of Horror*, and, as *Bloody Pit*'s running mate, *Terror Creatures from the Grave*. The director of both films, Massimo Pupillo, chose to blame *Bloody Pit*'s direction on "Max Hunter" and that of *Terror Creatures* on "Ralph Zucker," under which name he distributed both and acted a small role in *Bloody Pit*. For English release, most of the other Italian actors also assumed distinctly non-Italian names. And the films' lengths varied by several minutes, depending on where they were shown.

Movies like these defy ordinary analysis, which depends on at least some certainty as to the name of what's being analyzed, who made and appeared in it, and which scenes belong to it or do not. Such minor pitfalls, however, have not discouraged latter-day film scholars. *The Encyclopedia of Horror Movies*, for instance, waxes dire over the spectacle of Hungarian muscleman Mickey Hargitay in *Bloody Pit*:

> the viewer is invited to derive pleasure from contemplating the male body but the trouble such homo-erotic pleasures provoke for the supposedly macho viewer is diverted towards sadistic aggression against women who thus come to function as detour and safety valve within a circuit of homosexual narcissism established between the male viewer and Mr. Universe.

It's doubtful that this grim invitation would have meant much in the back of a '66 Chevy. *Il Boia*'s distributors had a better idea when they passed up any attempt to individualize that film or its companion. Instead, they tacked on purely generic buzzwords: "bloody," "horror," "terror," "grave." Dozens of other movies could have borne the same titles equally well; at the drive-in, all that counted was the familiar chill those words promised.

Such films do have individual features, of course; *Terror Creatures* even shows some flashes of style. But they make full sense only in the context of their genre, from which they dared not deviate too far. Their devices—dungeons, graveyards, maniacs, the living dead—are quite traditional and for the most part conventionally handled. Many Italian and Spanish horrors of the sixties and seventies are so old fashioned in this regard that they look like southern Europe's long-delayed revenge on Mrs. Radcliffe for setting her horrid novels there. Many are set in the north, like Mario Bava's *La Maschera del Demonio* (1960), best known in English as *Black Sunday*. Bava returned to spooky Saxon country several times, as did other Italian directors like Riccardo Freda and Antonio Margheriti. Recycling Hitchcock, Hammer, and Corman, their films also dug far into the past, dredging up scenes and character types that seemed to cast on motorized teenagers the same spell Catherine Morland had felt nearly two centuries before.

From 1960 through 1990, the sheer number of self-styled horror films grew so enormous that it's nearly impossible to trace any significant trends or developments among them. I'm inclined to agree with David Cronenberg, who remarked in connection with "splatter" films (of which he has directed several), "there's really nothing that new in them." Fashions have come and gone, but the stock types of horror now seem fixed, as does horror's source— the fear, in Cronenberg's words, of "the human body and the fact of aging and death and disease." The only clear development that all observers find in the last three decades of horror films is a movement toward extreme explicitness of bloodshed and mutilation. There's nothing new in this, either, except the special-effects technology that produces it, and even the technology has precursors in the stagecraft of the Grand Guignol and nineteenth-century melodrama.

But, unlike the mass of imitative horrors, the advance of gore threw up some landmarks, films that seemed to make a difference and form a chain of cause and effect. Hammer and Hitchcock came first, followed by *Blood Feast* (1963), *Night of the Living Dead* (1968) and its sequel *Dawn of the Dead* (1978), along with *The Texas Chainsaw Massacre* (1974) and perhaps a few others, like the infamous *Snuff* (1976). Certainly by 1980, what John McCarty calls "the last taboo of the screen" had been shattered for good: Gore was everywhere in movies, censors and parents were up in arms, and horror films had brought the whole mess on. The trouble with this familiar scenario is that, of course, it's much too simple. And, like everything else in the horror field, it was a repetition.

THE NEW PORNOGRAPHY

Time: 1954. Place: Anytown, U.S.A. Mrs. Jones tries to follow the advice of "child-psychiatry and child-guidance experts." She's been worrying about the effect of comic books on her seven-year-old son, Bobby; now she'll share the experience by reading one aloud to him. She selects a comic that must be intended for children because it sports "full-page advertisements showing forty-four smiling and happy children's faces." She begins with the cover, *The Battle of the Monsters!*:

> She describes the cover to her son. It shows an enormous bestial colored human being who is brandishing a club and carrying off a scared blonde little boy in knee pants. Then she goes on to the first story:
> "LOOK!! Their bodies are CRUMBLING AWAY!!"
> "KILL! K—AARGHH!"
> "YAIEE-E-E!!"
> Mamma has some difficulty in pronouncing these speeches. But her difficulties increase when in the course of the story a man encounters a big serpent: "WH-AWWOGG-HH-H!.! YAAGH-H-H-H!!" . . .
> Mrs. Jones thinks perhaps she had better switch to another story. So she turns a few pages and begins "Whip of Death!"
> "REVENGE!"
> "AIEEEEEEEEEEEEEEEEEEE!!" . . .
> Mrs. Jones gives up.

The comic book may have been real. But Mamma Jones and Bobby lived only in the imagination of Fredric Wertham, M.D., who brought them before the world in his 1954 best-seller, *Seduc-*

tion of the Innocent. Since 1946, Wertham had been studying and publicizing the havoc wrought by comic books on American youth. His articles had appeared in magazines like *Ladies' Home Journal* and *Reader's Digest*; *Time* had run a feature on his anti-comics campaign, and he'd been invited to serve as psychiatric consultant to the U.S. Senate Committee to Investigate Organized Crime. Judging from *Seduction of the Innocent*, Wertham was a frustrated man, despite his fame. The committee had judged comics harmless; the New York State Assembly had voted to enact a "crime-comic-book control bill," but Governor Thomas E. Dewey vetoed it. "Superman comes in many guises," muttered Wertham.

Forty years later, that remark makes little sense. It didn't make a great deal of sense in 1954 either, though it pointed to one of the many targets of Wertham's assault on the garish pamphlets that, according to him, were rapidly transforming America's children into murderers, drug dealers, and perverts. His gripe against Superman came from the equation of the caped crusader with the Nazi Aryan ideal, and that with Friedrich Nietzsche's *Übermensch*, literally translatable as "superman." In children who devoured tales about Superman, Captain Marvel, and their ilk, wrote Wertham, "there is an exact parallel to the blunting of sensibilities in the direction of cruelty that has characterized a whole generation of central European youth fed on the Nietzsche-Nazi myth of the exceptional man who is beyond good and evil." Wertham also had it in for Batman and Robin. "It is like a wish dream of two homosexuals living together," he said; "the Batman type of story helps to fixate homoerotic tendencies by suggesting the form of an adolescent-with-adult or Ganymede-Zeus type of love-relationship." Wonder Woman, "the Lesbian counterpart of Batman," was worse yet: "For boys, Wonder Woman is a frightening image. For girls she is a morbid ideal."

Wertham wasn't stupid, and not all his targets look silly forty years later. In retrospect, however, he seems typical of the 1950s, that curious episode of American history in which the most powerful nation the world had ever known fell into history's grandest fit of paranoid dementia. Wertham also joined the long line of doom mongers who, like Anthony Comstock fifty years before him, foresaw America's imminent collapse thanks to the debasement of her youth. Comstock's arch-vice was masturbation; Freudian Wertham wasted no ire on that old bugaboo. Instead, he ranted about *"the new pornography*, the glorification of violence and sadism." He saw violence and sadism everywhere in comic books, as well as in the delinquency of American children, which he documented with scores of lurid examples. The connection between the two, for Wertham, was direct and obvious.

Wertham's arguments are easy to pick apart, especially since the national debacle he predicted failed to occur on schedule. But the fears he expressed were genuine and not confined to him. Local citizens' groups had been agitating against comics long before Wertham hogged the limelight, staging public bonfires that recalled Nazi Germany far more vividly than Superman did. The magnitude of the comic-book craze, and its extraordinary growth, were scary in themselves. The first comic books in full color had appeared only in the early 1930s, recycling strips from Sunday newspapers. By 1948, Wertham estimated, about sixty million comics were being bought each month in the United States; the figure had risen to ninety million per month by 1954. The number is astonishing, given that in 1950 the country's total population was about 150 million. But later estimates range much higher: Comic-book historian Mike Benton puts the 1954 figure at closer to 150 million per month.

Later authorities disagree on what proportion of this vast heap actually went to children. It's likely that adults bought a far larger percentage than the crusaders recognized or the adults in question cared to admit. For Wertham and his sympathizers, however, comic-book reading was a children's disease. At a dime apiece, comics lay within the purchasing power of most American children; children also collected and traded them through an underground network that infuriated parents who wished to regard their offspring as wholly subservient to grown-up control. "The new pornography" aside, Wertham's most horrifying revelation was that America's children formed a tribe that had eluded parental surveillance until he exposed it. Naturally enough, the aim of this pint-sized conspiracy was wholesale debauchery and mayhem. Since long before Comstock's day, American parents have feared and mistrusted their children; Wertham seemed to prove how right the parents were.

Wertham adhered thoroughly to the American tradition of anti-smut crusading in both his rhetoric and his tactics. In substance, however, he broke with tradition. Despite his outrage at the big, pointy breasts of comic-book women (and the domestic bliss of Batman and Robin), Wertham's "new pornography" was not sexual; it was violent. Sex arose frequently, but only when it had been yoked with violence in what he called "sadism." Wertham exempted "harmless animal comics"—though there was no shortage of violence in the likes of Mickey Mouse, Bugs Bunny, and the Ducks, Donald and Daffy—but he saw sadism virtually everywhere else, in Westerns, jungle adventures, cops-and-robbers, even teen romances. He had rather little to say about "horror comics," lumping them with the rest as "a refined or rather debased form of crime comics," his catchall category. But it was on horror comics that Wertham's crusade had its most powerful effect.

They were, as Wertham noted, a "recent" development. Indeed, the horror-comic subgenre was hardly five years old when *Seduction of the Innocent* appeared. Thanks partly to Wertham, its days were already numbered. *Eerie*, which premiered in 1946, may have been, as Ron Goulart calls it, the "first out-and-out horror comic book," but it didn't last. In 1948, ads for *Adventures into the Unknown* cried, "For the first time—a magazine about GHOSTS!"—as if *Eerie* had never existed and the world were pining. Horror comics took off only in 1950, with surprising suddenness and volume. In that year alone, Entertaining Comics (E.C.) introduced *The Crypt of Terror* (soon retitled *Tales from the Crypt*), *The Haunt of Fear*, *The Vault of Horror*, *Weird Fantasy*, and *Weird Science*. Imitators sprang up like toadstools after rain: *Tomb of Terror*, *Weird Horrors*, *Weird Mysteries*, and many more. Overnight, it seemed, the corner drugstore had been drenched in gore and grue.

The phenomenon is extraordinary and hard to account for. Explicit bloodshed, along with the familiar horror-movie crew of vampires, werewolves, and ghouls, had shown up in comic books before. But now there were shelfloads of comics devoted exclusively to horror; the entire horrid warehouse got ransacked from top to bottom in a single raid. Goulart suggests that the horror-comic explosion came as a response to the very crusade that finally shut horror down. For artists and writers, says Goulart, it was a matter of "testing the limits," matching outrage with outrageousness until one side had to give in. Very often, horror comics convey the sense that their creators were replying to one another, not to any demand or desire in their readers. The heyday of horror comics also fits neatly between the petering out of horror movies in the late 1940s and their revival in the mid-1950s. It's as if, dead on the screen, fear rose again at the drugstore.

Horror comics featured full, bright color; blood was red and rot was green or purple, as they had never been in the few horror films that gave glimpses of such things. Cheap paper and (usually) small pictures made this foray into explicitness far less visceral than even the restrained Technicolor horrors that Hammer studios would soon provide. The manic style of many horror-comic artists, however, lent their strongest work a near-hysterical pace that was frightening all by itself. Scenes came at the reader from weird angles; figures in grotesquely contorted postures forced still pictures to portray frantic movement; bodies and body parts burst out of the frame, often intruding into other pictures. None of these techniques was new—hallucinated images had been a mainstay of comic strips since they began, in the late nineteenth century—but the rubric "horror" seemed to urge artists on to effects that were more cinematic than even the boldest moviemakers had tried for. Theirs was an art of fragmentation, disorientation, and delirium, a gross misfit in postwar America.

It was also the most hidebound, backward-looking art America or the world had ever seen. For their starting point, horror comics leapt straight into the eighteenth century, reviving the Graveyard chill nearly intact. From there, they went on to suck up and spew out virtually every variant of the horrid that had been devised in the intervening two hundred years. And they completed Monk Lewis's errand by driving horrid clichés to the ghastly limit they had always implied. Wertham believed that "crime comics" taught American children how to commit murder, but E.C.'s *Crypts* and *Vaults* gave them better instruction in obsolete burial practices. Precious few American children in 1954 had entered a crypt or a burial vault; fewer yet had seen a rotting corpse. E.C., however, could rely on a specific response to even the names of such things. In block capitals on their front covers, E.C. comics proclaimed it: HORROR, TERROR, and FEAR.

Along with stories about rotting corpses, *The Haunt of Fear*, *Tales from the Crypt*, and *The Vault of Horror* employed a trio of rather moldy hosts. The Crypt-Keeper, The Vault-Keeper, and The Old Witch introduced many stories and often came back on the last page to tie up loose ends. In this, they imitated radio voices like "Raymond" (Paul McGrath), whose sepulchral tones greeted listeners to the suspense series "Inner Sanctum" between 1941 and 1952. Alfred Hitchcock would imitate them all on television's "Alfred Hitchcock Presents" (1955–1962), and the device has been recycled frequently since then. E.C.'s hosts, however, spouted a distinctive jargon that would prove hard to copy.

Here, for instance, is the Old Witch, welcoming readers to a 1953 issue of *The Haunt of Fear*:

Hee, hee! GREETINGS, MY FINE FETTERED FIENDS. Time for another FOUL FEAST in THE HAUNT OF FEAR. This is your SHRIEK-CHEF, your DELIRIUM-DIETICIAN, THE OLD WITCH, ready with my bubbling cauldron filled with my latest REEKING RECIPE. So relax on that MARBLE SETTEE there and I'll BEGIN my MUCK-MAG by feeding you the TASTY TALE OF TERROR I call . . . "WISH YOU WERE HERE."

The story, drawn by Graham Ingels, turns out to be an arch twist on that anthologist's favorite "The Monkey's Paw"; the characters even discuss Jacobs's tale and name its author. But literary knowledge doesn't stop Enid Logan from using a "strange little jade statuette" to wish her husband back to life. Jason, unfortunately, has already been embalmed. Revived, he suffers horribly from the formaldehyde flowing through his veins. In answer to his frantic pleas, Enid hacks him into pieces, but even when there are "a million" of them, "each section still moved and jerked and quivered with life." The men in the white coats arrive to find Enid, in the penultimate panel, huge knife in hand, crouched madly above Jason's open coffin, which overflows with drippy, brownish-orange stuff.

"Wish You Were Here" is a typical horror-comic item, both in

its literary source and in the gruesome spin it puts on borrowed
ideas. The story steadily builds tension toward over-the-top ghastliness at the end; it is also ferociously moralistic, punishing the
transgressors (in this case both Jason and Enid) without mercy.
But it comes framed by the Old Witch, who returns in the last
panel to make a few more wisecracks. Her standard E.C. host's
fondness for silly puns and strung-out alliteration serves, to some
degree, the old purpose of comic relief. She and her companions,
however, are no bumbling cops or bug-eyed servants. If they
appeared within an E.C. story, these charnel-house refugees
would be objects of horror; as its framers, they ooze chumminess,
as if addressing fellow members of a secret society. Instead of an
antidote to horror, E.C.'s hosts offer something better: assurance
that horror *is* comical, a vastly amusing in-joke that only an idiot
(or a literal-minded adult) would take seriously.

There has never been a more literal mind than Fredric
Wertham's. He missed the horror-comic joke, of course, but he
dimly caught its characteristic tone, which he described as
"smart-alecky cynical." He wasn't far wrong. Horror comics invited their readers to giggle at drawings of extreme gore and rot
simply because they were extreme—and also because they were
drawings, not the real things at all. Where Wertham saw blue-
prints for mayhem, horror comics' intended readers found the
ultimate defense against real fear. It was a childish defense, no
doubt, and Wertham had little patience with childishness, especially from children. But it worked for grown-ups equally well:
Fear of the body's fragility and decay acknowledges no age limit.
In spite of Wertham, the horror-comic giggle would enjoy a long,
rich life. First, however, it had to die.

THE GORY TRUTH

Late in 1954, the boom in horror comics came to an abrupt end,
snuffed out by the comics' own producers. Though no legal action
of any magnitude had yet been taken against them, comic-book
publishers had grown skittish about attacks from Wertham and
others. Fearing censorship, they censored themselves, forming

the Comics Magazine Association of America in September of that year. The following month, the association issued a new code of self-taming. It read, in badly punctuated part, "No comic magazine shall use the word horror or terror in its title. . . . All scenes of horror, excessive bloodshed, gory or gruesome crimes, depravity, lust, sadism, masochism shall not be permitted. . . . Scenes dealing with, or instruments associated with walking dead, or torture shall not be used." A seal of approval was affixed to all comic books that passed muster; if they were not already, as Wertham maintained, a child-centered medium, the Code's enforcement made them one. The era of Jughead and Veronica had dawned, with a vengeance.

The death of horror comics, although it was self-inflicted, marked the first large-scale censorship of any medium on grounds of violence rather than sex. Movies, of course, had been submitting themselves for decades to such watchdogs as the British Board of Film Censors, formed in 1912, which began by stamping films either U ("universal") or A ("adult"). In 1932, H (for "horror") was added, thanks to the new onslaught of ghastliness out of Hollywood. Submission, however, was voluntary, and the ratings did not restrict attendance; they served merely as guidance for cautious parents. Five years later, when the first wave of Hollywood horror had passed, Britain imposed a moratorium on the import or production of H-rated films. It lasted till the end of World War II; in 1951, H was swallowed up in the larger class X, which compelled theaters to admit only patrons older than sixteen. Hollywood abided by its toothless Production Code till 1968, when an American version of ratings arrived: G ("general"), PG ("parental guidance suggested"), R ("restricted"), and a weakened form of the British X that let in no one under seventeen who was unaccompanied by somebody who claimed to be the child's parent or guardian.

The American system grew more baroque with time. In 1984, PG-13 joined the ratings roster, with little effect except to locate Hollywood's due date for puberty between ages thirteen and sixteen. In 1990, X got recoded as NC-17 ("no children under 17 admitted"), allowing films like *Henry and June* to obtain general distribution free of the stigma that had meant "pornography" for more than twenty years. In this, Hollywood imitated the Catholic Legion of Decency, whose original classifications of A, B, and C ("unobjectionable," "morally objectionable in part for all," and "condemned") suffered such balkanization that by 1970, when A alone sported four subclasses, the system had become virtually meaningless. Films of all sorts were variously clipped and trimmed under pressure from these and other agencies, but on the whole they had little effect, except to allow the eventual release of "re-stored" versions. Only in the case of horror comics did moral anxiety succeed in wiping out an entire genre.

Though all but the most infantile comics felt the wound, some of Wertham's "crime" varieties struggled on in attenuated forms. Superman thrived, as did the domestic duo Batman and Robin; William M. Gaines, publisher of E.C., forged ahead with *Mad*, which turned the Old Witch's wiseass gaze on the whole of American culture. "Horror" comics, however, had been denounced by name, and they disappeared. Deliberately ephemeral, meant to last no longer than the month it would take for the next issue to arrive, burned in bales by anxious parents, they soon grew scarce. In this way, too, they harked back to the throwaway novels that had chilled Catherine Morland. But the shrunken span of twentieth-century memory granted horror comics a gentler fate. In a sense, Wertham's nightmare of an America crawling with weirdos came exactly true; an entire generation had been "warped" by horror comics, as the victims would phrase it when they grew up. And some of them would bring their old victimizers, now turned "classic," back from the grave.

Stephen King, for example, was born in 1947, just in time to have reached an impressionable age when horror comics flowered. "I cut my teeth," he wrote thirty years later,

on William B. [*sic*] Gaines's horror comics—*Weird Science*, *Tales from the Crypt*, *Tales from the Vault* [*sic*]—plus all the Gaines imitators. . . . These horror comics of the fifties still sum up for me the epitome of horror, that emotion of fear that underlies terror, an emotion which is slightly less fine, because it is not entirely of the mind. Horror also invites a physical reaction by showing us something which is physically wrong.

King's memory was a bit faulty; he was also trying to distinguish between "horror" and "terror," a task that better heads than his had undertaken two centuries before him, with small success. Yet he remembered E.C. comics clearly enough to summarize two typical tales, and he placed their characteristic effect where it belonged, at the deep end, "the gag reflex of revulsion."

The influence of horror comics on King's own work is pervasive and obvious, especially in some of his short stories. But it is a diffuse influence, depending more on the recollection of a feeling than on any particular source. Starting with *Carrie* in 1974, and still gushing forth, King's novels all feature E.C. moments, which reviewers have sometimes, mistakenly, called "grand guignol." Those moments are few—like a horror-comics artist, King leads up to them slowly—but they exploit the traditional reservoirs of fear that E.C. made grossly explicit: bloodshed and bodily rot. King does not go in for the Old Witch's juvenile jokiness. He relies instead on what he calls "that comic-book *extravagance* of horror" to push matters over the line to where "it all starts to become rather funny." Combined with the lunch-counter gab of his prose, the excess of King's horror scenes perfectly conveys the message that the emotions he triggers are meant to be savored while they last, then wrapped up and shelved till the next call.

King advertised his fondness for E.C. by writing the screenplay for *Creepshow* (1982), an anthology of five short episodes that mimicked comic-book horrors. *Creepshow* wasn't the first movie to recycle E.C.; Hammer's chief British rival, Amicus, got there first with *Tales from the Crypt* (1972) and *Vault of Horror* (1973). If closeness of imitation gauges homage, the Amicus films were far more reverent, since along with their titles they borrowed E.C.'s stories, including "Wish You Were Here" (already "The Monkey's Paw" had won the award for most-recycled item in the horrid warehouse). But *Creepshow* paid homage of a more elevated order. King's screenplay didn't simply copy or adapt E.C.; it aimed to invoke, in new guises, the feeling King remembered, that adolescent delight in horror carried to a gross extreme. Its most faithful embodiment came in "They're Creeping Up on You," which displayed a roomful of two-inch cockroaches, crawling all over (and out of) villainous E. G. Marshall.

Creepshow—along with its 1987 sequel, *Creepshow 2*—was directed by George A. Romero, another grown-up admirer of E.C.'s prepubescent chills. "I think a great part of my aesthetic in the genre," Romero pompously began in an interview with Paul R. Gagne, "was born out of E.C. rather than movies." He soon slipped back into the gee-whiz idiom that both Romero and King like to put on: "The effects sucked. The E.C.s, on the other hand, were nitty-gritty, there was a lot going on in each frame, the stories were great, and the effects were sensational!" Romero had founded his horror-movie reputation with *Night of the Living Dead*, first released in 1968. The film's extraordinary success— made outside Pittsburgh for about $114,000, it had earned more than $30 million worldwide by 1987—seemed to mark a turning point in horror by displaying not only severed limbs and spilled innards but also cannibal zombies munching them. *Night* was not the most explicitly gory film ever made, but though it began on the lowly drive-in circuit, alongside Herschell Gordon Lewis's blood-soaked extravaganzas, it ascended before long into general distribution and critical esteem.

The film's success allowed Romero to finance two sequels, *Dawn of the Dead* (1978) and *Day of the Dead* (1985), which served up bloodshed in full color and took it to unprecedented extremes—unprecedented, that is, except in the horror comics of thirty years before. Both were released without ratings (dreaded X's would have been certain), and both made a great deal of money. As of 1987, *Dawn* alone had brought in $55 million. For many, perhaps most moviegoers, however, these films and their scores of imitators are simply unwatchable. Romero's, at least, are far from witless; they do not go in for nuances of acting or atmosphere—indeed, for nuances of any kind—but on their own horror-comic terms they are coherent, even polished products. They also contain an element of social satire that has made them respectable prey for strong-stomached academic cineastes. Yet their most distinctive feature, the primary focus of their attention and presumably their viewers' as well, excludes a larger audience than it welcomes.

That focus is gore, the ever more inventive rending and tearing of human flesh. For literal-minded fools—among whom, regret-fully, I include myself—the spectacle of heads split open, innards ripped out, and livers flying through the air is intolerable, because we cannot resist the illusion that such atrocities are really taking place. We know, of course, that they are not, that these make-believe orgies of pain and death exact no real penalty; they're only movies, after all. Confronted with all other transactions, on page, stage, or screen, we retain our critical faculties. We can evaluate the style, the performances, the direction, any aspect of artfulness; we remain effortlessly balanced between belief in the fiction and detachment from it. When a head explodes, however, or an arm gets yanked off, tendons dangling, our detachment shrinks to zero. We fail the Old Witch's test; we are hidiots.

We form the majority, perhaps. But, at the end of the twentieth century, fortunes can be made by persuading a tiny portion of the world to fork over, individually, tiny sums. Despite exceptions like King's novels and some of Romero's films, this has been the nature of most scary entertainments during the last two decades—specialized products aimed at audiences that know what to expect and what is expected of them. Particularly in movies, horror has become a narrower ghetto than ever. Since the days of Catherine Morland and Isabella Thorpe, scary entertainment has tended to foster coteries and in-groups; patrons of the Grand Guignol, fans of pulp magazines, and aficionados of horror comics also formed voluntary ghettos. Recent horror shows, however, have gone beyond these precedents by not just excluding but aggressively repelling the uninitiated. At bottom, the cat-and-mouse game remains what it always was, entertainers and audiences squared off in a battle of nerves. Only now, thirty years after *Psycho* shocked the world with a few gouts of chocolate syrup and a flashing blade, the game has taken on an air of "can you top this?" played with bleeding body parts.

From *Psycho* through *Blood Feast* and *Night of the Living Dead* to *Day of the Dead* (beyond which, in sheer emergency-room explicitness, it seems impossible to go), the moviemakers' gambit has been to render mutilation and rot ever more immediate. On their side, moviegoers have had to steel themselves increasingly against technical wizardry, countering each new foray into apparent realism with the assertion that the proceedings are pure artifice. The outcome has been the glorification of special-effects artists like Tom Savini, who worked on both *Dawn* and *Day of the*

Dead. (Quite appropriately, Savini also directed the 1990 color remake of *Night.*) Among Savini's most highly touted achievements is a moment in *Day,* when a zombie, breast and belly cut open by inquisitive scientists, rises from his bed and turns toward the viewer. Gagne describes the moment in appropriate terms:

> Savini and crew did the effect using a table with a lowered "pit" section cut into the middle. When the person playing the zombie (Mike Trcic) got on the table, his chest and torso would sink onto a platform below the pit, while his head and legs remained up on the level surface. The resulting "dip" where his chest and torso would be if he were lying flat was built back up with a false, hollow "chest cavity" made of foam latex, which was glued into place on his real chest. The chest cavity was painted black inside to give it the illusion of depth and was then filled with a variety of animal entrails . . . and chunks of foam latex "flesh." Trcic simply turned over to spill the guts onto the floor; the camera angle hid his real body and the hole in the table.

So the nausea a squeamish viewer feels becomes "nausea" for those who play the game correctly.

From the mid-1970s onward, horror films have cultivated a kind of audience well versed in artificial mayhem, willing to endure the utmost that technology can muster in order to rise above it with a laugh. The hilarity that prevails at showings of the most grotesquely ghastly films has shocked some observers, who mistake it for callousness in the face of carnage. In fact, it is nothing of the sort. You laugh—if you can—in delight at the sheer excess of an art devoted to nothing but outdoing itself, and also in triumph at your own ability to resist such clever illusions. The response is rather sophisticated, since it entails gauging the emotion aimed at, perhaps even feeling it to some degree, then stepping back to seal it up in quotes and get free of it, all in an instant. But today's horror-film audiences, predominantly under thirty-five, possess far more sophistication about images than they are usually given credit for. They have been raised on television and movies, movies on television, TV movies, and the mass recycling brought on by home video. They may be next to illiterate, but they know artifice when they see it, and they see it everywhere.

QUOTH THE MAVEN

Excessive gore is generally taken to be the hallmark of the last two decades' horror movies; it has become conventional in them and may already be suffering the senility that inevitably overcomes conventions. Gore, however, is not essential to horror in any genre, nor did horror films singlehandedly pioneer it in movies. During the sixties and seventies, the most widely publicized blood was shed in films like *Bonnie and Clyde* (1967), *The Wild Bunch* (1969), and *The Godfather* (1972); since then, adventure films of every sort have steadily heightened the level of bloodshed, until the lily-livered moviegoer ends up staying home most nights. The process has run parallel with a trend in all media toward increased explicitness, including sex, language, and sheer wonder as well as violence.

After 1970, pornography (not Wertham's "new" kind but the familiar sexual variety) made rapid advances in both vividness and breadth of distribution. By 1980, thanks to videotape, it had acquired unprecedented immediacy of picture and sound; it had also, thanks to the VCR, become a familiar guest in many ordinary homes. The same development occurred in nature photography, which achieved pictures of animal behavior (sometimes sexual, rather often violent) that would have been unthinkable a decade earlier. In the 1980s, TV cable connections, stereophonic sound, high-resolution picture tubes, and videodiscs all worked toward making that medium ever clearer and more explicit. Compact discs did the same for music, virtually annihilating LP records along the way. Pocket-sized tape players allowed their owners to carry easy listening through hostile crowds; cellular telephones abolished the isolation of plane and car trips; fax machines let documents cross the world in minutes. And all these devices continue to race after sharper pictures, more lifelike sound, every trait of being there for real.

This has been the double route, for at least the past 150 years, of what's often called communications—toward steadily sharper detail and ever wider accessibility. "Communications," however, is a misleading label, despite its enshrinement in college departments. The word suggests that two human beings or groups have come together for the purpose of conveying information from one to the other, perhaps back and forth. One may argue about cellular phones and faxes, but for the most part the purpose of recent technology seems to be not conveyance but the presentation of images, establishing a relation not of dialogue or even sender and recipient, but rather of entertainer and audience. At the end of the twentieth century, when images of unprecedented explicitness had become commonplace in middle-class homes all over the world, American television belatedly acknowledged the fact by coining the word *"infotainment,"* an ugly but accurate name for news shows that simulate on-the-spot reportage. The heightened gore in the last two decades of horror films—and in film's pale copy, horror fiction—represents the genre's participation in a universal drive toward the realizing of images.

Despite the jitters of moralists, realism in gore has not led to widespread blood lust, or even to callousness, among those who consume a heavy diet of scary entertainment. Instead, film gore has become a carnival of technology, and its aficionados are likely to be experts in the manipulation of latex and computerized puppets. At least two large-circulation American magazines, *Cinefantastique* and *Fangoria*, are devoted to exploring the technical marvels of make-believe mayhem. Their pages are packed with about equal parts of breathless praise for the latest gory illusion and plaintive sighs that the thrill is gone. In a 1990 article recalling the ancient impact of *Night of the Living Dead*, Thomas Doherty struck a typical note: "when, gentle viewer," he archly inquired, "was the last time you were shocked—really freaked—by a scene of violence or grossness at the movies?" For most readers of *Cinefantastique*, the answer was probably: "A long time ago." And though they might have lamented their lost innocence, they had only acted out, in high-tech form, the same muffling of fear that Mrs. Radcliffe had offered her readers two centuries earlier, when she revealed that the worm-eaten corpse behind Udolpho's black veil was really made of wax.

The most remarkable feature of late-twentieth-century horror is not its gore but the tremendous inventiveness it manages to display while maniacally recycling a tiny roster of scenes and situations. For all its technological wonders, horror still depends on the old chill of the walking dead and their cobwebby precincts, along with their usually unexplained malice against the living. Vampires, werewolves, zombies, and ghouls predominate, along with the occasional homicidal maniac or nasty extraterrestrial. Indefatigably, they go on rising from graves, enduring weird transformations, and stalking frightened young women down dank corridors. Classics get dug up yet again—as in the 1990 film *Two Evil Eyes*, which dusted off Poe's "The Black Cat," "The Pit and the Pendulum," and "The Facts in the Case of M. Valdemar." *Two Evil Eyes* was directed by George A. Romero and Dario Argento, international grand middle-aged men of horror. It showed off special effects by the "King of Splatter," Tom Savini, including close-ups of a blade slicing through a naked woman's midriff. *That* had never been filmed before—but it was only more of the same, after all.

This is not to say that all recent horror films are just gorier repetitions, or that all who attend them feel the maven's ennui. But the years after 1970 saw a remarkable tightening of the bounds of the horror ghetto, along with the rise of a new kind of horror fan, one who makes a cult of the whole business and revels in arcane information that only fellow fans share. During the same period, of course, several mass-market films borrowed horror techniques and subjects: The list runs from *Rosemary's Baby* (1968), *Jaws* (1975), and *The Omen* (1976), with their various sequels, to *Alien* (1979) with *its* sequel, David Cronenberg's remake of *The Fly* (1987), and beyond. Deliberately serious directors, such as Brian De Palma and David Lynch, imported horror into films with artistic pretensions, including Lynch's *Blue Velvet* (1986) and *Wild at Heart* (1990), perhaps inuring high-minded moviegoers to matters they would have disdained if the vehicle had been *Bloodsucking Freaks* (1976). A few novelists also achieved mass success with straight-out horror: Stephen King became an institution, while Anne Rice, Clive Barker, and Peter Straub won critical recognition along with popularity.

As usual, despite its ghetto, horrid entertainment remained tied to culture at large, feeding it as well as battening on it. But horrid fictions have always been exceptionally conservative, even retrograde. At their origin, in the late eighteenth century, they were already nostalgic, harking back to a Gothic age grander and spookier than their own. Ever since, the past has always obsessed them. If they convey any lesson, it is that the past does not die, the dead are never really dead, and those who ignore this truth are doomed to enact it. Even the most nauseating latter-day ventures preserve the grim warning intact; for all their technological bravado, they form our closest link to the very past they seek to scare us with. Horrid conservatism has also led to the apparently endless recycling of a few scant materials, all assembled two hundred years ago. Since the lesson, apparently, can no longer be learned—since that unfortunate fact is what makes it frightening—horror fiction can neither die nor change except in the incidental ways its history shows. Because horror fiction's original and evidently permanent home is the vault, that uncanny place where the dead still lie in our imaginations even if we have incinerated them in fact, it is appropriate that horror fiction should itself become, figuratively, a chamber full of rotting corpses, none of which is dead.

The adulthood of the E.C. generation, the unleashing of cinematic gore by Hammer and *Psycho*, and the invention of the VCR conspired to turn horror fiction back on itself in a way that no genre, indeed nothing in human history, had ever known. Not only did every implication of horror now become possible; virtually every prior instance of it, in whatever form, also became present and available for working over. The archiving of horror had begun in the 1920s, with the arrival of horrid anthologies and the first scholarly inquiries into the primary horrors of the eighteenth century. From the twenties through the forties, film and radio solidified horror's typology: graveyard, haunted house, man-made monster, vampire, zombie, werewolf, ghoul, and homicidal lunatic. In the fifties, horror comics packaged these types in capsule form; then television brought the movies back, and both movies and television recycled them. When the VCR arrived, in the seventies, these media joined the printed word in a vast archive at the disposal of anyone with sufficient interest and money. Similar developments occurred throughout Western culture, of course: Our next age is the first in human history that will have all prior ages to gaze upon at will. But the horrid genre, as usual, has taken the lead when it comes to looking back. It has spawned a creature whom other genres envy and who foreshadows our future: the horror maven.

This character exists in various subspecies, though he is most likely to be male, between fifteen and forty-five years old, and American. To some degree, he is a by-product of the craze for nostalgia that plagues the United States in the last years of the twentieth century; he is also a kind of cultist or collector, what the eighteenth century called a virtuoso, a pedigree that leads back to Horace Walpole. The horrid virtuoso shares with Walpole a fondness for things that mainstream culture regards as trash or worse. Like any stamp or coin collector, perhaps most of all like a bibliophile, he loves to gather minutiae—the exact date when a film was released, for instance, or its precise original running time, or the trailer that announced its imminent arrival. And he has a mania for filmographies, bibliographies, discographies, any sort of list that can be quibbled about with fellow devotees.

The horror maven isn't quite an underground man, though the publications that cater to his tastes seldom show up on ordinary newsstands. Dozens of such magazines have appeared, some lasting only a couple of issues; many have been virtually single-handed efforts, like *Crow* (which apparently died in 1988), spawn of Bill Dale Mancinko's New Jersey–based brain. They range from the sniggering *Gore Gazette* to the far more sophisticated *Psychotronic Video*, launched in 1988 by Michael J. Weldon as a spin-off from his *Psychotronic Encyclopedia of Film*. Though "psychotronic" (Weldon's coinage) applies mainly to horror films, it can also be attached to movies featuring Hell's Angels, rebellious teens, and Annette Funicello, along with certain kinds of rock 'n' roll, science fiction, and exploitation—"projects of overall general weirdness," as a 1989 issue of *Psychotronic Video* sums it up. "Weird" counts among Weldon's favorite words—as it does for other mavens like King and Romero—along with "demented," "degenerate," "sick," and simply "bad." Like "psychotronic," which subsumes them all, these are terms of praise; they name not only things that high culture rejects but also whatever goes too far in any direction, especially toward ineptitude.

Similar standards govern the output of suppliers to the maven, most of which specialize in videotapes, though some sell audio, too, and a few even offer books. They fill the range from near-mainstream to members-only. Rhino Records (Santa Monica, CA) specializes in music of the fifties and sixties, with a small selection of weird videos. Sinister Cinema (Pacifica, CA) purveys video only, in a thoroughly psychotronic style that embraces science fiction, horror, exploitation, "Jungle Thrills," and "Weird Westerns." From Video Mania (Chicago, IL), you can obtain—you could, at least, in the summer of 1989—the farthest reaches of hard-core gore. Like the maven's magazines, his suppliers come and go. In the last years of the twentieth century, markets and merchants have multiplied far beyond the tally of products they buy and sell; it's impossible to keep track of them.

"Psychotronic" defines the maven's territory by lumping horror together with the lame, the would-be, and anything fired to fury by a foolish cause. Mavens do recognize quality and even seek it out in little-known places, but they also cherish an inverted scale that awards top value to the absolute worst of its kind. There is no better field for this exercise than horror films, where by the 1950s all the playing pieces were on the board, ready for stupid gambits. Scary entertainments never did call for experience and reflection on the part of either their makers or their audiences; all they require is knowledge of their conventions, which can easily be gained without any reference to meaning. This is one reason why the horrid has traditionally appealed to the young, from M. G. Lewis and Catherine Morland to the readers of horror comics who refused to grow up. Horror's insulated, ghettoized nature has also encouraged a special sort of bungling that no other genre can quite manage: the mindless manipulation of clichés in the absence not only of meaning but even of common sense. And horror spawned the arch-bungler of cinematic history, Edward D. Wood, Jr.

Wood's ineptitude worked in such wondrous ways that he has become a strange sort of classic. His efforts enjoyed their first revival in the late 1960s and early 1970s, chiefly on American college campuses, where the accompaniment of drugs lent a special savor to any entertainment that fell on its face without knowing it. This was the probable birthplace of the maven and his upside-down aesthetic; in the last two decades, with or without chemical enhancement, it has permeated American culture, threatening to push the Wood cult up into the mainstream. Not all of Wood's works belong to the horror genre: *The Violent Years* (1956), for instance, seeks to exploit the fad for troubled teens, while *Jail Bait* (1959) does what it can about women behind bars. And *Glen or Glenda?* (1953) presents an impassioned, goofy plea for justice to heterosexual male transvestites (of whom Wood was one).

But Wood hit his limping stride in horror, from *Bride of the Monster* (1953) and *Night of the Ghouls* (1959) to *Plan 9 from Outer Space* (1959) and *Orgy of the Dead* (1966). Horror's modest economic demands no doubt drew him to it: Wood's films were obviously made on something slimmer than a shoestring, and he became an inadvertent auteur, producing, directing, and scripting his films, sometimes under aliases. Horror also appealed to him, however, because such films could be put together in the modular way invented by nineteenth-century melodrama: a ghoul here, a zombie there, a coffin creaking open, a graveyard by night, and the desired chill ought to be automatically invoked. Unfortunately for Wood—the T. J. Horsley Curties of his day—even the hardiest clichés can be defeated by fatuous dialogue, patently phony sets, and wretched acting. This was certainly true in the 1950s, when few Americans were so naive about film that they could succumb to Wood's ham-handed manipulation. Wood blundered exactly where Hitchcock triumphed in *Psycho*: Wood's horrors treated their viewers like hicks, while Hitchcock recognized his viewers' sophistication and hoisted them on it.

Twenty years later, sophistication had grown, at least for some, into jadedness, and new audiences derived a kind of pleasure from Wood that Hitchcock cannot offer. It is the pleasure of watching earnest vapidity at work, missing every step but stumbling doggedly to the end of the dance. The masterpiece in Wood's oeuvre is undoubtedly *Plan 9*, which purveys such delights as a flying saucer that's plainly a dangling pie plate, police cars racing from broad daylight into a pitch-dark cemetery (containing a cardboard mausoleum), and the same short sequences shown over and over, as if Wood had forgotten he'd used them before and hoped the audience would catch his amnesia. These are decadent delights, perhaps, but they also form the stock in trade of a serious business: Along with more recent gory excesses, once-obscure failures like Wood's fill the horror maven's archive, and he compiles endless inventories of them. By the end of the twentieth century, it seems, the sloppy bookkeeping that has distinguished the horrid genre for two hundred years will be tidied up at last. By then, of course, the whole of Western culture will have become an archive, and for the first time in its history, the horrid will have led the way.

THE WORLD'S A VAULT

The wellspring of horror remains, as it was in the eighteenth century, the fear of death—or rather the fear of being dead, of the body's losing form, turning slimy, melting away. This source shows no sign of abatement; it seems so self-evident and natural that it has come to be regarded as eternal, part of the universal human inheritance. Perhaps our remotest ancestors feared death much as we do; perhaps it is uniquely human to know that death will come and to brood on it. Our ancestors certainly feared dying, and they often feared the dead, as old tales of vengeful ghosts amply testify. If they feared being dead, however, if the very idea of a corpse, especially a rotting one, made their healthy flesh creep, they left no evidence. The aftermath of the plagues that ravaged late-medieval Europe brought a boom in artistic ghastliness, especially sculpture, that seems to prefigure the worst of twentieth-century horror. All the icons are there: grinning skulls, beckoning skeletons, putrid tableaux that virtually reek. Yet these images were both realistic (because those who saw them had very likely seen the real things) and monitory (because they meant to chasten the observer, to remind him of life's brevity and urge him toward salvation).

In the late seventeenth century, Western culture began a slow turn away from the fact of being dead that has continued for three hundred years. The reality of corpses, their sight and especially their smell, came to seem disgusting, obscene, dangerous to health. The spectacle of rot—for centuries a familiar spectacle—was moved from the centers of cities to their peripheries. Cemeteries lost their charnels and their stink, becoming clean, airy places where the dead, safely ensconced underground, benignly fed the roots of trees and grass, though visitors tried not to think about that. The banishing of deadness moved unevenly but inevitably; a few old charnels remain even now, in Europe and South America, to the astonishment of tourists who fancy themselves more enlightened than those who constructed such grisly things. Today, at least in Europe and North America, no one ever sees or smells a rotted corpse except by lamentable accident; even morticians and gravediggers evade the experience, thanks to the chemicals that are routinely pumped into the dead to postpone their reunion with the earth. The horror that accompanies portrayals of the trenches of World War I, Nazi extermination camps, and the killing fields of Cambodia has surely been bolstered by the twentieth-century sense that the last obscenity is not so much death as it is decay.

On the threshold of our long recoil from deadness, images of rot rose up in art. Earlier art had not wholly neglected them, but with the Graveyard poets of the mid-eighteenth century, a new aspect of connoisseurship arrived, holding rot at intact arm's length to savor its horror, gauging its score on a scale of emotive power. Blair, Young, and company stood with one foot in the old camp, the other in the new: They admonished their readers as funerary verse, sculpture, and painting had done for centuries, but they also offered their wares in the literary marketplace. Their considerable vogue all over Europe owed little to piety. Perhaps unintentionally—though Young knew just what he was doing— the Graveyard poets served themselves up as one of the more piquant dishes on the smorgasbord of Sensibility. As Ann Radcliffe's novels demonstrated, readers of the late eighteenth century could savor graveyard gloom and mountain glory side by side, sensing no incongruity. They could savor, indeed, just about any emotion, so long as it was coaxed from them in a genteel manner that rounded its potentially raw edges. With a blitheness that baffles and annoys latter-day observers, late-eighteenth-century people felt to the utmost, watched themselves feeling, and felt *that* to the utmost as well.

The late eighteenth century also witnessed the first stirrings of an entertainment industry. Slow-moving, small, and tentative by comparison with its gargantuan twentieth-century descendant, the market for horrid novels and melodramas nevertheless exhibited the same appetite for small changes on proven successes that would characterize horror movies two hundred years later. And it debased its currency with remarkable speed. Mrs. Radcliffe's formula wore out in less than thirty years; horrid melodrama was more adaptive and durable, but it had become hopelessly passé by the middle of the nineteenth century. Like the fear on which it drew, scary entertainment never faded away or even, at bottom, changed much. But, as the industry grew, the shelf life of its wares shrank steadily. New sources came in constant requisition: legends from Scotland, Germany, Transylvania, the Caribbean, anywhere; reports of urban atrocities; accounts of ghosts that had been seen, spoken to, even photographed. Worn-out devices got retooled: The Gothic castle became the cursed country house, then the mansion permanently to let on a gloomy city street; the devilish monk turned into a debauched nobleman, a mad barber, an unmotivated psychopath wielding a cleaver.

Everything changed, yet nothing did. After more than two centuries, the horror industry remains devoted to cultivating the same skin condition *Udolpho* coaxed out of Catherine Morland—the hair-raised state called gooseflesh. And it employs the same means, the invocation of the body's dreadful softness, its horrid habit of dissolving once life has left it, or even before. Until quite recently, of course, there was no "horror industry." There were poets, novelists, playwrights, short-story writers, and filmmakers who specialized in gooseflesh, along with others who went after it now and then. Until recently, too, they never went after horror unalloyed. Humor or romance always joined the brew, as it still does in all but the most blinkered efforts.

Scores of essays and books (including this one) notwithstanding, there was also, until recently, no horror tradition. Fiercely, even suicidally imitative, the devisers of scary entertainments exploited what seemed fresh and therefore lucrative; when one set of tricks grew boring, they went after another, sometimes reviving the past without knowing it. But not until the 1920s, when anthologists and scholars began their horrid labors, did workers in the genre gain easy access to the genre's past. In part, this amnesia was due to horror's hybrid nature: With a few exceptions like the stories of Hoffmann, Poe, and Le Fanu, chills had tended to come bound together with many other responses in most fictions that sought to arouse them. Dickens's *A Christmas Carol*, for example, offers a considerable dose of graveyard spookiness, yet it has never been considered a horror tale; cozy warmth obliterates its chills. Since straight-out horror was so rare before the turn of the twentieth century, only the sketchiest of traditions could have been assembled from it.

Also, of course, most novels, stories, and plays that showed significant streaks of fear had been ephemeral, low-grade stuff, unlikely to be preserved. Again except for Poe—an anomaly on this count as on others—the canon of polite literature contained few horrors. Romantic forays like Coleridge's "Christabel" or Keats's "La Belle Dame Sans Merci" could be considered experiments by writers whose hearts really lay elsewhere; Hawthorne could be excused on allegorical grounds; for the rest, the field belonged to the second-rate or worse. When the Gothic novel fell into disrepute among polite readers, it seemed to take the whole scary enterprise with it. Though chills abounded in melodramas, magazine stories, and penny dreadfuls, these were at best momentary diversions, at worst mere trash. In part, there was no horrid tradition before the 1920s because no one had bothered to preserve one.

From the twenties till now, however, horror has grown steadily more self-aware. A succession of technological developments—film, which recycled books and plays; sound film, which recycled silents; television, which recycled them all; videocassettes, which made them immediately available—has led to the construction of a vast horror archive, a universal vault. At least if he confines himself to the twentieth century, the browser can now have a look at almost everything that has been or might be called horrid. The avid (and rather well-heeled) collector can even acquire, in fifty-three hardbound volumes, the complete output of E.C. Comics—"printed in black and white," an advertisement intones, "so the fine craftsmanship of the E.C. artists can be studied and enjoyed to its fullest." When these works were new, barely forty years ago, craftsmanship was on no one's mind but the artists'. At the end of the twentieth century, however, the past has come to seem the only place fine work resides, whatever form it takes.

In less than seventy years, scary entertainment has been transformed from a forgetful, slapdash diversion, hardly a genre at all, into a serious, highly reflective pursuit that exhibits a rigor that any academic discipline might envy. This, I think, is a far more important development than the boom in explicit gore that has run in tandem with it. Gore was always possible; lately it has been a fashion. But the source that fuels artificial fear remains potent whether the spilling of guts is shown or only implied. Chills have traditionally taken whatever vehicles the time provides: When ruined abbeys were popular, chills lurked there; when domesticity reigned, chills went domestic; now that explicitness is in season, guts spill. Like prior fashions, this one will not so much pass as take its place in a warehouse full of alternatives for future exploiters.

An October 1990 issue of *TV Guide*, faultless monitor of American taste, noted a "backlash" by parents and therefore by advertisers against the "graphic, gory, state-of-the-art special effects" that had lately invaded the small screen from the big one. "As a result, TV horror may be returning to its roots—when psychological terror and subtlety had more impact than an ax to the head." There are, of course, no such roots, in television or anywhere else. The horrid tradition began in *The Castle of Otranto*, with a boy crushed under a gigantic helmet—nothing subtle or psychological about *that*. But the explosion of cinematic gore from the 1960s through the 1980s, and its eventual seepage into television, had no essential link to horror and made no fundamental change in it. Explicitness invaded all media and genres during the same years; as usual, horror merely went the way the wind blew. Subtlety may replace explicitness for a while, though such a trend seems unlikely, especially on television. Subtlety, however, is irrelevant, too; its presence may elevate one work or another in the estimation of critics, but it makes no difference at the source.

If any change at all can be expected from scary entertainment, it will come as a by-product of the expansion and eventual completion of the horrid archive. When turn-of-the-century writers wished to raise gooseflesh, they had more or less to reinvent their techniques, since too few past efforts had been preserved for copying or adaptation. But already by the 1940s, Dracula, for instance, had spun off so many sons, daughters, and cousins that overwork seemed to have achieved what no sharpened stake could manage. A glut of copycat horrors in print, radio, and film had made audiences so familiar with the likes of vampires that the vein had apparently dried up. In the early 1950s, horror comics were able to exploit this very satedness by forging a condensed, rapid-fire version of the same old thing. Horror comics expected their readers to know all about ghouls and animated corpses; comic-book horrors won novelty not only from unprecedented gore but also from a snide, joky attitude that winked at their readers' wisdom. The stories themselves were tired; the style, however, looked new.

Twenty years later, when writers and filmmakers like King and Romero sought to revive the E.C. formula, they gave it an ironic twist: Fresh yet stale, it offered the shock of the old. There was some novelty in that, though of an arch, allusive kind that made the heavily derivative E.C.s seem original. King, Romero, and company enjoyed the advantage that those originals were not widely available for inspection; they were known more by repute and dim memory than by firsthand contact, and they bore the vaguely titillating aura of having been suppressed. Twenty years later still, facsimiles of the original E.C.s can be pored over in detail, along with the works of their imitators and of those who imitated *them*. Forgetfulness, which once characterized the genre, seems impossible now. Even the lowest-grade entry, even *Bloody Pit of Horror*, can be screened and rescreened at will, studied, and perhaps imitated. Forgetfulness used to provide fresh life; that sort of freshness will never be seen again.

In this, of course, scary entertainment keeps pace with Western culture at large, which seems bent on preserving, cataloguing, and copying everything the past leaves behind. The late twentieth century has become a new collector's age, a vast resurgence of the campy spirit that led Walpole to cram Strawberry Hill with medieval garbage. The future, should there be one, will inherit from the twentieth century far more junk than it can have any use for; it will also, very likely, inherit no standards for distinguishing junk from nonjunk. The burden seems crushing; perhaps it has become so already, as allusiveness and quotation replace what was formerly called creativity. Scary entertainment has never worried much about that intangible quality, nor has it spent much energy separating the fine from the shoddy. In a sense, our new archival world was horrid fiction's permanent dream. At last someone takes inventory in the horrid warehouse; not only that, the list is computerized, instantly accessible, and scrupulously kept current. Like death and decay, the past is as scary as it ever was. Only now the past is present. The future is already here.

Notes

Introduction

Chapter One: Into the Crypt

12 "a more perfect example": Draper, 81.
13 "there is a representation": Meiss, 74.
13 "Ascetic meditation": Huizinga, 140–41.
14 "I believe": Hoever, 1293.
14 "Where Wisdom's surely taught": Parnell, line 8.
14 "Whilst some affect": Blair, lines 1–5.
15 "At this hour": Porteus, lines 5–11.
16 "In his": Boswell, 1111.
17 "The knell": Young, Night IV.
17 "Lorenzo! no": Young, Night III.
17 "The Man how bless'd": Young, Night V.
18 "a sort of cross": Pinney, 337–38.
18 "is never bent": Pinney, 367.
19 "The sweet garden-breath": Pinney, 358.
20 "The curfew tolls": Lonsdale, *Poems*, 117.
20 "yonder ivy-mantled tower": Lonsdale, *Poems*, 119–120.
22 "yet regarded": Summers, *Quest*, 114.
23 "an ancient pile": Hervey, 46.
23 "The next thing": Hervey, 50.
23 "I found the memorials": Hervey, 51.
23 "these confused relics": Hervey, 52.
24 "Yonder entrance": Hervey, 86.
25 corpses did not linger: Ariès, 360.
25 When the process: Ariès, 54.
26 "In the seventeenth": Ariès, 69.
28 "The whole Army": Fielding, 135.
29 "On April 20, 1773": Ariès, 481–82.
30 "Some, I know": Hervey, 77.
33 "Should one of these": Hervey, 93–94.

Chapter Two: Feelings for Sale

page

35 "Thro' yon dark Grove": quoted in Sickels, 51.
36 "Let others draw": Freneau, lines 9–12.
37 "Old castles": Lonsdale, *New*, 168.
37 " 'Tis now the raven's": Lonsdale, *New*, 169.
37 "Yet time has seen": Lonsdale, *New*, 169.
39 "Strawberry Castle": W. S. Lewis, 9:102.
39 "a little Gothic castle": W. S. Lewis, 20:111.
39 "I give myself": W. S. Lewis, 37:406.
39 "ancient": W. S. Lewis, 1:90.
40 His garden gate: W. S. Lewis, 1:178.
40 "a pretty little sarcophagus": W. S. Lewis, 24:462.
40 "conventual gloom": W. S. Lewis, 25:532.
40 "this *old, old*": W. S. Lewis, 28:28.

40   an owl: W. S. Lewis, 32:193.
40   "Gothic towers": W. S. Lewis, 31:316.
41   "The Abbot of Strawberry": W. S. Lewis, 10:127.
41   "in all the glory": W. S. Lewis, 10:168.
41   "all the air": W. S. Lewis, 21:306.
42   "In their buildings": quoted in Germann, 5–6.
45   "Under the rubric": Goethe, 6:248.
46   "How often I went": Goethe, 6:248.
48   "I thought of": Wordsworth, lines 43–49.
48   "secular priest": Chatterton, 7.
48   age of eleven: Chatterton, 7.
49   "Systers in sorrowe": Chatterton, 19–20.
49   "Distraughte": Chatterton, 22.
49   *levynde* means: Chatterton, 20.
50   "This is the most": Boswell, 752.
51   "A nation that": Boswell, 578.
51   "What would you have": Boswell, 579.
51   "Sir, when he leaves": Boswell, 306.
51   when Macpherson sent: Macpherson, 1:462n.
52   "It is night": Macpherson, 1:454–55.
53   "All, all is over!": Goethe, 4:69.
53   "He smiled": Goethe, 4:97.
53   "A stream": Goethe, 4:103.
55   "the curious": Price, 344–45.
55   "the theater of mind": Price, 343.
56   "this woman's nature": Eliot, 691–92.
58   "Ten times in a day": Sterne, 24.
59   "I can't get out": Kuhn, 65.
59   "I was going": Kuhn, 66–67.
59   "He gave a deep sigh": Kuhn, 67.
60   "poor Maria": Kuhn, 104.
61   "MARIA made": Sterne, 484.
61   "I sat down": Kuhn, 105.
61   "Nature melted": Kuhn, 106.
62   "—Dear sensibility": Kuhn, 107.
62   "a man, sensible": Kuhn, 220.
63   "There is a certain": Kuhn, 222.
63   "It is perhaps": Kuhn, 224.
63   "He seized": Kuhn, 224–25.

Chapter Three: Fear among the Ruins

page

67   "a rather solemn tone": Austen, 5:112.
68   "Miss Morland": Austen, 5:113.
68   "The public": Austen, 5:12.

69   In 1780: Griest, 11.
70   "provided that": Austen, 5:15.
71   "Dear creature!": Austen, 5:40.
73   "Shall I even": W. S. Lewis, 1:88.
73   "as a matter": Bleiler, *Gothic*, 17.
74   "nature": Bleiler, *Gothic*, 22.
74   "that *the Castle*": Bleiler, *Gothic*, 27.
74   "dilated": Bleiler, *Gothic*, 104.
75   sometime between: Bleiler, *Gothic*, 17.
75   "hollowed into": Bleiler, *Gothic*, 35.
75   "a chain": Bleiler, *Gothic*, 73.
75   "the fleshless jaws": Bleiler, *Gothic*, 99.
76   "preternatural": Bleiler, *Gothic*, 18.
76   "the gloomiest shades": Bleiler, *Gothic*, 74.
78   "congenital and indigenous": Summers, *Quest*, 189.
78   "With all the chances": Austen, 5:141.
78   "a fine old place": Austen, 5:158.
79   "suddenly expires": Austen, 5:160.
80   " 'There,' said Montoni": Radcliffe, *Udolpho*, 227.
80   "Suddenly I became": Stoker, 14.
80   "It was huge": King, *'Salem's*, 6.
81   King suggests: King, *'Salem's*, 1.
81   "At first glance": Bloch, 39.
83   "some dark towers": Radcliffe, *Romance of the Forest*, 14.
83   "He approached": Radcliffe, *Romance of the Forest*, 15.
83   Gothic gate": Radcliffe, *Romance of the Forest*, 15–16.
84   It has been uninhabited: Radcliffe, *Udolpho*, 229–30.
84   "such a strange": Radcliffe, *Udolpho*, 231.
84   "Annette, perceiving": Radcliffe, *Udolpho*, 232.
85   "a suite": Radcliffe, *Udolpho*, 232.
85   "hung with pictures": Radcliffe, *Udolpho*, 232–33.
85   "Have you gone": Austen, 5:39–40.
85   "proud irregularity": Radcliffe, *Udolpho*, 245.
85   "ancient grandeur": Radcliffe, *Udolpho*, 248–49.
86   "It may be remembered": Radcliffe, *Udolpho*, 662.
87   "monkish superstition": Radcliffe, *Udolpho*, 662–63.
87   "a terror": Radcliffe, *Udolpho*, 248.
88   "a tall figure": M. A. Radcliffe, 1:4.
89   "a human hand": M. A. Radcliffe, 1:10.
89   picks up: M. A. Radcliffe, 1:11.
89   "In our next": M. A. Radcliffe, 2:212.
89   "And thus": M. A. Radcliffe, 2:226–27.
89   "The breathless body": M. A. Radcliffe, 4:64.
90   "he had but one hand": M. A. Radcliffe, 4:126.
90   "the waves": M. A. Radcliffe, 4:148–49.
90   *"To be good"*: M. A. Radcliffe, 4:222.
92   "spacious and lofty": M. A. Radcliffe, 1:1–2.

92   "In this, however": M. A. Radcliffe, 1:8.
93   "Rosalino [*sic*] felt": M. A. Radcliffe, 1:30.
93   " 'A few years' ": Radcliffe, *Romance of the Forest*, 16.
94   "in their most flamboyant": Summers, *Quest*, 341.
94   "more legitimate": Curties, 1:vi–vii.
94   "the youthful illustrious": Curties, 1:1.
95   "gamester": Curties, 1:6.
95   "the Father Confessor": Curties, 1:11.
95   "a nameless sensation": Curties, 1:19.
95   "His stature": Curties, 1:23.
95   "nameless horror": Curties, 1:33.
95   "with an expression": Curties, 2:23–24.
95   "shuddered, a faint": Curties, 2:43.
96   "here Sanguedoni": Curties, 2:141.
96   "He seemed": Curties, 3:7–8.
97   "On a lofty eminence": Curties, 3:42.
97   "fearful abode": Curties, 3:43–48.
97   "middle aged woman": Curties, 3:48–49.
97   "ascended a once noble": Curties, 3:51–52.
98   "the remains": Curties, 3:66–67.
98   "moist and unwholesome": Curties, 3:68–69.
98   "Heaven may": Curties, 4:232.

Chapter Four: Stages of Fear

page

101   "beautifully bossed": Green, 1:107.
103   "was spoken of": Summers, *Quest*, 213.
103   "success and scandal": Summers, *Quest*, 212.
104   "Have you ever": Austen, 5:48.
106   "He sat": Lewis, *Monk*, 109.
106   "I was oppressed": Lewis, *Monk*, 385.
107   "reptiles": Lewis, *Monk*, 390.
107   "I vowed": Lewis, *Monk*, 393–96.
108   "[T]he auditorium": Nicoll, *History*, 4:11.
109   "Castle and City": *Siege of Troy*, 16.
110   "sudden Convulsion": Summers, *Bibliography*, 345–46.
110   First: Levine, 21–22.
111   "a horrid ghost story": Tieck, 19.
112   "What on earth": Tieck, 23.
112   "In what time": Tieck, 24.
112   "FISCHER: Ah": Tieck, 29–30.
112   "*The pit*": Tieck, 59.
112   "rotten pears": Tieck, 62.
113   "fierce glare": Nicoll, *History*, 4:35.
115   "close imitation": Jephson, 4.

115   "The owl": Jephson, 17.
115   "recourse to supernatural agency": Boaden, 1.
116   "Our Bard": Andrews, 3.
116   "an old Castle": Andrews, 26.
116   "SICILIAN GIRLS": Andrews, 5.
117   "most typical": Summers, *Quest*, 254.
117   "*The folding-doors*": Lewis, *Spectre*, 43–44.
117   "REGINALD *kneels*": Lewis, *Spectre*, 52.
117   "lie still unburied": Lewis, *Monk*, 181.
118   " 'We meet again' ": Lewis, *Spectre*, 37.
118   "*Instantly*": Lewis, *Spectre*, 44.
119   Lewis wrote: Summers, *Quest*, 284–85.
119   "must have been": Nicoll, *History*, 4:79.
121   "a kind of drama": Hartog, 40.
122   "*the humorous dancing*": Holcroft, 2:1.
122   "Whither fly?": Holcroft, 2:2.
123   "*Music loud*": Holcroft, 1:1.
124   "Much as a maker": Mayer and Scott, 4.
126   "*glides across*": Boucicault, 28.
126   "old crusted grizzly": Newton, 19.
128   "The most divergent": Weber, 12.
129   "*Frightful forest glen*": Weber, 102.
129   "Invisible Spirits": Weber, 104.
130   "*bends and breaks*": Weber, 116.
130   "*The whole sky*": Weber, 118.
131   "*dreary site*": Kerr, 25.
131   "*mistic sword*": Kerr, 27.
131   "*adders—toads*": Kerr, 27.

Chapter Five: Fear Comes Home

page

135   Thurtell bashed: Borowitz, 53.
135   Hunt's evidence: Borowitz, 233.
136   "distraught": Borowitz, 218.
136   "the life and characters": Altick, 25.
136   Thomas Boyle has seen: Boyle, 51–54.
137   "The Identical": Borowitz, 129.
138   "WOODVILLE": *The Gamblers*, 5.
138   "AMELIA": *The Gamblers*, 10.
138   "BRADSHAW": *The Gamblers*, 13.
139   "drama": S. N. E., iii.
139   staged at Norwich: Nicoll, *History*, 4:507.
139   "in after-years": Newton, 97.
140   "freezing": Newton, 62.
140   "horrifying shrieks": Newton, 272.
140   the unlucky barn: Altick, 31.

140   "most popular of all": Altick, 96.
140   "How well": *Maria Martin*, 4.
141   "universe of death": Boyle, 13.
141   He relies heavily: Boyle, 7–8.
142   "On which murders": De Quincey, 326.
142   "To her astonishment": De Quincey, 292–93.
143   "and this time": James and Critchley, 12–13.
144   "Dr. Bowen found": Radin, 69.
144   "There was blood": Spiering, 41.
145   "Rapidly": De Quincey, 295.
145   Henry Mayhew reported: Mayhew, 1:284.
146   "A highly popular": Dickens, *Great*, 160.
147   "long cosy talks": Gosse, 80.
147   "who killed": Gosse, 80.
147   "the Carpet-bag Mystery": Gosse, 81.
148   "but clear enough": Gosse, 81.
148   "in addition": Altick, 133.
150   "liquid blue eyes": Braddon, 44.
150   "A fierce": Braddon, 23.
151   "a disease": Balzac, 364–65.
151   "What lay": Zola, 470.
153   "One must have": Ellmann, 469.
156   "He considered": Radcliffe, *The Italian*, 225.
157   "Which way": S. N. E., 21.
158   "Ha! what form": S. N. E., 43.
159   "What is this": Rowell, 481–82.
160   "The Bells!": Rowell, 499.
161   "Everything that": Ibsen, 334.
162   "the strange human craving": Woolf, 217.

Chapter Six: Genrefication

page

167   "the blurred": Homer, 186.
168   "earliest masterpiece": Cox and Gilbert, xii.
168   "But they werena": Scott, 156.
168   "too easily": Summers, *Omnibus*, 26.
169   "comfortable, but": Cox and Gilbert, 4.
170   "Here, contrary": Cox and Gilbert, 5.
170   "gloomy chamber": Austen, 5:158.
170   "seemed in motion": Austen, 5:167.
170   "haggard and ghastly": Cox and Gilbert, 5.
170   "indispensable business": Cox and Gilbert, 6.
170   "an old-fashioned gown": Cox and Gilbert, 8.
170   "all firmness": Cox and Gilbert, 9.
171   "an experiment": Cox and Gilbert, 10.

171 "the accursed hag": Cox and Gilbert, 11.
171 "That is the picture": Cox and Gilbert, 11–12.
174 "one of the dullest": Davidson, viii.
174 "With all due": James, *French*, 60.
176 "a cloud": Poe, 308.
176 "excessive antiquity": Poe, 89–90.
176 "numerous vaults": Poe, 94.
176 "an influence": Poe, 91.
177 "True!": Poe, 259–60.
177 "vulture eye": Poe, 261.
177 "I was sick": Poe, 50.
177 "I cannot": Poe, 79.
178 "There is in man": Baudelaire, 125.
178 "a reasonably sufficient": Baudelaire, 125.
179 "grievous tragedy": Baudelaire, 24.
179 "many strange tales": Summers, *Omnibus*, 548.
180 "Ingoldsby enthusiasts": Summers, *Omnibus*, 26.
180 "pretty harmless": Freeman, 224.
181 "good spooky yarn": Summers, *Omnibus*, 33.
181 "on Christmas eve": James, *Turn*, 7.
181 "Certainly": Briggs, 41.
181 "from time immemorial": Dickens, *Pickwick*, 475.
182 "round that pretty": Dickens, *Selected*, 126.
182 "we all remember": Dickens, *Selected*, 127.
182 "lobster eyes": Dickens, *Selected*, 127–28.
182 "a middle-aged": Dickens, *Selected*, 135.
182 "old houses": Dickens, *Selected*, 137.
182 "the branches": Dickens, *Selected*, 141.
183 "Brave lodgings": Dickens, *Pickwick*, 482.
185 "he suddenly stopped": Bleiler, *Supernatural*, 162–63.
185 "*I never awoke*": Bleiler, *Supernatural*, 167.
185 "nothing has prospered": Bleiler, *Supernatural*, 172.
185 "subterraneous passage": Bleiler, *Supernatural*, 228.
186 "at last we found": Bleiler, *Supernatural*, 184.
187 "I deplore fear": Jackson, 183.
188 "that which no": Bleiler, *Five*, 98.
189 "I remember": Crawford, 219.
190 "There is very": M.R. James, 66.
190 "dampish": M.R. James, 150–51.
190 "the hideous smell": M.R. James, 152.
191 James's individual volumes: Briggs, 125.
194 "appropriately ghostly": Sullivan, 32.
194 "an ideal introduction": Sullivan, 12.
197 "Around me": Dziemianowicz, 13–14.
198 "wan, pallid": Dziemianowicz, 14.
198 "One morning": Dziemianowicz, 17.
198 "Warm, fresh blood": Dziemianowicz, 20.

Chapter Seven: Scream and Scream Again

page

201 "That is reality": Becker, 208.
202 "pseudo-gothic designs": Gordon, 14.
202 "a place where": Gordon, 18.
203 "unexpected brutalities": Gordon, 41–42.
203 Gordon would like: Gordon, 43.
204 "soothing system": Poe, 598.
204 "very good friends": Poe, 603.
205 "a perfect army": Poe, 606.
205 "highly valued collaborators": Gordon, 129.
205 "The blood is flowing": Gordon, 137.
205 *"At this moment"*: Gordon, 141.
206 "the vogue": Hardy, 31.
206 "standard haunted-house": Hardy, 34.
207 "popular school": Nicoll, *Beginnings*, 200.
210 "Drawing on": Hardy, 37.
214 *"loved* cobwebs": Riley, 23.
216 "three-engined": Deane and Balderston, 41.
216 "The place smells": Deane and Balderston, 73.
217 *"there are such things"*: Deane and Balderston, 74.
217 "more like something": Mank, 15.
221 "horror film": Bojarski, 68.
221 "go for this": Bojarski, 167.
224 "to make": Mank, ix.
227 "Since the 1950s": Doherty, *Teenagers*, 3.
227 "Without the support": Doherty, *Teenagers*, 1.
227 "52 of Universal's": Doherty, *Teenagers*, 149.
228 director George Melford: Skal, 159–63.
231 "how profitable": Rebello, 22.

Chapter Eight: Splat!

page

237 "Poe cycle": Corman, 78.
238 "the viewer": Hardy, 169.
239 "there's really nothing": McCarty, 81.
239 "the human body": McCarty, 80.
240 "She describes": Wertham, 270–71.
241 "Superman comes": Wertham, 350.
241 "there is an exact": Wertham, 97.
241 "It is like": Wertham, 190.
241 "the Lesbian counterpart": Wertham, 192–93.

242 *"the new pornography"*: Wertham, 329.
242 By 1948: Wertham, 37.
242 the figure had risen: Wertham, 307.
242 Mike Benton puts: Benton, 53.
243 "harmless animal comics": Wertham, 51.
243 "recent": Wertham, 106.
243 "first out-and-out": Goulart, 255.
244 "testing the limits": Goulart, 266.
246 "smart-alecky cynical": Wertham, 67.
247 "No comic magazine": Goulart, 273.
248 "I cut my teeth": King, *Danse*, 34–35.
249 "the gag reflex": King, *Danse*, 37.
249 "that comic-book": King, *Pet*, 225.
250 "I think": Gagne, 126.
250 made outside Pittsburgh: Gagne, 31, 38.
250 As of 1987: Gagne, 2.
252 "Savini and crew": Gagne, 184.
254 "when, gentle viewer": Doherty, *"Night,"* 21.
257 "projects of overall": Hertz, 24.
264 "backlash": Lieberman, 3.

Bibliography

Altick, Richard D. *Victorian Studies in Scarlet*. New York: Norton, 1970.

Andrews, Miles Peter. *The Mysteries of the Castle: A Dramatic Tale*. London: T. N. Longman, 1795.

Ariès, Philippe. *The Hour of Our Death*. Trans. Helen Weaver. New York: Vintage, 1982.

Austen, Jane. *The Novels of Jane Austen*. Ed. R. W. Chapman. 3d ed., rev. 5 vols. Oxford: Oxford University Press, 1969.

Balzac, Honoré de. *Cousin Bette*. Trans. Anthony Bonner. New York: Bantam, 1961.

Baring-Gould, Sabine. *A Book of Ghosts*. 1904. Reprint. Freeport, NY: Books for Libraries Press, 1969.

Baudelaire, Charles. *Baudelaire on Poe: Critical Papers*. Trans. and ed. Lois and Francis E. Hyslop, Jr. State College, PA: Bald Eagle Press, 1952.

Becker, George J., ed. *Documents of Modern Literary Realism*. Princeton, NJ: Princeton University Press, 1963.

Benton, Mike. *The Comic Book in America: An Illustrated History*. Dallas, TX: Taylor Publishing Co., 1989.

Blair, Robert. *The Grave: A Poem*. London, 1743.

Bleiler, E. F., ed. *Five Victorian Ghost Novels*. New York: Dover, 1971.

Bleiler, E. F., ed. *Three Gothic Novels*. New York: Dover, 1966.

Bleiler, E. F., ed. *Three Supernatural Novels of the Victorian Period*. New York: Dover, 1975.

Bloch, Robert. *Psycho*. 1959. Reprint. New York: Warner Books, 1982.

Boaden, James. *Aurelio and Miranda*. 3d ed. London: J. Bell, 1799.

Bojarski, Richard. *The Films of Bela Lugosi*. Secaucus, NJ: Citadel Press, 1980.

Borowitz, Albert. *The Thurtell-Hunt Murder Case: Dark Mirror to Regency England*. Baton Rouge and London: Louisiana State University Press, 1987.

Boswell, James. *Life of Johnson*. London: Oxford University Press, 1953.

[Boucicault, Dion]. *The Corsican Brothers, A Dramatic Romance, in Three Acts and Five Tableaux*. New York: Samuel French, n.d.

Boyle, Thomas. *Black Swine in the Sewers of Hampstead: Beneath the Surface of Victorian Sensationalism*. New York: Viking, 1989.

Boyse, Samuel. *Deity: A Poem*. 3d ed. London: C. Corbett, 1752.

Braddon, Mary Elizabeth. *Lady Audley's Secret*. London: Simpkin and Co., n.d.

Briggs, Julia. *Night Visitors: The Rise and Fall of the English Ghost Story*. London: Faber, 1977.

Chatterton, Thomas. *Poems, Supposed to Have Been Written at Bristol, by Thomas Rowley, and Others, in the Fifteenth Century*. 1777. Reprint. Menton: Scolar Press, 1969.

Collins, Vere H., ed. *Ghosts and Marvels: A Selection of Uncanny Tales from Daniel Defoe to Algernon Blackwood*. 1924. Reprint. Freeport, NY: Books for Libraries Press, 1972.

Corman, Roger, with Jim Jerome. *How I Made a Hundred Movies in Hollywood and Never Lost a Dime*. New York: Random House, 1990.

Cox, Michael, and R. A. Gilbert, eds. *The Oxford Book of English Ghost Stories*. Oxford: Oxford University Press, 1989.

Crawford, F. Marion. *Wandering Ghosts*. New York: Macmillan, 1911.

Curties, T. J. Horsley. *The Monk of Udolpho: A Romance*. 4 vols. 1807. Reprint. New York: Arno Press, 1977.

Darwin, Charles. *The Expression of the Emotions in Man and Animals*. 1872. Reprint. Chicago: University of Chicago Press, 1965.

Davidson, Edward H., ed. *Selected Writings of Edgar Allan Poe*. Boston: Houghton Mifflin, 1956.

Deane, Hamilton, and John L. Balderston. *Dracula: The Vampire Play in Three Acts*. New York: Samuel French, 1927.

De Quincey, Thomas. *Confessions of an English Opium-Eater and Other Writings*. Ed. Aileen Ward. New York: New American Library, 1966.

Dickens, Charles. *Great Expectations*. Ed. Angus Calder. Harmondsworth: Penguin, 1965.

Dickens, Charles. *The Posthumous Papers of the Pickwick Club*. Ed. Robert L. Patten. London: Penguin, 1972.

Dickens, Charles. *Selected Short Fiction*. Ed. Deborah A. Thomas. Harmondsworth: Penguin, 1976.

Doherty, Thomas. "*Night of the Living Dead:* The Original." *Cinefantastique* 21 (Dec. 1990): 20–21, 60.

Doherty, Thomas. *Teenagers and Teenpics: The Juvenilization of American Movies in the 1950s*. Boston: Unwin Hyman, 1988.

Draper, John W. *The Funeral Elegy and the Rise of English Romanticism*. New York: New York University Press, 1929.

Dziemianowicz, Stefan R., Robert Weinberg, and Martin H. Greenberg, eds. *Weird Tales: 32 Unearthed Terrors*. New York: Bonanza Books, 1988.

Eliot, George. *Daniel Deronda*. Ed. Barbara Hardy. Harmondsworth: Penguin, 1967.

Ellmann, Richard. *Oscar Wilde*. New York: Knopf, 1987.

Fielding, Henry. *Tom Jones*. Ed. Sheridan Baker. New York: Norton, 1973.

Freeman, Mary E. Wilkins. *The Wind in the Rose-Bush and Other Stories of the Supernatural*. 1903. Reprint. Chicago: Academy Chicago, 1986.

Freud, Sigmund. *The Standard Edition of the Complete Psychological Works of Sigmund Freud*. 24 vols. London: Hogarth Press and the Institute of Psycho-Analysis, 1953–1974.

Gagne, Paul R. *The Zombies That Ate Pittsburgh: The Films of George A. Romero*. New York: Dodd, Mead, 1987.

The Gamblers: A New Melo-drama, in Two Acts. London, 1824.

Germann, Georg. *Gothic Revival in Europe and Britain: Sources, Influences and Ideas*. Trans. Gerald Onn. London: Lund Humphries with the Architectural Association, 1972.

Goethe, Johann Wolfgang von. *Werke*. 6 vols. Frankfurt am Main: Insel, 1970.

Gordon, Mel. *The Grand Guignol: Theatre of Fear and Terror*. New York: Amok Press, 1988.

Gosse, Edmund. *Father and Son: A Study of Two Temperaments*. 1907. Reprint. Harmondsworth: Penguin, 1970.

Goulart, Ron. *Ron Goulart's Great History of Comic Books*. Chicago: Contemporary Books, 1986.

Green, William Child. *Abbot of Montserrat; or, The Pool of Blood*. 2 vols. 1826. Reprint. New York: Arno Press, 1977.

Griest, Guinevere L. *Mudie's Circulating Library and the Victorian Novel*. Bloomington: Indiana University Press, 1970.

Hardy, Phil, ed. *The Encyclopedia of Horror Movies*. New York: Harper and Row, 1986.

Hartog, Willie G. *Guilbert de Pixerécourt: Sa Vie, son mélodrame, sa technique et son influence*. Paris: Libraire Ancienne, 1912.

Hertz, Gary. "A *Psychotronic* Interview with Sid Haig." *Psychotronic Video* 3 (Summer 1989): 24–27.

Hervey, James. *Meditations and Contemplations*. Philadelphia: Willis P. Hazard, 1863.

Hoever, Hugo H., ed. *Saint Joseph Daily Missal: The Official Prayers of the Catholic Church for the Celebration of Daily Mass*. rev. ed. New York: Catholic Book Publishing Co., 1963.

Holcroft, Thomas. *A Tale of Mystery*. London: J. Dicks, n.d.

Homer. *The Odyssey*. Trans. Robert Fitzgerald. Garden City, NY: Anchor, 1963.

Huizinga, Johan. *The Waning of the Middle Ages*. Trans. F. Hopman. Garden City, NY: Anchor, 1954.

Ibsen, Henrik. *Correspondence*. Trans. Mary Morison. 1905. Reprint. New York: Haskell House, 1970.

Jackson, Shirley. *The Haunting of Hill House*. 1959. Reprint. New York: Penguin, 1984.

James, Henry. *French Poets and Novelists*. 1878. Reprint. New York: Grosset and Dunlap, 1964.

James, Henry. *The Turn of the Screw and Other Stories*. Harmondsworth: Penguin, 1969.

James, M. R. *Ghost Stories of an Antiquary*. 1904. Reprint. New York: Dover, 1971.

James, P. D., and T. A. Critchley. *The Maul and the Pear Tree: The Ratcliffe Highway Murders 1811*. New York: Mysterious Press, 1971.

Jephson, Robert. *The Count of Narbonne, a Tragedy. In Five Acts. With Remarks by Mrs. Inchbald*. London: Moon, Boys, and Graves, n.d.

Kerr, John. *Der Freischutz; or Zamiel the Spirit of the Forest, and the Seventh Bullet. A Melo-Drama in Three Acts. (Founded on the Terrific Northern Legend.)* London: John Lowndes, n.d.

King, Stephen. *Danse Macabre*. New York: Everest House, 1981.

King, Stephen. *Pet Sematary*. New York: Doubleday, 1983.

King, Stephen. *'Salem's Lot*. 1975. New York: New American Library, 1976.

Kuhn, Albert J., ed. *Three Sentimental Novels*. New York: Holt, Rinehart and Winston, 1970.

Levine, Lawrence W. *Highbrow/Lowbrow: The Emergence of Cultural Hierarchy in America*. Cambridge: Harvard University Press, 1988.

Lewis, Matthew G. *The Castle Spectre*. London and New York: Thomas Hailes Lacy, n.d.

Lewis, Matthew G. *The Monk*. Ed. Louis F. Peck. New York: Grove, 1952.

Lewis, W. S., ed. *Horace Walpole's Correspondence*. 48 vols. New Haven: Yale University Press, 1937–1983.

Lieberman, David. "Horrors!" *TV Guide* 38:43 (October 27, 1990): 3–7.

Lonsdale, Roger, ed. *The New Oxford Book of Eighteenth-Century Verse*. Oxford: Oxford University Press, 1984.

Lonsdale, Roger, ed. *The Poems of Gray, Collins, and Goldsmith*. New York: Norton, 1972.

McCarty, John. *Splatter Movies: Breaking the Last Taboo of the Screen*. New York: St. Martin's, 1984.

Macpherson, James. *The Poems of Ossian, &c. Containing the Poetical Works of James Macpherson Esq. in Prose & Rhyme*. Ed. Malcolm Laing. 1805. Reprint. Edinburgh: James Thin, 1871.

Mank, Gregory William. *It's Alive!: The Classic Cinema Saga of Frankenstein*. San Diego: A. S. Barnes and Co., 1981.

Maria Martin; or, The Murder in the Red Barn. A Drama in Two Acts. London: Samuel French, n.d.

Mayer, David, and Matthew Scott. *Four Bars of 'Agit': Incidental Music for Victorian and Edwardian Melodrama*. London: Samuel French and the V & A Theatre Museum, 1983.

Mayhew, Henry. *London Labour and the London Poor*. 4 vols. 1861–1862. Reprint. New York: Dover, 1968.

Meiss, Millard. *Painting in Florence and Siena after the Black Death: The Arts, Religion, and Society in the Mid-Fourteenth Century*. Princeton, NJ: Princeton University Press, 1951.

Milton, John. *Complete Poems and Major Prose*. Ed. Merritt Y. Hughes. New York: Odyssey, 1957.

Newton, H. Chance. *Crime and the Drama; or, Dark Deeds Dramatized*. 1927. Port Washington, NY: Kennikat Press, 1970.

Nicoll, Allardyce. *English Drama 1900–1930: The Beginnings of the Modern Period*. Cambridge: Cambridge University Press, 1973.

Nicoll, Allardyce. *A History of English Drama 1660–1900*. 2d ed., 5 vols. Cambridge: Cambridge University Press, 1952.

Parnell, Thomas. *Poems on Several Occasions*. London: Bernard Lintot, 1726.

Pinney, Thomas, ed. *Essays of George Eliot*. New York: Columbia University Press, 1963.

Poe, Edgar Allan. *The Short Fiction of Edgar Allan Poe: An Annotated Edition*. Ed. Stuart Levine and Susan Levine. Urbana and Chicago: University of Illinois Press, 1976.

Porteus, Beilby. *Death: A Poetical Essay*. 4th ed. Philadelphia: Robert Bell, 1773.

Price, Martin. *To the Palace of Wisdom: Studies in Order and Energy from Dryden to Blake*. Carbondale: Southern Illinois University Press, 1964.

Radcliffe, Ann. *The Italian; or, The Confessional of the Black Penitents: A Romance*. Ed. Frederick Garber. London: Oxford University Press, 1971.

Radcliffe, Ann. *The Mysteries of Udolpho: A Romance Interspersed with Some Pieces of Poetry*. Ed. Bonamy Dobrée. London: Oxford University Press, 1970.

Radcliffe, Ann. *The Romance of the Forest: Interspersed with Some Pieces of Poetry*. Ed. Chloe Chard. Oxford: Oxford University Press, 1986.

Radcliffe, Mary-Anne. *Manfroné; or, The One-Handed Monk: A Romance*. 3d ed. 1828. Reprint. New York: Arno Press, 1972.

Radin, Edward D. *Lizzie Borden: The Untold Story*. New York: Dell, 1962.

Rebello, Stephen. *Alfred Hitchcock and the Making of* Psycho. New York: Dembner Books, 1990.

Riley, Philip J. *London after Midnight*. New York: Cornwall Books, 1985.

Rowell, George, ed. *Nineteenth Century Plays*. 2d. ed. London: Oxford University Press, 1972.

S. N. E. *The Murdered Maid; or, The Clock Struck Four!!! A Drama. In Three Acts*. Warwick: Heathcote and Fodden, 1818.

Scott, Sir Walter. *Redgauntlet: A Tale of the Eighteenth Century*. Boston: Dana Estes, 1894.

Sickels, Eleanor M. *The Gloomy Egoist: Moods and Themes of Melancholy from Gray to Keats*. New York: Columbia University Press, 1932.

The Siege of Troy; or Giant Horse of Sinon: A Grand Spectacle, in Two Acts. London: Orlando Hodgson, n.d.

Skal, David J. *Hollywood Gothic: The Tangled Web of* Dracula *from Novel to Stage to Screen*. New York: Norton, 1990.

Spence, Ralph. *The Gorilla: A Mystery Comedy in Three Acts*. New York: Samuel French, n.d.

Spiering, Frank. *Lizzie*. New York: Random House, 1984.

Sterne, Laurence. *The Life and Opinions of Tristram Shandy, Gentleman*. Ed. Ian Watt. Boston: Houghton Mifflin, 1965.

Stoker, Bram. *Dracula*. Ed. A. N. Wilson. Oxford: Oxford University Press, 1983.

Sullivan, Jack. *Elegant Nightmares: The English Ghost Story from Le Fanu to Blackwood*. Athens: Ohio University Press, 1978.

Summers, Montague. *A Gothic Bibliography*. London: Fortune Press, n.d.

Summers, Montague. *The Gothic Quest: A History of the Gothic Novel*. London: Fortune Press, 1968.

Summers, Montague. *The Supernatural Omnibus*. 1931. Reprint. New York: Causeway Books, 1974.

Tieck, Ludwig. *Der gestiefelte Kater: Kindermärchen in drei Akten mit Zwischenspielen, einem Prologe und Epiloge*. Ed. Helmut Kreuzer. Stuttgart: Reclam, 1965.

Weber, Carl Maria von. *Der Freischütz. Romantische Oper in drei Aufzügen*. Wittingen: Polydor International, 1973.

Wertham, Fredric, M.D. *Seduction of the Innocent*. New York: Rinehart, 1954.

Willard, John. *The Cat and the Canary: A Melodrama in Three Acts*. New York: Samuel French, 1927.

Woolf, Virginia. *The Essays of Virginia Woolf*. Ed. Andrew McNeillie. vol. 2. San Diego: Harcourt Brace Jovanovich, 1987.

Wordsworth, William. *The Poems*. Ed. John O. Hayden. 2 vols. New Haven: Yale University Press, 1981.

Young, Edward. *The Complaint; or, Night Thoughts on Life, Death, and Immortality*. London: Thomas Tegg, 1837.

Zola, Emile. *Nana*. Trans. George Holden. Harmondsworth: Penguin, 1972.

Index